DROP THE BALL

DROP THE BALL

Expect Less from Yourself
and Flourish in Work and Life

Tiffany Dufu

PENGUIN LIFE

AN IMPRINT OF

PENGUIN BOOKS

PENGUIN LIFE

UK | USA | Canada | Ireland | Australia
India | New Zealand | South Africa

Penguin Life is part of the Penguin Random House group of companies
whose addresses can be found at global.penguinrandomhouse.com

First published in the United States of America by Flatiron Books 2017
First published in Great Britain by Penguin Life 2017
This edition published 2018
001

Printed in Great Britain by Clays Ltd, St Ives plc

A CIP catalogue record for this book is available from the British Library

ISBN: 978–0–241–97312–7

Obviously for Kojo

CONTENTS

FOREWORD

Bringing the Revolution Home

Gloria Steinem

There are two ways that a system of power stays in power. The first is obvious—unequal laws, unequal opportunity, very unequal money, and violence or the threat of violence—but the second is more internal and difficult to uproot. It's the idea of what is normal; how we ourselves behave to earn equality and power, and how early in our lives these norms are introduced. Since women are half of every population, and unlike other secondary groups, not only live and work with men but give birth to boys as well as girls, there is a constant danger that we will recognize our shared humanity and rebel. That's why gender roles have to begin so early and go so deep. Those are the inequalities we grow up with, from a pink or blue blanket to the invention of "masculine" and "feminine." We see these roles all around us, assume they are inevitable, and come to expect conformity even of ourselves.

When a belief punishes the believer—for instance, when women believe that for us, "having it all" must mean "doing it all"—it becomes what psychologists call *internalized oppression*.

Tiffany Dufu's *Drop the Ball* is crucial because it takes on that

deeper system. We've spent the last fifty years trying to democra-
tize the external one—and come far enough to know that we can
and must go much further—yet we have not uprooted the inequality
that begins in the family. For instance, the old logic says that a
woman spends a year or so bearing and nursing a child, so she must
be more responsible for raising that child to adulthood. Yet the truth
is that children have two parents; thus if a mother spends a year bearing and nursing a child, why is a father not responsible for spending
much more than half that time in child-rearing? Logic is in the eye
of the logician.

The good news is that once we open this door of shared humanity, all kinds of new possibilities come in, not only for women but
also for men and children.

For instance, until I was ten or so, my father played a bigger role in
my upbringing than did my mother. This was because she was sometimes ill and incapacitated, and also because he was an itinerant an-
tiques dealer who worked at home and could take me with him as he
drove around to roadside shops. Certainly, it was not because he was
a conventional parent. He let me eat all the ice cream I wanted—he
himself weighed over three hundred pounds—and took me with him
to see the Hollywood movies of the day. He never once told me to go
to bed, and he let me sleep by the fire or near our dog when she was
nursing a litter of puppies. He himself often fell asleep on the couch
while reading me the funnies. All I knew was that he loved my company, treated me as well or better than he treated himself, and asked
for and listened to my opinions. What more could any child want?

Spending so much time with this gentle and loving man taught
me there were gentle and loving men in the world. As an adult, I was
never tempted by the distant or dominating ones—unlike women
friends I saw trying to reenact and transform their childhoods with
distant, absent, or even cruel fathers. I always understood that men
could raise children just as well as women and that they could be just
as kind. My father gave me a huge gift. I have been grateful ever
since.

It is the genius of this book that Tiffany focuses on the internal paths to equality. She questions why women—as wives, daughters, or just citizens—are more or even solely responsible for home care; meals; raising children; caring for the elderly or ill; maintaining social, school, health, and family networks; and doing pretty much everything that isn't paid. Though there are now more nurturing fathers and equal partners than there were in my father's day, our nation is still far behind other modern democracies when it comes to family-friendly policies. We do what we see, not what we're told; hence the saying "You have to *see* it to *be* it." We haven't demanded enough change, so a man with children is still thought to be more responsible and employable, while a woman with children is still viewed as less responsible and employable. Now that women are 50 percent of the paid labor force, and 40 percent of primary breadwinners— and men are not anything like 40 or 50 percent of the workers at home—there may be enough pain and frustration to bring the revolution home.

I know from our time together as organizers, working on ways to empower women and girls, that Tiffany is the right author and activist for this important moment in time. She has raised money for girls' education, run a national women's leadership organization, advised Fortune 500 companies on the best diversity practices, and pushed for family-friendly policies in the workplace. But perhaps even more important, she has, as a parent and partner, navigated an intimate and brave journey from an unequal family dynamic to a truly democratic one. Along the way, she has learned valuable lessons to share with us—lessons that relate to the workplace and the kitchen table. She offers actionable wisdom to pass from one woman to another, from her family to yours.

Having watched and shared in her work, I also know that she succeeds because, like Eleanor Roosevelt, she always "draws a wider circle." She not only shows that we all gain when women become part of, contribute our talents to, and are ourselves changed by the world *outside* the home, but also how we will all gain when men become part of, contribute their talents to, and are themselves changed by the world *inside* the home.

To defeat barriers that are both internal and external, it's leadership by example that counts. No matter how long each of us has worked for greater fairness—and how well we know that gender, race, caste, and class are all made-up categories that can be unmade—what we need are examples of people who live in a new and equal way. Tiffany is that example herself, and she shows us many more. Because gender tends to be the unequal division that we see first—and that also normalizes all other birth-based inequalities—this is radical. But if we learned about the 90 percent of human history that we usually ignore as "prehistory," we would know that it is not too radical to be true. Men did share child-rearing in our migratory past. As Dorothy Dinnerstein and many other scholars have pointed out, men then developed the full circle of human qualities, with no artificial idea of "masculinity" to prove, just as women developed that circle by being equal outside the home, with no concept of "femininity."

Inspired by Tiffany's power of example, here is a story from my own life that may hint at the new possibilities she will bring into yours.

Early on, I was saved by the writings of everyone from Simone de Beauvoir to Andrea Dworkin and Florynce Kennedy. They gifted me with the knowledge that I was neither crazy nor alone in hoping that women could be safe, use our talents, and be treated as whole human beings. This was huge. Yet all three assumed there had never been a society in which women were truly equal. That's why they didn't quite still my fear that we were working for an impossible goal.

Then in 1977, I went to the National Women's Conference in Houston. Though the media barely covered it, this was a gathering of two thousand delegates, elected from every state and territory, to vote on issues that also had been democratically proposed. Because it brought a diverse national movement together on a shared agenda, it probably is still the most important feminist event ever. While listening to the many Native American and Alaskan Native delegates, I realized that I knew nothing about the history of the land I lived on. While the rest of us hoped for an unknown and equal future, these activists cited a known and equal past. In Indian country, women once decided when and whether to give birth by using their knowledge of herbs, abortifacients, and timing; men were present at childbirth and active in child-rearing; women controlled agriculture and men hunted, but both were equally necessary; female and male elders made decisions, and spiritual figures were as likely to be female as male. To this day, many Native American languages have no gendered pronouns, no "he" and "she." People are people. What a concept.

Now, we may be reinventing the past by declaring our right to control our own bodies and destinies—outside *and* inside the home. We need a vision of how to live this revolution every day. We need women and men who lead by example, as those women from Indian country did for me almost four decades ago, and as Tiffany does for readers of these pages.

When I was growing up, my mother dropped the ball because she had no choice, and my father picked it up out of love and necessity. Now, women and men can again share all of life and explore our whole human selves.

Webster's Definition:

drop the ball: to make a mistake especially by failing to take timely, effective, or proper action

My Definition:

Drop the Ball: to release unrealistic expectations of doing it all and engage others to achieve what matters most to us, deepening our relationships and enriching our lives

DROP THE BALL

INTRODUCTION

I used to be the queen of domesticity, a *Good Housekeeping* cover model in the making. I was also an ambitious professional. These two identities had always been on a collision course. But I was oblivious to that fact until after the crash.

Eight years into my marriage and six months after giving birth to my first child, I started a new job, fully expecting to be the power-house perfect working wife and mother who had it all and did it all. I was joyfully wedded to my college sweetheart, we had a beautiful baby boy, and we were committed to changing the world together. I knew that juggling the demands of a growing family, reaching the highest levels in my career, and supporting my husband as he climbed his own professional ladder wouldn't always be easy—but we were ready.

Many women find it difficult to leave their infants on that first day back from maternity leave, but I was not one of them. I loved my work. I have always been a passionate advocate for the empow-erment and advancement of women and girls, and I had been of-fered my dream job directing the fund-raising efforts of a national women's leadership organization. I would be doing work I cared about while learning from a pioneer in the women's movement, Marie Wilson, cocreator of Take Our Daughters to Work Day and former president of the Ms. Foundation for Women. On top of all that, the salary was enough to allow me the peace of mind that comes with leaving a child in the hands of a skilled and loving caregiver—a privilege too many working mothers cannot afford—and I had negotiated for a private room where I could pump breast milk. My maternity leave came to an end, and I joyfully prepared to go to work.

I had grown up being told I could do anything I put my mind to, and as I got dressed that first morning back, I couldn't imagine I'd have to compromise on anything: career, marriage, raising a family, keeping our homelife running smoothly while advancing the cause of women and girls. I left my apartment confident I would be successful doing it all.

That illusion lasted six hours.

My first day back at work was a whirlwind. I was so consumed with getting up to speed and running from meeting to meeting that by the time I realized I'd forgotten to pump, my breasts were engorged. With each passing minute, they became more swollen and painful. Milk started leaking through my blouse onto my suit jacket.

To add insult to injury, the "private room" I had negotiated turned out to be a bathroom stall. Having no experience with engorged breasts, I tried to pump, but the machine suction couldn't latch on to what now appeared to be two throbbing bowling balls on my chest. To relieve myself, I applied warm paper towels and tried expressing the milk by hand. That worked—but it meant I couldn't hold the empty bottle. And the good Lord didn't exactly design women's breasts so they would be easy to aim.

There I was, kneeling on the floor of a bathroom stall in my drenched silk blouse and designer suit, emptying my baby's milk into the toilet. Tears were streaming down my face as the milk streamed from my body. My breasts had exploded, and my vision of a future in which I gracefully managed both career and home had been obliterated.

On the suffocating train ride home from Wall Street to 125th Street in Harlem, the reality of my new circumstances began to sink in. If I was too consumed at the office to remember to do something as essential as pump milk for my baby, what else was going to fall through the cracks? When would I sort the pile of mail or pay the bills? How was I going to keep up with the laundry and cooking? When would I have time to go to the grocery store? My floors were going to turn into a health hazard as soon as my son started crawling; how would I keep them pristine? I had missed two e-mails from the caregiver while I was in meetings. How would I make sure her questions were answered promptly? What would I do about getting the car inspected? Would my book club ever see me again? Would I ever read another book? When would I buy all the Christmas gifts for my family and friends? How would I have *time* for family and friends? How would I have time for *me*? All of a sudden, the idea of scaling the professional ladder, being strong and vibrant, and making a difference in the world—all while nurturing a wonderful marriage and raising a healthy and happy child—went from inevitable to overwhelming.

My sorority sisters used to call me Trapper Keeper because I was so well organized. But now, when I looked at my situation, I felt trapped by competing demands. I wanted to be the perfect working mom—not a milk-soaked, stressed-out mess. But there was no way I could organize my way out of this. Something would have to give.

I knew that many women solved this dilemma by simply outsourcing their domestic responsibilities. There is a robust supply of professionals (mostly other women) who can be hired to do everything from cooking to cleaning to carpooling. But this is largely the solution for women who can afford an in-home staff—women at senior levels who earn big salaries or are married to men who earn them. That wasn't my husband and me. We were making just enough money to cover our living expenses, child care, retirement, and student loans, with occasional support to members of our extended family. How was all of this going to get done? The enormity of the challenge reduced me to tears.

I was still sniffling in bed at 10:00 P.M. when my husband got home. It was early for him, as he regularly pulled all-nighters at the bank where he worked. I listened to him kick off his shoes and leave them in the hallway instead of putting them in the closet. I knew the exact moment he was hanging his jacket because I could hear the rustle of the dry-cleaning bag I had picked up for him on my way home. He headed straight to the fridge for the dinner he knew would be waiting there. After he'd eaten, I heard the familiar clatter of his plate and cutlery being placed in the kitchen sink instead of the dishwasher. Then a thud—his body hitting the blue couch. I had seen him in this position countless times. His right hand would be resting lazily on his thigh as he used his thumb to awaken the remote. As I heard the TV click with the usual drumbeat of ESPN highlights, a tinge of resentment tickled my toes. By the time it reached my knees, it had become jealousy, which turned to anger inside my stomach. By the time the anger crawled up my chest, it was full-blown rage. Clearly he and I were on the same highway, but somehow he had managed to detour around the crash scene.

I was his solution to having it all.

What would be mine?

I wish I had known then that I was far from being the only woman struggling with competing work-life demands. In a recent Pew survey of millennial working mothers, 58 percent said that being a mother made it harder for them to get ahead in their careers compared with 19 percent of millennial fathers.[1] The reason for the disparity is obvious. Just as women reach middle management and their leadership responsibilities at work increase exponentially, they are simultaneously starting families and taking on a larger share of labor at home. It is a cruel confluence of a college-educated woman's career and her biological clock. By the average age of thirty,[2] whether it is as part of a team at the office or in caring for a baby at home, women are shouldering more responsibility than ever before in their lives. This collision of bad timing then combusts with two other external forces. First, workplaces are still organized around the myth of an ideally supported worker. The professional world assumes that every full-time employee has someone else managing his or her home. Second, the heightened demands of modern child-rearing make the burden of parenting and household management heavier than ever. The myth of the ideally supported worker and the expectations of extreme parenting conspire to communicate a clear message to a new generation of women: you can have it all, as long as you do it all. Sooner or later, we discover that doing it all is impossible.

The most commonsense solutions to the work-home conundrum are national affordable child care, paid family leave policies, evolved workplaces, and a culture that values caregiving. Anne-Marie Slaughter makes a powerful and persuasive case for this in her book *Unfinished Business*.[3] Iceland, along with many European countries, has subsidized nurseries and has the longest parental leaves of any nation. It is ranked as the best place in the world to be a woman.[4] In contrast, most American women can't find time to go to the gym, let alone to wait for Washington bureaucrats to pass this type of forward-thinking legislation that would support working families.

So in addition to calling our senators and dreaming of an in-home staff, women (and the men who love them) are left to solve this problem for themselves. The most traditional solution is to drop out of career pursuits altogether. Women who choose this path are a small, affluent group representing only 5 percent of married mothers.[5] This solution is economically impractical for the vast majority of women whose families rely on their income. In fact, women are now the sole or primary breadwinners in 40 percent of U.S. households with children under eighteen.[6]

The second solution involves slowing down career pursuits. Seventeen percent of women reduce or adapt their work commitments so that they will have the bandwidth to take care of demands at home.[7] This path is commonly referred to as the "mommy track" because it involves working part-time or reduced hours, or taking advantage of flex policies—all of which carry a stigma of noncommitment in most work cultures today.[8] In recent years, the slowing-down solution has been referred to as the "nonlinear track."[9] In a Harvard Business School alumni survey, 37 percent of millennial women and 42 percent of those already married said they plan to interrupt their careers for family. By age thirty, nearly half of them had already chosen more flexible careers or had intentionally stepped off the fast track. Nine percent had declined a promotion because of family responsibilities.[10]

The third solution is to not have children at all. In 1992, nearly 80 percent of female Wharton business school graduates said they planned on having children. By 2012, this had dropped to 42 percent.[11] Millennial women who choose not to have children as their career success strategy, or who can't have children, do have a precedent: at this point in time, 49 percent of women at the highest levels of corporate leadership have never had children, compared with only 19 percent of their male counterparts.[12]

None of these three solutions worked for me. I didn't marry a very rich man, but even if I had, I was too risk averse to compromise my economic viability (and that of my son) to stop working. My mother had stalled her career to raise her children, and I'd seen the cruel result: when she and my dad divorced, she soon fell into poverty. I spent my young adulthood struggling to help her, and I vowed that I would never be financially dependent on anyone. Opting out— leaving the paid workforce—was unacceptable, especially now that I had a child. So was working anything less than full-time, since that would leave us unable to cover the cost of child care. And, as a brand-new employee, I wouldn't dare ask for a flexible arrangement. Besides, I loved my job. I didn't want to quit or work less. I didn't want to tamp down my ambitions.

And as for not having kids, that train had already left the station.

That left me with the recourse that most women take: trying to do it all at work and at home. Unfortunately, these attempts take their toll, primarily on our health and mental well-being. Those of us committed to our careers and our families, who are unable or don't want to pause or slow down our career pursuits, end up more exhausted, stressed out, depleted, and sick than any previous generation of women.[13]

The night after my first day back from maternity leave, lying in bed as this dilemma was hitting me, I realized I needed a better solution. It would take me years to find an answer. And the journey was not always easy and conflict-free. But I did eventually find an answer for myself.

Today, I can report that I am flourishing in my career and I am doing work that matters deeply to me. I've maintained my health. And I'm focused on the aspects of parenting that are most important to me. It wasn't easy or automatic to get to this place, but the results have been life-changing. I'm not burdened by the anxiety that so many working mothers feel—and that I once felt myself. I average seven hours of sleep a night and work out four days a week. I'm not bogged down with child-care logistics. I can RSVP to evening work events and know that my husband will either cover for me or coordinate a babysitter. Most importantly, I'm not plagued with guilt. My life is far from perfect, as the clutter bursting out of my apartment closets can attest, but on most days, I feel that everything I am and everything I do is enough.

I have devoted my career to exploring the best strategies for addressing the dearth of women in American leadership—as head of the White House Project, a national women's leadership organization, and currently as chief leadership officer at Levo, a technology platform founded to help millennial women elevate their careers. I've seen that despite climbing to new heights on the professional ladder, women still rarely get to the top. We are 51 percent of the population,[14] and by 2020, we are projected to be 47 percent of the labor force,[15] yet we still command only an 18 percent share at the highest levels of leadership.[16] Smart executives are committed to changing this trend. Many Fortune 500 companies and major nonprofits have hired me to advise them on retaining and advancing women, and I do a lot of public speaking on the benefits of diverse leadership.

Over the course of my career, I've been heartened by the growing support for women's empowerment in the workplace, but I'm mindful that most of the efforts involve either encouraging women to keep their feet on the gas pedal of their professional lives, equipping workplaces to support their female employees more robustly, or changing public policy to incentivize workplaces to do so. I'm a fierce proponent of each of these approaches (as we all should be), but I've come to realize that they don't give guilt-laden, anxiety-ridden, and exhausted women a practical, actionable solution to juggling the competing demands of work and home.

This realization—and the inspiration for this book—came to me at the end of 2013. That year, I spoke on sixty stages to nearly twenty thousand women, usually about what individuals and organizations can do to diversify leadership. Regardless of the content of my talk or the composition of my audience, the most common question at the end of my lectures was always personal: "How do you manage everything you do?"

In response, I would say, "I expect far less of myself and *way* more of my husband than the average woman!" That always got a laugh. Then I'd solicit what I thought were more pressing questions about how to navigate office politics or reform corporate and government policies. Despite my best intentions, women were inevitably eager to return to the logistics of my personal life. Details that seemed mundane to me—like how my husband and I coordinated school drop-offs or camp shopping lists or evening work events—seemed fascinating to them. One day, after yet another experience like this, I made the connection. I finally understood that when women kept asking, "How do you manage it all?" they were really wondering, "How can *I* manage it all?"

Drop the Ball is my honest answer to their question. It is the story of my three-year journey to figure out what really mattered to me, how to achieve it, and what structures of support I needed to put in place to make it possible. The situation I was in on my first night back from maternity leave—feeling helpless and confused, angry and resentful of the person who was actually in the best position to help me—is not uncommon. Many women experience the struggle of home lives that become more demanding and time-consuming right at the point when their careers need the most attention, energy, and creativity. This is the story of how I learned to excel at a purpose-driven career, nourish my marriage, raise happy children, give back to my community, sustain meaningful friendships, and be healthy and fit—all at the same time.

But *Drop the Ball* is more than a personal memoir; it's also a manifesto. I want women to know that their individual problem is a collective one, too. The research is unequivocal: the most complex problems are best solved by a diverse group of people. Yet the highest levels of leadership are glutted with the same type: male, white, straight, able-bodied, and wealthy. This has been true since the dawn of our country two and a half centuries ago. Don't get me wrong. Like many of our founding fathers, today's corporate decision makers are accomplished, smart, and well meaning. It's just that now that it's the twenty-first century, their lens is too narrow to address gigantic problems like economic inequality, climate change, terrorism, or the decline of America's educational system. If we care about these problems, we have to care about the women whose help we need to solve them.

Today, women are half of the workforce, but at our current rate, it will take one hundred years for women to be half of our leaders.[17] The very future of our society rests on women's ability to get past middle management and to thrive in the process. We need a *Drop the Ball* movement—not just to prevent working mothers from crashing but to fast-forward history.

PART ONE

—✦—

Doing It All

CHAPTER 1

A Woman's Place

I was going to do it all. I would have a high-flying career, and so would my husband. We would have an incredible marriage, more substance than romance, but still storybook. We would change the world together and raise beautiful children along the way. Oh, and we would be happy. Very, very happy. We'd have problems, but they wouldn't last for long, and they would only serve one purpose: to make us stronger. Little did I know the problem with fairy tales: they never address logistics.

I was groomed to manage a home for as long as I can remember. My thirteenth birthday card featured a cartoon of a girl rushing into the kitchen with a bag of groceries. Inside was a handwritten note from my parents, thanking me for all my contributions to our family. When I was sixteen, my parents divorced, and my fourteen-year-old sister, Trinity, and I moved in with our dad. Because I was the oldest, I automatically became the woman of the house. While my friends were at the mall, I planned meals and grocery shopped.

Once, burned out from juggling my household responsibilities and schoolwork, I announced that we would all share the cooking. I assigned weekend evenings to my dad and Tuesdays and Thursdays to my sister. I was hoping for at least the minimum: a protein, a starch, and a vegetable, preferably from scratch. On my dad's first night, he boiled Top Ramen, toasted bread, and opened a can of pears. The best you could say about my sister's first meal, Hamburger Helper Cheesy Macaroni Beef, was that it was cooked all the way through. Clearly, no one else shared my commitment to well-balanced, nutritious meals. From then on, I abandoned the rotating cooking plan and just did it myself.

Doing it myself became my mantra—and not just doing it myself but doing it perfectly. I changed my fingernail polish each day to match my outfit. I rewrote my college admissions essay eight times. I made my own senior prom dress on the day of the dance because I didn't like the job the seamstress had done on my original dress when I'd picked it up that morning. I was an opinionated, driven girl who loved being given leadership roles at school and in church. My parents always encouraged me to speak my mind, to stand up for what was right. But at the same time, I was clear about my future responsibilities at home. I knew that when I grew up I would be in charge of housekeeping (which included food shopping, cooking, arranging the linen closet, cleaning, and decorating), social coordination (everything from tracking special occasions and buying gifts to making potluck dishes and preparing for houseguests), and child-rearing (the pressure of which I felt long before I ever had children). No one ever *told* me all these tasks were my future job. When speaking about the future, mostly people told me I would go to college and that I should follow my passion. They never alluded to what eventually hit me unexpectedly—a conflict between fulfilling all these household duties and fulfilling my dreams.

Many women experience a sense of pressure that men rarely do—the pressure to succeed at work *and* to keep things running smoothly at home, especially when children arrive on the scene. This is not to say that men don't feel the stress of fulfilling household duties. On the contrary, many men today are up to their ears in laundry. But after mentoring, coaching, speaking, and listening to thousands of women, I have observed a deeper anxiety specific to women. In addition to fulfilling our professional responsibilities, we feel we are in charge on the home front—we are the ones primarily responsible for managing child care, household chores, and generally keeping our homes and family lives running smoothly. According to the American Time Use Survey, half of the women in America did some form of housework, like cleaning or laundry, on an average day. Only 20 percent of men can say the same.[1] And even in the homes where we aren't the ones doing all the work, we are the ones thinking about all the work, as Judith Shulevitz pointed out in her 2015 *New York Times* op-ed, "Mom: The Designated Worrier." "I don't mean to say that she'll be the one to do everything," Shulevitz explained, "just that she'll make sure that most everything gets done."[2]

Although the fact that women do more work than men at home has remained true since the 1950s, women today often feel lucky because, unlike the husbands of yesteryear, ours chip in. Women tend to think we should feel grateful for how far men have come. Indeed, more men are contributing to child care and household management than ever before. But even with these strides, the truth is that men still do not share an equal amount of the work and worry that accompanies managing a home. In her seminal book *The Second Shift*, sociologist Arlie Hochschild attributed women's appreciation for men who did less at home to their use of the "going rate tool."[3] As long as our husbands are doing relatively more than their peer group or what our society seems to expect of them, then we're happy they've done their fair share. This inequitable division of labor has psychological repercussions: when men change a diaper, they feel like they're helping us out; when we change a diaper, we feel like we're just doing our job.

And it isn't just any job. It's one that carries a lot of emotional freight. No matter what we achieve in our careers, if our home lives aren't taken care of, we experience it as a moral failure. How often have we heard a female colleague, lamenting over missing a school

event or not making dinner for her kids, say, "I'm such a bad mom"?
Even if the kids are perfectly well fed by someone else, mothers often feel personally accountable in a way that fathers generally don't.

A 2014 *Harvard Business Review* article detailing interviews
conducted with more than four thousand C-suite executives,
44 percent of whom were female, reveals the stark difference in the
way men and women view work-life balance. "When you are paid
well, you can get all the [practical] help you need," one female re-
spondent explained. "What is the most difficult thing, though—what
I see my women friends leave their careers for—is the real emotional guilt of not spending enough time with their children. The
guilt of missing out." Overwhelmingly, female respondents spoke of
feeling "torn" between home and work; they commented on the feelings of inadequacy and failure that accompanied pursuing their
careers. In contrast, male respondents saw themselves as economic
providers and were far less emotional in response to questions about
guilt brought on by not spending enough time with their families.[4]
They were comfortable seeing themselves as breadwinners. Several
of the male executives felt that not spending adequate time with
their children was an "acceptable price" to pay for providing them
better opportunities than they themselves had as children. But for
the women executives, though they were proud to be a role model
for their children, they associated their professional success with
negative emotions about their performance at home. Women set for
themselves a higher bar to achieve success because they were expected to do well both at work and at home.

Where did we get the notion that "doing it all" is our job in the
first place?

The simple answer is our childhood homes provide our earliest
coaching about domestic roles. The examples set by our parents and
extended families become models for our own adult lives. A 2014
study by the University of British Columbia revealed that mothers'
behaviors and explicit beliefs about domestic gender roles predicted
the beliefs held by their children.[5] The more that mothers fulfilled
traditional household duties and subscribed to the assumption that

most women will, the more their children, especially their daughters, imagined themselves fulfilling gender-stereotypical roles in the future. This indoctrination is solidified by the time a child reaches adolescence.[6] Though a mother might be a positive role model for her children's perception about what women can achieve outside the home, what her children observe her doing directly at home is even more powerful. Even the daughters of mothers who leave for the office each day grow up believing they'll be responsible for the bulk of responsibilities at home if that's what their mothers are doing—our children don't see us leading meetings, making presentations, or mentoring young colleagues—they do see us rushing around to prepare dinner, do the laundry, and load the dishwasher while their fathers respond to work e-mails or check the score on a baseball game.

There's no question that my belief that I needed to be in charge at home had its roots in the way my mother managed our household when I was a little girl. My mother grew up in the Watts neighborhood of Los Angeles, a rough place during the mid-1970s, and she was resolved to escape it. Against the odds, she excelled academically and artistically; she loved fashion and designed and sewed her own clothes. She was on track to attend UCLA when she became pregnant with me at nineteen. Plans had to change, but she was determined to find a way to keep moving forward.

My father was one of eleven kids, born into a housing project not far from where my mother lived. He experimented with drugs but otherwise stayed out of trouble and always had a desire to help people. At my mother's urging, he joined the army as a way to break free of his addiction and get out of the projects. They got married in the summer of 1973, and I was born nine months later at Fort Lewis in Tacoma, Washington. My parents broke a vicious cycle of poverty, substance abuse, and violence in one generation, and in the process, they taught me a fundamental truth: if you want something you've never had before, you'll have to do something you've never done before in order to get it.

In retrospect, the first sixteen years of my life were close to perfect—though, like most teens, I thought my life was terrible at the time. I wasn't allowed to go to parties; I was expected to do chores like start making dinner when I came home from school; and I was constantly being told by my mother that I was smart, beautiful, and loved—something that annoyed me to no end—when all I wanted was bigger boobs. But my family was proving the American dream. My father, the same man who kicked a heroin addiction to pass a military physical exam, eventually went to college on the GI bill, earned a Ph.D. in theology, worked as an elementary school guidance counselor, and pastored churches. When I was in middle school, my mom began a career as a social worker, but her primary roles were as a mother and a preacher's wife, and she played her parts beautifully.

One of my earliest childhood recollections is the smell of frying chicken and collard greens simmering in ham hocks wafting underneath my bedroom door on Sunday mornings. My mom would wake early to start cooking so that the meal between the morning and evening church services could be served expeditiously. All she had to do when we got home was whip up a batch of corn bread. In the summertime, she'd make homemade vanilla ice cream on the porch. I can't recall a sink full of dirty dishes or a store-bought birthday cake. And my hair was always beautifully styled. My younger sister, Trinity, and I spent countless hours between my mother's knees. By the time she removed the cornrows, washed, blow-dried, then braided and beaded one head, six hours could have easily passed (which partly explains black women's endurance—as young as five years old, we could sit that long to have our hair done!).

My father worked hard, too, but mostly outside the house. He started each day with a neighborhood jog. Our family car was always gleaming. Our yard was immaculate. The garbage bin was brought to the curb and the gutters were cleared like clockwork. Occasionally, my father would wash the dishes or do the laundry. These tasks seemed to bring him joy, and he literally whistled while he worked. But we all understood these weren't his jobs; my mom just got lucky that she married a man who liked to do them. Mostly when my dad was inside, he was studying in preparation for a sermon, watching episodes of *Star Trek* or *The Twilight Zone,* or dancing to Lou Rawls or Earth, Wind & Fire. When he wasn't home, he would be at school or church, tending to the flock. My mother and father fulfilled their ordained family responsibilities—she as homemaker and he as provider—and we moved upward from inner-city apartments to a suburban house with a white picket fence.

When I was growing up, the church was my community. Because my parents had uprooted themselves from their childhood homes in California, church folk became our family. Even though we were in the Pacific Northwest, many of the African Americans we knew had roots in the South, so food was always the centerpiece of any gathering. I remember these feasts of my childhood with great affection, but I also remember the gendered division of labor: in our church, women were the caregivers who cooked for, set up for, and served the men. Even as a little girl, it was clear to me that while women were central to making the church community function, their role was to serve.

Sometimes I chafed against this arrangement. I was frequently told that I was bright, college bound, and that the world was my oyster, but I'll never forget the time I was reprimanded by a Sunday school teacher for praying loudly and heartily at the end of class. Apparently, when she asked for a volunteer to pray, she'd meant a boy. I stared at her dumbstruck as she scolded me. That was the day I learned that our church doctrine didn't allow women to lead men in prayer. I was eleven years old, and nothing about the teacher's comment that "boys are the leaders" sat right with me. I am quite sure my future passion for advancing women and girls first stirred to life in that moment.

Fortunately, I had the kind of father who didn't believe that this "boys lead" rule applied to *his* daughters, even though he preached it to others. He would turn a booster seat upside down on a chair during our weekly family meetings and coach my sister and me in delivering sermons. But because our public speaking was done in the privacy of our home and kept separate from the church, even his encouragement reinforced the community's stronger message:

women should concern themselves primarily with quietly caring for others.

—◆—

Gender role indoctrination starts early, passed down to us in the conscious and unconscious attitudes and actions of even the most progressive and well-intentioned parents. So it was for Jun, a sales director I met when I was consulting for a Fortune 500 pharmaceutical company that was launching a women's initiative. Jun had been tapped to lead the new program—the executives in the C-suite thought she was a superstar. She had always believed she could achieve anything she worked hard for. From her elementary school spelling bee trophy to her Yale acceptance letter, Jun had accumulated compelling evidence that her relentless work ethic was the key to her success. Yet, at the age of thirty-nine, working harder than ever, she felt like she was failing miserably—and she was miserable.

She had exceeded her sales goals for three consecutive quarters and was widely respected by colleagues, but in talking with her, it became clear she was hanging on by a thread. Despite her belief in the power of hard work, she couldn't seem to find enough hours in the day to meet the demands of her job and her family.

"My house is a complete wreck," she confessed. "I haven't cleaned for weeks. Things are growing in my fridge." She smiled ruefully. "I'm afraid they'll open the door and walk out if I don't chuck them soon."

That was just the beginning. When Jun and I discussed any hesitations she might have about leading the new program at work, she never once mentioned feelings of professional anxiety. Instead, it seemed that what was holding her back at work was her to-do list—and the feelings that came with those obligations—at home. Just as my mother's example had shown me that I should be responsible for the efficient management of my household, Jun's upbringing had influenced her beliefs about her role at home.

Jun's parents, both Japanese, were professionally ambitious and successful and enjoyed some flexibility when it came to their schedules. Her father was a professor of history and her mother an anesthesiologist. Jun's father had summers off from teaching and was not expected to be on campus at night or on the weekends. Yet Jun recalled the household responsibilities being clearly divided along gender lines. "My father never cooked, cleaned, or took me to my after-school activities," she said. "It sounds weird, but I don't think he ever answered our telephone. I'm thinking now that maybe my mother worked part-time, because when I recall everything she did, I can't fathom how she managed it all."

Jun was joking about her mother working part-time; the reality is that her mother had two full-time jobs—her profession outside the home and the management of the home itself. Jun attributed some of her own struggle to her effort to emulate her mother. "I guess I never appreciated the complexity of what my mom was juggling," she mused. "She made it look so easy."

When Jun and I met, she ticked off a long list of her "failures," the worst of which (according to her) was missing her oldest son's baseball games. "I want to be there, but it's impossible with my work schedule." No matter how hard she tried, Jun never felt like she was doing enough.

Scheduling challenges were also a cause of stress for Susan, another woman I know. I first met Susan at a community festival in Harlem. Our sons bonded by kicking a ball back and forth in a pretend World Cup match, and we bonded over our non–soccer mom status. Recently divorced with nine- and five-year-old kids, Susan was constantly trying to navigate a tug-of-war between her livelihood and her duties at home. She worked as a city bus driver, which meant she and her kids had to get up at 4:30 A.M. to make her punch-in time at the depot. The kids' school had been on her morning route, which meant she got to drop them off herself. But the day we met, her route had been changed, and she didn't know how she'd manage. "This route change is just my work-life conflict flavor of the week." She sighed. "Next week it will be something else."

When I asked her why she felt she had to be the one to drop off her kids at school, Susan looked at me aghast. "I can't imagine asking a friend or a neighbor to drop them off," she said. "They'll think I'm a terrible mother." I probed a little deeper and learned that, like so many of us, Susan understood what it meant to be a "good mom" by watching her own. "My mom would always be up and about," she told me.

Her father was a police officer, and Susan remembered him doing chores outdoors, like washing the car and mowing the lawn, but she had trouble recalling what he did inside of the house. "I mostly remember him watching TV from his recliner," she said. "My mom would serve him dinner on one of those old metal TV trays."

Jun, Susan, and my early childhood experiences had a lasting impact on how we understood our future roles. If women are doing twice the amount of housework as men, it means that the children in those households are being sent a clear message that taking care of the home is mostly a woman's responsibility, even if no one articulates it explicitly.[7]

But we do not just learn from our own homes. The culture at large communicates expectations about what our roles should look like. From episodes of *Modern Family* to women's magazines to Pinterest, we're bombarded with external messages about where we should be spending our time and energy.

As a child, my favorite cartoon was *The Flintstones*. In 2013, *TV Guide* ranked it as the second-greatest TV cartoon of all time, behind *The Simpsons*. Both shows depict the buffoonery of working-class men whose very capable and intelligent wives are homemakers. Classic children's book series such as *The Berenstain Bears* also feature the mom character working in the home. Disney movies from *Cinderella* to *Snow White* to *The Princess and the Frog* reveal young women toiling away at domestic chores before being discovered by a handsome prince. Not surprisingly, participants in a study by the National Institute on Media and the Family found that both boys and girls described female characters as "domestic, interested in boys, and concerned with appearances."[8]

We internalize the messages we see and hear about how our family lives should look at very early ages. And those messages are so powerful that they often influence our decisions even before we're in a position to really make them. I mentor a young woman named Maria who is already anxious about her future work-life challenges. Out of college for only two years, Maria is in her first job in marketing and isn't planning on starting a family for at least a decade; she doesn't even have a boyfriend. But already, she is concerned about how she will be able to manage it all. "It scares me every day, the idea of having kids and having to give up my career," she admitted to me in one of our mentoring sessions. "I feel like I've been told my whole life that I can have it all, but now that I'm working seventy hours a week, I just don't see how that's possible. The women who are successful here don't have kids."

When I asked Maria whether she was making career decisions now in anticipation of needing to balance work and family in the future, she said, "Not really, but only because I don't know what decisions I *should* be making now. All I know is I couldn't do this job and be a good mom at the same time."

I probed Maria to describe what she meant by being a "good mom." She detailed the things her mother used to do for her and her siblings: tasks like shuttling them to their sporting events, making their lunches, and sewing their Girl Scout patches onto their uniforms. Just as Jun, Susan, and I had internalized the idea that management of the home was our responsibility because that was the example we had been given by our mothers, Maria seemed incapable of imagining a kind of motherhood for herself that would differ from the one her mother modeled for her.

The pressure Maria was putting on herself was only compounded by messages being sent to her by her community. Despite her academic achievement in college and her professional success as a marketing manager, when she is on her Dominican stomping ground, neighbors always want to know when she plans to settle down. "Now that I've graduated from college, people seem less excited about my career and more concerned with me fulfilling my duty to find a husband and start a family," Maria told me.

Maria is articulating something countless women experience but rarely voice out loud: it's not just that we think it is primarily our responsibility to manage things at home, but at some level—often an unconscious one—we believe that things at home should be our primary responsibility. While a strong majority of youth (82 percent) agrees that girls and boys are equally good at being leaders,[9] and young women like Maria grow up thinking that they can achieve success at work and at home, as they get older, they perceive there's a catch to the "have it all" ideal: home and family must come first. Women have internalized the message that we cannot be successful in the public sphere unless we're superstars on the home front as well. That's why we all wanted to be Clair Huxtable, one of the most beloved and popular TV moms of all time—she was a fierce partner at her law firm *and* she raised five perfectly well-behaved children.

Just as Maria's Dominican culture communicated to her that her professional accomplishments aren't as important as settling down and fulfilling domestic duties, many religious traditions convey these same values to women. Christian sermons and wedding ceremonies remind women that God created them to be man's helpmate. Jewish women, not men, are expected to clean before Passover to remove hametz, or leavened products. And though the Koran espouses the spiritual equality of men and women, Islamic practice encourages women to dutifully serve as the primary caretaker of their homes.

Even more insidiously, popular culture warns of a terrible price to be paid by women who ignore traditional domestic duties. When a woman is in a position of power, as portrayed in *The Proposal* starring Sandra Bullock or *Disclosure* starring Demi Moore, she is frequently portrayed as a coldhearted, detached career woman with sociopathic tendencies. "The witch is on her broom," the office assistants text each other as Bullock's character walks into the office in *The Proposal*. More often than not, her power comes at the price of her personal or family life. In *How to Get Away with Murder*, Viola Davis, the first black woman to win an Emmy for Best Actress in a Drama Series, plays Annalise Keating, a brilliant defense attorney and highly respected criminal law professor with a terrible marriage. Similarly, Miranda Priestly, Meryl Streep's character in the film version of *The Devil Wears Prada*, is a star at work and a mess at home. When she is caught crying by her young assistant, Miranda explains that her husband has left her: "Another disappointment, another letdown," she weeps. These comments send the message that powerful women must sacrifice healthy relationships, family, and possibly even their sanity to rise to the top in their careers. Even tabloids like *Us Weekly* and *People* give more coverage to women enacting maternal roles, such as escorting their children to and from school, than they show women completing professional tasks. More female celebrities are featured on the cover of these magazines when they get married or have a baby than when they star in a film or launch a new business.[10] After Marissa Mayer became CEO at Yahoo, more attention was given to her building a nursery in her office and how she planned to manage her domestic responsibilities than her vision for the direction of the company. As of this writing, there are one hundred thousand more Google search engine results for "Marissa Mayer baby" than there are for "Marissa Mayer leader."

The models we see in our own families, in our cultural and religious traditions, and in popular culture have communicated to women time and again that their primary role is to care for others—the family and the home—and that when they don't fulfill those obligations, everyone suffers.

—◆—

Like Jun, Susan, and Maria—indeed, just as all women do—I came of age with a clear understanding of what was expected of me as a girl (and what would be expected of me as a woman) at home. But it wasn't until I was in high school that I understood how important it would be for me to excel professionally as well.

My drive and determination to have a successful career outside the home solidified for me the year I turned sixteen, which was when the proverbial picket fence came crashing down. My parents dropped me off at summer camp together, but at the end of the summer, my mom came to pick me up alone. On the long drive home, she explained that she and my dad were getting divorced. She didn't actually use the word *divorce,* but I knew what she was trying to say. When we got home, I ran to Trinity's room only to have my worst fears realized. My little sister shared all the details, including the fact that my father had already moved out of the house.

Trinity and I lived with our mom for a few months until the situation at home deteriorated. Within weeks of the divorce, my mom's new boyfriend moved in. I had a bad feeling about him from his first toothy smile, and his behavior soon confirmed my assessment. He smoked and drank and swore, and worst of all, he hit my mom. I hated what was happening to her but didn't know how to help. Finally, one day, I packed my things and called my dad to come and get me. Trinity joined me within the week.

That is how my sister and I came to be two teenagers living with a single dad.

This is also how I came to be obsessed with working my butt off. I was aspiring to spiral upward as I watched my mom spiral down. In what seemed like the blink of an eye, her existence went from stable as a suburban housewife to volatile as a domestic violence victim. I'd seen how my mom's economic viability had been jeopardized by her reliance on men. Our relationship taught me one thing more surely than any other lesson: a woman should always have control over the income she earns, and it should be enough to provide for her and her children. I knew the chances of my ending up in my mother's situation were slim. And yet her situation after the divorce fueled my drive to succeed. I vowed that I would have a successful career that would ensure my independence. I didn't know exactly what it would be, but I was committed to helping all women and girls lead powerful, self-determined lives.

During my last two years of high school, I poured myself into getting good grades and engaging in extracurricular activities that would make me attractive to a college admissions committee. My junior year in high school, I was elected class representative. Because I was a student leader, the teachers and administrators knew me. One day I was walking in the hallway during a class period when our vice principal boomed from behind me, "What are you doing out of class?" I just kept walking as I heard another kid explaining that he was on his way to the bathroom. Moments later, it struck me that I hadn't even turned around when I heard the vice principal's question because no adult at my school would ever be asking me why I wasn't in class. My student leadership gave me a permanent hall pass. In other parts of my life, being a girl meant coloring in the lines. *Don't pray in front of the boys. Don't brag. Don't be so nosy. Don't play on the monkey bars. Don't get your braids wet. Don't have sex. Don't talk too loud.* For me, leadership was the only part of my life in which I wasn't expected to follow the rules; I could even make them.

But even with the freedom leadership afforded me at school, just like in church, being a girl leader meant being a worker bee. The boys were great at brainstorming homecoming themes, but the girls largely managed the logistics and details. At one point, we prohibited the boys from making banners because their block bubble letters weren't sufficient. Even then, the girls had a specific way we wanted things done. The irony that strikes me now, too, is that for all of my school leadership passion, I never aspired to run for the top spot. The role of class president usually went to a boy, and it never occurred to me to question that.

There is only one college that any high-achieving black girl who grew up in the Pacific Northwest during the late eighties wanted to go to: Spelman. The historically black women's college is nestled in the heart of Atlanta, conveniently located next to its historic male counterpart, Morehouse. Historically black colleges were made especially popular by the hit TV show *A Different World* and Spike Lee's film *School Daze.* For me, going to Spelman represented the epitome of accomplishment. I was a voracious reader, and along with Sweet Valley High novellas, I devoured books by authors like Alice Walker, Pearl Cleage, and Tina McElroy Ansa—all Spelman alumnae. The most blissful moment in my life was receiving my Spelman acceptance letter in the mail. I slept with it under my pillow for weeks.

My first year at Spelman was magical. Each dormitory had a council, and I was elected vice president of Abby Hall, so I was in

my student leadership element. Student government may have felt
familiar to me, but in every other way, my life at Spelman was pushing me to grow and learn. For one, in high school I did my homework by myself at the kitchen table. I could take sole credit for my
academic achievement, but when I got stuck, it was frustrating. At
Spelman, I was always studying with my sisters. I quickly realized
that if I helped them with their composition papers and they helped
me with chemistry, we'd all get much further in our academic pursuits. It was my first time truly experiencing the benefits of women
helping other women, and it would prove vital later in my life. The
biggest change for me, though, was that for the first time I was surrounded by black people at school. And the guys at Morehouse were
the icing on the cake.

From elementary school through high school, I was always one
of two black girls in my public school classes. There were other black
kids in my schools, but I was tracked into the gifted program, which
was predominantly white, so my interaction with them was limited.
By the time I was in high school, my propensity to have a high GPA,
conjugate all of my verbs when talking, run for office instead of
playing sports, and my diverse group of friends meant that the black
kids accused me of "acting white." The taunting was painful, and I
became highly conscientious about only dating black guys in order to
affirm my identity. I was so sensitive about my blackness being called
into question that I planned my entire junior prom but didn't attend
because no black guy had asked me to go. The night of the dance, I
went to the venue to set up and decorate, went back home and
watched two movies, then returned at the end to clean up and pay the
DJ. To this day, I still feel terrible about that night because I turned
down a really nice Jewish guy who had asked me to be his date.

Morehouse men were manna from heaven for me. And since, unlike my blackness, my girlness was never questioned, I knew my job
was to make one of them my husband. Of course, my first priorities
were my studies and community service. But the recesses of my
mind were on the hunt for a bachelor made eligible by his spiritual

grounding, appreciation for strong women, good looks, and postcollege job prospects.

Unfortunately, I wasn't at Spelman long enough to find him.

If I thought my world had been turned upside down by my parents' divorce, the call I received from my father toward the end of my first year at Spelman was about to obliterate it. In short, he'd been crunching the numbers and determined he couldn't afford to keep me at Spelman and also send Trinity to her choice college. He asked me if I'd consider coming home and attending our state school. Shards of glass pierced my heart as I said softly, "Of course, Daddy. I'll come home. Don't worry."

All the social conditioning had worked. I was a determined girl. The kind that decided what she wanted and knew how to make it happen. I was also a good girl. The kind who understood when what she wanted didn't matter. I was a young woman now, and women sacrificed for their families. There wasn't time to cry. I had a final the next day, and I needed to start packing my dorm room.

CHAPTER 2

Prince Charming

The first time I laid eyes on Kojo, I was in the lobby of my new college dormitory at the University of Washington. He was laughing with his friends, and the brilliance of his smile, the ivory white against the cocoa-skinned canvas, captured my peripheral vision. Then I saw him walk. He seemed the physical embodiment of self-assuredness. His gait was pure brown-boy swagger. *He walks like he comes from a place where black people are on the money,* I remember thinking. I wasn't surprised to learn that I was right. I was the new girl on campus, so I had to get the intel on Kojo from my roommate. She explained that he was an international student from Ghana and an electrical engineering major. He ran track. She said he was a little cheesy but really nice—"Everyone loves Kojo."

That was all the information I needed to quickly sum him up. If he had an African mother, he was accustomed to strong women, so I knew he could handle me. I was striving, stubborn, and trusted my own decision making. It was a lethal combination, and I liked that he would know better than to try to keep an eagle in a shoe box. An engineering major plus an athlete meant he was smart, was hardworking, and had earning potential. Finally, if people thought he was a little cheesy (he still sported a flattop even though they had gone out of style), I wouldn't have to compete with the popular girls to win his affection.

I immediately came up with a plan to get Kojo to notice me. I prided myself on my intellect, tenacity, and altruism, but I knew these qualities wouldn't necessarily attract a guy. And I wasn't willing to sexualize myself—which is the easiest way to get a guy's attention in college—so I figured I'd have to win him through repeat exposure, like a TV ad you have to see several times before it occurs to you to buy the product.

I quickly learned that Kojo was a resident advisor in my dorm. All the RAs took shifts manning the front desk, so I checked the schedule to find out when he would be working. Before long, I had also figured out his breakfast and dinner routine in the dorm cafeteria. I would walk by the front desk during his shift or go grab fries in the cafeteria when I knew he'd be there. Sometimes I smiled and said hi, but mostly I'd just act nonchalant, as if I was minding my own business. I did this for an entire semester, but Kojo never asked me out. Girls weren't supposed to ask guys out, so I was frustrated. I'd have to step up my game.

When we returned from winter break, I was in the throes of another courtship—pledging my sorority, Delta Sigma Theta. Since I was an English major, I had volunteered to write the script for the Black History Month program that our chapter produced each year. It was the perfect opportunity to take Operation Kojo to new heights. As I envisioned it, the program would chronicle each decade of black history through songs and short scenes, and I intentionally curated the 1980s segment to include Kojo. The scene involved two young black men sitting at desks on the stage, writing letters about what was happening in their lives. As the spotlight shone on each one of them, the audience would hear a voice-over of what they were writing. One was a young man in Detroit. The other was in a village in Ghana.

As luck would have it, one of my pledge sisters was also an RA in my dorm, and she had Kojo's phone number. I told her I needed it to interview him for the scene. I wanted a firsthand account of what it was like to grow up in Ghana in the 1980s. Finally, a real conversation with Kojo! But after the interview, I hung up and realized it hadn't gotten me anywhere. I'd have to find a reason to talk to him again. So I called him back to ask if he'd be willing to play the role of the Ghanaian boy in the skit. "And do you think you could make the rehearsal next week?" He said yes!

He'd caught the bait at last, and all I had to do now was reel him in. I offered to pick him up from our dorm in my car, a 1988 white Ford Escort, and drive him to the rehearsal. I assumed he'd realize that since our dorm was in easy walking distance from the theater, the offer to pick him up was my way of telling him I was attracted to him. The night of the rehearsal, I wore my usual jeans and Spelman sweatshirt but decided to add a cowrie shell necklace that I was hoping would scream "I am your African queen!" Sure enough, after the rehearsal, in the lobby of the theater, Kojo looked down at my neck. I could tell it was the first time he had really noticed me. "Nice necklace," he said. "Do you have any plans tonight? Wanna go to Red Robin?" I smiled and exhaled.

I should note that when Kojo is asked how we met, this is not the story he tells. He says that we met at a seventies-themed Halloween party.

A few months before the sorority skit rehearsals, my new friend Toyia and I were invited to a Halloween party. Toyia said we were supposed to dress up in seventies gear, but I had nothing to wear. I found a flowery funkadelic dress at a secondhand store and asked one of my mom's old friends, a very fashionable woman who was like an aunt to me, if it would work for the party. She said the dress was cute but that it needed some alterations. She then proceeded to cut off the bottom half of the dress! Insisting that legs were popular in the seventies, she helped me find high-heeled platform shoes, neon-pink tights, hoop earrings, and an Afro wig to complete the look.

Outside of getting to know Toyia, who later became my sorority line sister and one of the most generous people I know, the whole night had been forgettable to me. I spent it in the corner, awkwardly trying to pull my dress down while everyone else was on the dance floor pulsating to Heavy D's "Got Me Waiting." But for Kojo, this party had been pivotal. When he noticed my cowrie necklace in the theater lobby, he suddenly realized I was the same hot seventies chick from the Halloween party. That's when he asked me out.

Years later, I now realize that my plan to lure Kojo into the sorority skit would not be the first time I'd spend enormous energy trying to get him to do something I wanted, only to later discover there would have been a faster route if I had been willing to compromise.

That first dinner at Red Robin set the tone for our future relationship. Kojo and I talked for hours over Banzai burgers and endless fries. We covered politics and current events, our families, the latest campus drama, and which movie was better—*Boyz n the Hood* or *Menace II Society*. He totally impressed me with his grasp of world history. As an English major, I'd wrongly assumed that an engineer wouldn't be interested in the humanities, but that wasn't true when it came to Kojo. We both led student organizations and had lobbied for change on campus through protests and staged events. Once, we blocked an interstate highway to bring attention to the fact that the university needed to hire a more diverse faculty. It wasn't long before we were seeing one another almost every day. Our relationship became the sum of our long, late-night conversations combined with our passionate campus activism. We dreamed each other's visions. He would eventually return to Ghana to help build the telecommunications infrastructure. I would be a social justice champion, probably teaching or working at a nonprofit.

Kojo referred to me as his friend, but as far as I was concerned, he was my boyfriend. I knew he agreed after our first summer. He landed an internship in Denver, and when I wasn't at my summer

job cashiering at Nordstrom, I spent every waking moment meticulously crocheting a blanket in the colors of his national flag. Every
loop was my way of letting Kojo know how much he mattered to me.
He was pleased when I surprised him with it upon his return. A few
weeks later, I noticed him packing the blanket when he was going
on a trip to see his parents. I knew that he was going to introduce
me to them by showing them the blanket. That made me very happy.

When Kojo asked me to marry him in the spring of 1997, just a
few weeks before graduation, a wry smile crept across my face. "I
thought we were just friends," I teased. "I think friendship's the best
way to start the rest of our lives," he answered seriously. As much as
I adored Kojo and wanted to spend my life with him, we were still
very young, so I didn't answer right away. Instead, I consulted the
women I eventually came to call my Sage Mentors—relatives and
other older, more experienced individuals whose opinions and advice I trusted. They all gave me some version of the same advice:
marry him now, but wait to have children. With that condition, I
ran back to tell Kojo yes, making it clear that we'd have children
when *I* was ready. He agreed easily. We loved each other. More importantly, we were confident we'd change the world together. I got
right to work designing our wedding invitation and embossed all 150
of them by hand.

After Kojo and I got married, we bought a cute little starter house
in Seattle and set about creating our domestic kingdom. Our biggest negotiation was over our first major furniture purchase, an $800
sectional couch from IKEA. Outside of our futons, everything we
owned as recent college graduates was small enough to fit inside suit-
cases or large duffel bags. For us, the sectional couch was a huge
investment. Kojo, always prudent about finances, kept insisting we
didn't have a lot of money, and it had taken some convincing on my
part just to get him on the IKEA showroom floor. I had my heart
set on light gray and hadn't considered the possibility that Kojo
would care one iota about the color of the couch. It was a poor assumption on my part, one I'd have to live with for nearly two decades. "We're interested in this couch in dark blue," my husband said

definitively as the associate was approaching. *No, we're not!* I thought to myself, quickly calculating my situation. I had spent my newly-wed capital convincing Kojo that we needed a new couch, but I'd neglected to negotiate the color in advance. *Damn! Now he thinks he's already given me everything I wanted.* The color was his, I decided. If I insisted on light gray at that point, it might jeopardize the entire purchase. I stayed silent, and two weeks later, the blue couch arrived.

As spouses, Kojo and I continued our long conversations about everything, usually while curled up together on that blue couch. We talked about our values, about the impact we wanted to have on our local and global community. We talked about our finances—conversations that got very tense when I insisted on having a separate bank account. When I was a little girl, I once overheard my mom and her friends pitying a woman at the church who was in a terrible marriage because she didn't have her own bank account. At least that's how my young mind interpreted the situation. I never wanted to be pitied, and I wanted control over the money I earned. Kojo reluctantly acquiesced. We talked about our careers, agreeing that he'd support me through graduate school first, and then I would support him through business school. We talked about the number of children we wanted to have—when I was ready; our children were still in the distant future. For all the time that Kojo and I spent talking, it's amazing to me now that we never talked about one fundamental aspect of our lives: who would do what at home.

For the first eight years of our marriage, our household responsibilities fell along traditional gender lines. It was like the default ringtone on our smartphones. It worked so well it never occurred to us to change it. I did most of the cooking, and when Kojo took over, it was largely to operate the grill. The only exception was that he regularly made a traditional tomato-based dish from West Africa called jollof rice. Like any good American woman who marries a Ghanaian, you learn to cook his traditional food. I had mastered Kojo's favorite, kelewele, which is ripe plantain sliced, spiced, and deep fried to golden delicacy. But I could never get the jollof quite right.

In the beginning, it bothered me—that he could cook it better—but over time, it became the one dish I loved for him to make.

The perfectionistic, controlling tendencies I developed when I was living with my father and sister remained strong in my early years as Kojo's wife. I scrubbed our kitchen floor on my hands and knees with a sponge because I thought a mop was insufficient. I dusted furniture and changed bed linens weekly. Even after I developed a deadly shellfish allergy, I still insisted on making Kojo's favorite seafood gumbo from scratch—wearing latex gloves to peel the shrimp—because I couldn't imagine him eating anyone else's but mine. Kojo mowed the lawn and made sure the oil in our car was regularly changed. I coordinated our social calendar. He coordinated the refinancing of our house and paid the bills. I used weekends to clip, test, and file Martha Stewart recipes. He used weekends to watch football.

I didn't think much about this arrangement. After all, I *enjoyed* cooking and baking and keeping an impeccable home. Professionally and publicly, I was an advocate for women's empowerment, but privately I was on Stepford wife autopilot. I would never have described myself as the queen of domesticity, but I had always assumed that women were just better equipped for it. I even took pride in it, as anyone who's ever tasted my potato salad could attest. Though you wouldn't have known from our household division of labor, I thought Kojo and I were a progressive and thoroughly modern couple.

One day in March 2003, I woke up to the first tick of my biological clock. It was my twenty-ninth birthday. I had completed my master's degree in English and was working as a fund-raiser for Seattle Girls' School, a new social venture aimed at empowering girls to be leaders and innovators. Kojo was a wireless communications engineer for Qwest, a major telecom company. I rolled over and woke him up for my announcement. "I'm ready to have a baby," I whispered. He had been so patient for the first six years of our marriage that I'd assumed I was the one holding up the timeline, so his response surprised me. "Not yet," he said. "I want to go to business school first."

I'd always known he wanted to get an M.B.A., so this made sense to me. That day he brought home *The Wall Street Journal*'s guide to top business schools. By the summer of 2004, we had rented our Seattle starter house and were packing up our Jetta for the cross-country trip to Boston, where Kojo had been accepted at the MIT Sloan School of Management. I wasn't thrilled with the move to Boston. I had grown up in the Pacific Northwest, and I loved my home. Only the seduction of Spelman had pulled me to Atlanta. But I had walked down the aisle with a man who was from another continent, so I'm not sure what had made me think we would be in Seattle forever. Remember, fairy tales don't address logistics.

Even though the move to Boston was, at first, emotionally difficult for me, it ended up being one of the best decisions of my life. I got a job as a fund-raiser at Simmons College, which turned out to be an important stepping-stone in my career. I was a big proponent of girls' and women's education, and raising major gifts was the next step to eventually becoming a director of development. I had my own portfolio of alumnae that covered Detroit, Chicago, Philadelphia, and their surrounding areas, and I traveled frequently, which was fine with me since Kojo was consumed with business school. I had all the resources I needed to be successful. On top of all this, Simmons was a wonderful community. I became an adviser to the Black Student Organization and adored the students and my colleagues. Some of them have been friends ever since.

Boston was also where I caught the political bug. One morning, I heard an NPR interview with Deval Patrick, an unlikely prospective candidate for Massachusetts governor. An African American, he had been raised by a single mother in very humble circumstances, and yet here he was, poised to make history. His message of opportunity for all people resonated with me, perhaps because he spoke with a sincerity and optimism I had seldom heard in politics. I remember being moved by a story he told about attending a private boarding school in Massachusetts. A letter had been sent home telling parents to have students bring a jacket with them to school. Deval arrived with a bomber jacket, thinking school administrators meant an outer layer to protect against the elements. But no, they had meant a dress jacket for the social occasions he would now be required to attend. It was one of the candidate's earliest insights into the cultural disconnect that must be bridged to bring about meaningful change. Deval seemed to truly believe that a few committed people working for the greater good could transform the world. It was electrifying.

A few days later, I was talking about the candidate with friends at a cocktail party. Deval's wife, Diane, happened to be at the same party, and she overheard my enthusiasm and invited me to introduce her husband at her upcoming Women for Deval Patrick launch event. Talk about being in the right room at the right time! I immediately said yes. I have always believed that when a person of influence asks you to step up, you accept, and you do your level best.

This was how I came to be standing before a packed room at Copley Plaza on November 17, 2005, introducing the man who would eventually become the next governor of Massachusetts. It was a huge honor, and I had never been so nervous in my life. But I knew that my anxiety in the moment was only one reason for the butterflies in my stomach. I was three months pregnant. My commitment to controlling things had extended into family planning. Our first child would be born just weeks before Kojo's business school graduation.

I began my maternity leave, and two weeks later, on April 28, 2006, our son arrived. He was breathtaking. In Ghanaian culture, the father names the child, and I agreed to honor this tradition. His first name would be Kofi, the name given to a boy born on a Friday. His middle name would be Abiam, Kojo's father's appellation. Like all new parents, Kojo and I settled into a blissful yet numbing routine of feedings, diaper changes, and intermittent naps. One morning, the question hit me: *How am I going to do my job at Simmons and take care of this baby?* My job required frequent travel to meet with potential donors, and I was nursing Kofi every few hours. I hadn't factored this new reality into my career plan.

Just as I began contemplating exactly how I'd work things out, Kojo got offered a job with a topflight investment bank in New York. As he shared the good news with me that evening, I experienced something new and strange: in my mind and heart, I knew I should be happy for Kojo and for us, but deeper, in the pit of my stomach, there was a rumble of jealousy—something I had never felt in the eleven years Kojo and I had known each other. It wasn't a good feeling. Though I wouldn't have been able to fully articulate it at the time, the feeling stemmed from how easy it seemed for Kojo to be making big career decisions; it felt like it was a given that I'd handle the details, let alone figure out how I'd do my job and care for our child. For the first time, I was confronting the reality that new parenthood might have very different kinds of impact on Kojo's and my careers. I tried to brush the feeling off, telling myself it was nothing and that Kojo's good news was good for all of us.

Feeling overwhelmed and sleep deprived, I told Kojo that we should go to New York. He should take the job. But secretly, I was heartbroken. Leaving Boston meant giving up two opportunities that I was sure would have taken me to the next level—my job as a major gifts officer at Simmons and my growing involvement with Deval Patrick's gubernatorial campaign. Moving to New York felt like a huge career setback for me, and yet I didn't see another choice. I didn't see how, with a newborn, I could go back to my old job with its extensive travel. Plus Kojo didn't have any job offers in Boston. Even though I knew the move to New York was the next right step in Kojo's career—and that it was what was best for our family at the time—that intellectual understanding still came with some emotional difficulty. It was as if Kojo and I had been running a 4×100 relay, gracefully passing the baton back and forth to each other until our son was born. Now, suddenly and without warning, there was a hurdle in my lane but none in Kojo's. His career path rolled out ahead of him free and clear.

It felt unfair.

CHAPTER 3

Working Mom

That summer after Kofi was born, I quit my job and arranged our move from Boston to New York, confident that I'd find something new in due time. In the meantime, life was rosy. I cleaned and cooked, decorated our new apartment in Harlem, sleep-trained and breast-fed Kofi, and got his genius on track through Baby Einstein CDs. All I needed to solve my working-mom dilemma was a caregiver I could trust and a position that didn't require a demanding travel schedule.

As I had anticipated, finding a job was not difficult. I had chosen to work in the nonprofit sector because I was committed to helping women and girls lead powerful, self-determined lives, and I knew that nonprofit fund-raisers would always be in high demand. Everyone has a great idea about how to make the world a better place, but few people know how to secure the money to make it happen. My former colleagues in Seattle and Boston generously made introductions to nonprofit leaders in New York, and after several meetings, I had my dream job offer as director of development at the White House Project.

I had always assumed that as a working mother, I'd take my baby to a day care, but I quickly learned that high-quality day cares in New York City were extremely expensive. The cost of hiring a private caregiver was reasonable in comparison, but that idea made me uncomfortable. In my worldview, only rich people had nannies. Since I still religiously planned my family's meals based on Fine Fare's weekly sale items, it took psychological adjustment for me to accept that I would be hiring another woman to care for my son in my home. Plus, who would I find that could nurture him the way I did?

I soon discovered that the world of mom LISTSERVs was chock-full of candidates. I quickly responded to one mom who posted a rave review of her nanny, Lucinda, whom she was only letting go because she had decided to stay home full-time. Lucinda made a nice first impression, but then the interview got bumpy. My heart gushed when she immediately took off her jeweled sandals and washed her hands when she walked through our apartment door. Her Barbadian lilt was soothing and infectious. But once we sat down on the blue couch and I put Kofi in my lap, it felt awkward. She kept answering my open-ended questions as if they were true or false.

"What are the things you feel uncomfortable with or prefer not to do?"

"Dogs."

And she took no interest in returning my smiles or peppiness. When she told me she had two children of her own, I was slightly surprised. She didn't feel like the kid-friendly type. Which is why I lied and told her that Kofi didn't take well to new people when she asked if she could hold him. I felt saved by the bell when our home phone rang and I had to excuse myself. Without thinking, I put Kofi on his bright-colored Fisher-Price play mat on the floor at Lucinda's feet, then walked away.

No sooner than I said hello did I realize that I had just left my baby with a perfect stranger. But by the time I turned to dash back and save him, I could hear the two of them squealing with delight.

In less time than it took me to walk ten feet and answer the phone, Lucinda had gotten down on the floor and started a coofest with Kofi. And they were beaming at each other! Sure enough, her references panned out: "Oh yeah, she's shy with adults . . . but she's a baby whisperer." In the end, I decided that the best caregiver for Kofi would be the one *he* had chemistry with. I offered Lucinda the job before Kojo ever met her.

Having accepted my job offer and having lined up Lucinda, I was on cloud nine. The way I saw it, I would just continue climbing the career ladder and simultaneously provide my son with everything he needed. I went off to my first day with such optimism. But after my exploding boobs disaster, things fell back down to earth. As I realized that night after my first day back at work, it became increasingly difficult to stay on top of things at home while I was working full-time. Lucinda handed Kofi off to me as soon as I walked in the door, and by the time I cooked, fed, bathed, played with, read to, and put him to bed, there wasn't enough time to do a full cycle of laundry. Or it would be too late to return my doctor's phone call. Our car was soon plastered with bright orange parking tickets because I'd forget to move it to the alternate side to accommodate the city's street-cleaning ordinance. On top of that, it was a serious adjustment for me to have a hard stop to every workday. I was used to working as long as I needed to get everything done. Now, I had to be sure to leave the office early enough to make it home in time to let Lucinda go by 6:00 P.M. I was constantly frustrated by the fact that I never seemed able to get done all that I needed and wanted to in a day at the office. I was used to always being prepared and being ahead. But with each passing day, I began to feel that I was losing an imaginary race. In the beginning, I simply did what I had always done to achieve results—work harder. I'd stay up late or wake up early to respond to e-mails or finish work tasks. I'd spend Sundays prepping all the dinners for the week ahead. I stopped exercising— who had the time? But as the weeks wore on, one thing became clear: if I was to be successful at work, my domestic reign would have to end. I had no time to figure out how, though. I was distracted by a new dynamic that was permeating my marriage, and it wasn't good.

———✦———

Kojo and I adored each other, and for most of our marriage, we would have been great candidates for *People*'s Happiest Couple of the Year award. We had struck a healthy balance between independence and togetherness. It wasn't unusual for us to vacation separately to connect with our different friends, but we wouldn't dare indulge in our weekly *24* television show addiction without being curled up next to each other on the blue couch. We relished our deeply intimate conversations and moments of playfulness in between.

Yet after Kofi was born, a new set of emotions began intruding on my relationship with my husband. Put bluntly, I was pissed off an inordinate amount of the time. Publicly, I would brag about what a wonderful husband and father Kojo was, but inside, I often found myself annoyed, and I couldn't articulate why. I tried valiantly to suppress my frustration, but it was always there, a stealth submarine of Kojo-focused hostility, ready to surface and fire an attack at any time.

Kojo might innocently inquire, "Hey, babe. Where's the pacifier?" and I'd fly off the handle. "Where's the pacifier?!" I'd spew back. "It's in the same place it *always* is!" Or while dusting, I would find he'd left a pile of receipts on our dresser, and I'd become so irritated with his pack-rat tendencies that I'd throw them away, even though I knew he had wanted to save them. One weekend, I sorted all the laundry and then put his back into the dirty hamper and only washed mine. When he complained on Monday morning that he didn't have any clean underwear, I commented sarcastically that his wife only had the time to do her own. Some of my behavior was downright mean, though I suspect he chalked most of it up to my sleep deprivation. He certainly had no clue about the real source of my passive aggression, and initially, neither did I.

In retrospect, the reason I was out of touch with my own emotions was because I felt conflicted having them. After all, Kojo's investment banking job demanded more face time than my gig at the nonprofit, and it paid more, too. Didn't his longer hours and bigger paycheck compensate for my additional hours at home? Didn't they give him the right to expect that I would wash his clothes? This line of thinking would calm me temporarily, but not for long. I'd overhear him give someone advice about how to make home-made baby food when he hadn't puréed a carrot in his life, and the stealth submarine would surface again; I'd shoot Kojo a pointed look of disgust.

Of course, the stealth submarine was pent-up resentment, and the reason I directed it so squarely at Kojo was because, from what I could see at the time, he had it much easier than I did. Both of us worked full-time outside the home, but inside the home, I worked harder. And, maddeningly, he seemed unaware of half the things I did to keep our household running smoothly. In other words, not only did he do less, he didn't appreciate that I did more.

To save money on grocery bills, Kojo and I usually bought our meat in bulk from Costco. For years, I assumed the laborious task of painstakingly cutting and seasoning meat portions, inserting them into dated bags, and arranging them in the freezer. Each Costco run required an additional hour at home just to prep and store the meat. Kojo and I never discussed this; I just naturally took on the task myself.

One Sunday I got an idea. Kojo and I went to Costco together, shopped, came home, unloaded the car, and then headed in separate directions. I immediately went into the kitchen to begin preparing the meat while Kojo headed to the blue couch to turn on his 49ers game. Shortly after my post-maternity-leave breakdown, I was feeling particularly overwhelmed, and as I was standing at the kitchen counter, sprinkling salt on the beefsteak, it hit me: *Kojo could do this*. In fact, our apartment was so small that he could easily stand at the kitchen counter in full view of the television. He could watch the game *and* prep the meat at the same time. Scooooooore! Everybody would win!

That's it, I thought. *I'm not doing this anymore. My meat prep days are done. Starting with our next Costco trip, this will be Kojo's job, and I'll get to sit on the couch.*

It was a great idea. The problem was, I never actually voiced it.

I'd had an epiphany, but it hadn't occurred to me to share it. Nor had I signaled through my behavior that I expected things to change. So, sure enough, the next time Kojo and I returned from Costco, he headed straight to the blue couch as usual. And I failed to communicate my needs. I took a passive approach. Instead of prepping the meat as I usually did, I left it in the refrigerator. My hope was that Kojo would see it and step up—that he would realize it was *his* job now. I'd done it for years without being asked, so why not him?

I might as well have been hoping for a windfall in the lottery without ever buying a ticket.

Over the next several days, I grew frustrated, then furious, as the beef turned from a bright red to a purplish brown, without Kojo even seeming to notice. I fantasized about him complaining about the rotting meat so that I could snap, "Well, why don't *you* do something about it?" But even after two days of a rancid-smelling refrigerator, he never said a word. I finally decided I couldn't take it any longer. I threw out all the meat in a fit of rage. I'd thought I could have my meat and get it prepped, too! Instead, two weeks' worth of dinners were in the garbage, and I was down in the dumps. The most infuriating part came later that evening when Kojo thanked me for putting the meat away in the freezer. It didn't even occur to him that I had thrown it away. "It was starting to smell bad, babe," he said. All I could do was stomp into our room and slam the door behind me.

There are many ways to ask for help with household responsibilities, but the key is that we *do* have to ask. My problem was that I had fallen into a trap of *imaginary delegation*. This is when we mentally assign our partners a task but never take the step of telling them. We assume that they will intuit our needs or that they'll naturally step forward if we hang back. In an interview published in *The Atlantic*, one woman noted that she didn't want to feel like she was micro-managing her husband, but she became frustrated when he failed to see a task through that she expected him to realize was his responsibility.[1]

But men aren't mind readers, nor are they wired like women. Research shows that, in general, men aren't as attuned to nonverbal cues.[2] If we don't clearly express that we want them to pick up the slack, they proceed with business as usual, while the metaphorical beefsteak turns brown. And we silently seethe—or angrily lash out—while our husbands wonder, "What's going on?" We wait for apologies that never come because our partners have no clue they've let us down.

According to a 2007 Pew Research poll, "sharing household chores" now ranks as the third most important factor to a successful marriage behind "faithfulness" and a "happy sexual relationship."[3] And in *Fast-Forward Family: Home, Work, and Relationships in Middle-Class America*, UCLA researchers uncover that it's common for women to feel resentment toward their husbands for their home management burden.[4] If Kojo's ability or willingness to share the burden of my to-do list at home was so crucial to my happiness, you'd think I'd just tell him what I needed or wanted him to do. But no, I continued to keep my frustration to myself. One day, Kojo made a joke about needing to go to the spa more than I did. The comment made me furious. I sent him the following e-mail:

Your comment about you needing to go to the spa more than me really bothered me. I tried to cover it up with my response that you "sit around" at work, but I really just should have said that my feelings were hurt. Even though my job doesn't require as much face time as yours, I do have enormous responsibility there and most nights continue working after I put Kofi to bed. More importantly, I bear most of the time-intensive responsibilities that keep our home functioning. THAT is the reason why you're able to work the schedule you do and still have a valuable family experience. Anyway, don't expect you to "get it" but you have always cherished my feel-ings so just wanted to share them with you.

When I hit Send on this e-mail, my expectation was that Kojo would read it, be stricken with guilt, and rush to my side with a long list of tasks he was going to take off my plate. I waited for it . . . waited for it . . . but Kojo never responded. Reading it now, I'm not surprised. After all, my e-mail manages to ask for absolutely noth-ing. To the contrary, my last line implies that my only goal in writ-ing was to share my feelings. I had even written that I "didn't expect him to get it." Kojo wasn't going to feel guilty about something we had both always taken for granted, that, as I wrote, "I bear most of the time-intensive responsibilities that keep our home functioning." If I expected those circumstances to change, I would have to learn to say so directly.

But for a long time, I couldn't. For months after I reentered the workforce as a new mom, I used imaginary delegation tactics like these to try to motivate my husband to do more at home. Kojo always seemed willing in theory, but things never worked out in practice. Either he wouldn't follow through on one of my imaginary delegation tasks, which exacerbated my resentment, or he would do it all "wrong," which reinforced my need to be controlling. Not surpris-ingly, for most of that first year after Kofi was born, I ended up doing the work myself anyway.

Kojo was working so hard at the bank that part of me felt badly for wanting him to do more. But I was working hard, too, and trying to perform what felt like two full-time jobs—one at the office and the other at home. I found myself appreciating Kojo one day and feeling exasperated by him the next. I'm sure he felt the same way about me, given my behavior that first year. One week, I'd cook dinner each night, and the next, I wouldn't cook anything. If Kojo dared to ask what we were going to eat, I'd rail at him about how I couldn't keep up with these things anymore. Then, when he made jollof rice, I'd be upset that he didn't serve vegetables. I could've earned a Ph.D. in passive aggression—and it wasn't getting me anywhere. Imaginary

delegation was just that—*imaginary*. I needed a concrete solution.
But I had no idea where to begin.

By our son's first birthday in April 2007, I was so filled with resentment toward Kojo that I found it increasingly difficult to suppress.
The sad part is that Kojo was, and has always been, my biggest
cheerleader. If I had been able to talk to him about my dissatisfaction
and the role he played in it, he would have likely responded with
sympathy and tried to fix it, even if he didn't fully understand. But
I never gave him the opportunity. Instead, I just kept lobbing passive-
aggressive grenades in his direction.

Finally, and as I often do when I feel I've reached a crossroads,
I sought the counsel of my Sage Mentors. One of them, a woman
who had been married for longer than I'd been on the planet, said
something I'll never forget: "Resentment is like drinking poison and
expecting the other person to die." Her comment forced me to ac-
knowledge why I had never spoken directly and thoughtfully about
my feelings to my husband: wallowing in resentment ensured that I'd
remain the uncelebrated martyr in my own story. But it was a dangerous game I was playing. The longer I allowed myself to accept a
story line in which Kojo was the bad guy, the more evidence I looked
for to support my case.

In the simplest terms, I was resentful because I was doing most
of the work at home. My situation was typical, even in an era when
70 percent of women with children work or are looking for work outside the home.[5] Studies show that 76 percent of wives who work
full-time are still doing the majority of the housework.[6] Even as
women are going to work in almost equal numbers as men and sharing all the responsibilities of busy professional lives, for the most
part, men aren't cooking dinner (only 39 percent compared to
65 percent women),[7] driving to soccer practice, scheduling home repairs, and paying bills (82 percent of women do this every day compared to 65 percent of men),[8] joining the PTA, or keeping tabs on
whether the kids have outgrown their shoes. In 2008, only 30 percent

of women reported that their partners took on as much or more responsibility for child care as they did.[9] Those things remain in the women's purview.

Because of my deep sense of responsibility as a woman, I kept trying to sublimate my feelings. To be openly resentful would fly in the face of expectations that "good women" serve and sacrifice. I couldn't recall my mother ever complaining about all the things she did for her family. But one has to look no further than the blogging world for examples of the closeted resentment women harbor because they feel obliged to captain the ship dutifully at home. Whether it's one woman who believes that her feelings of resentment might undermine her love for her family[10] or another who rails at the fact that she is unable to put in as many hours as her male coworkers at her law firm because of child-care duties, we can see that it is *obligation* that motivates women to keep these feelings under wraps.[11] Their most common lament: "It all falls on me."

The problem with repressing our resentment is the way it builds and curdles. Take Janelle, a chief diversity officer at an insurance company, who had been struggling with her anxiety and overall health, in large part due to personal and professional demands. I met her at a conference, where her intellectual rigor and accessibility had made her the most memorable participant in my session. Soon afterward, Janelle invited me to help her formulate a women's retention strategy at her company. A friendship blossomed.

Janelle was eager to ensure that her twin sons would get into a good kindergarten, and she was spending countless hours trying to navigate the New York school system. She had gained weight and admitted that although she was hyperaware of the food her sons ate, she wasn't nearly as responsible about her own diet. She was also under a lot of pressure to overhaul the firm's diversity initiatives after a new class of promoted executives included no women or people of color. When I asked her whether her spouse might be able to chip in a little bit more to help her manage, she looked at me like I was crazy and replied, "*That* spoiled fucker isn't lifting a finger."

Janelle's resentment toward her spouse had mutated into deep hostility. I asked what impact her feelings toward her husband were having on her marriage. "I feel like my resentment stands in the way of our intimacy," she confessed. Not only that, but her resentment was fueling a vicious cycle. "I don't want to be vulnerable with him or close to him," she reflected. "So I don't ask him for help. I just do more, which makes me even more stressed at work." And, not surprisingly, more resentful, too.

My own situation wasn't too dissimilar from Janelle's. It wasn't what Kojo *did* that made me resent him, it was more what he *didn't* do. For example, if we both received an Evite party invitation, he would never RSVP for us, even if it was from a couple we both knew. Or if we missed a UPS or FedEx package and they left a sticky note on our door, he would just leave it there, even if he came home before I did.

I also came to see that I was resentful not only for what Kojo wasn't doing but for what I felt I had to do. More than I hated doing the laundry, I hated the fact that I *had* to do it—that somehow, this household task, along with so many others, was on my plate even though I'd never signed up for it. And yet, I would feel guilty if I didn't get it done. Among working mothers, I had plenty of company. Indra Nooyi, the CEO of PepsiCo, is one of the most successful businesswomen in the world. But when asked about balancing work and family, she admitted, "I'm not sure [my daughters] will say that I've been a good mom. You have to cope. Because you die with guilt."[12] Guilt is defined as a feeling of remorse for having committed an offense or violated a moral law. In saying she feels like she has to cope with the guilt of not having been "a good mom," one of the world's most accomplished women is articulating an unspoken cultural truth: if women let their home lives suffer for the sake of their careers, they have effectively committed a moral transgression.

Guilt is a word I've heard countless times from women in the workforce, but it is only used when we feel like we're failing at home. We don't use the word *guilt* to describe how we feel when we're not thriving at work. Mediocrity at work can bring feelings of inadequacy and anxiety; we worry that we're not measuring up or fulfilling our potential, but rarely do we express those feelings as a sense of guilt. We want to excel at both our professional and home lives, but it's only when we fail in the latter that we feel we've committed a moral offense.

I resented Kojo's freedom from this sense of obligation. I resented that he had society's permission to put household and familial duties on the back burner, while I could not. If I missed Kofi's doctor appointment for being at the office, I was a bad mother, whereas if Kojo missed Kofi's doctor appointment, he was being a good and responsible provider. It just didn't seem fair. But then, neither did it seem fair to hold Kojo accountable for society's shortcomings.

I gained another insight about my resentment when I read Anna Fels's book *Necessary Dreams: Ambition in Women's Changing Lives*. Fels defines ambition as a desire to achieve mastery of one's craft combined with a desire to receive public recognition for it. I had always been ambitious: I was the little girl who was eager to demonstrate her knowledge, to raise her hand, to sit in the front of the class, to be on time, to be smart, to be seen. My proudest accomplishment was that at all my alma maters, from McCarver Elementary School to the University of Washington, there was a plaque with my name on it. I wanted credit.

What I discovered was that my resentment toward Kojo was in large part an expression of my frustration with the fact that my role at home wasn't fueling my ambition. No matter how hard I worked to develop my baby's language capabilities, redecorate our apartment, and scrub the grime off the bathroom tile, on Mother's Day, I was going to receive the same Hallmark card as the next busy woman. I had to admit to myself that I didn't enjoy this aspect of home management. No matter how good at it I was, no matter how fully I mastered the demands of the home front, I'd never be publicly recognized for it. As Anne-Marie Slaughter argues, our society doesn't value care the way it values competition.[13]

Now that I was finally facing the true source of my resentment toward Kojo, I knew I'd have to let go of the latent fear of what exposing it would say about me, about Kojo, and about our marriage.

One reason we women try so hard to suppress our resentments is that we like to believe that, as modern women, we have married modern men. No woman wants to think she married a man who is stuck in the cultural norms of the 1950s. But if our husbands seem to assume that household tasks default to us, it says less about the quality of our decision making and more about the fact that men are as susceptible as we are to social conditioning.

For Kojo, the impact of gendered stereotypes was particularly powerful because he grew up in a matriarchal society in Ghana. In his culture, children belong to the mother's clan, and women are the heads of their families. Kojo's mother, Irene, was a superwoman on steroids. At sixteen, she left her village and traveled alone on a ship to London for nursing school. It was there, years later, that she met Kojo's father, an engineer, and the two of them wed, but not before Irene had established her career as a nurse. Irene gave birth to her first child in her early thirties, which was late even for a Western woman in the mid-1960s. She had two more children before the family migrated home to Ghana.

Kojo, the fourth child, was born there in 1973. During the first part of Kojo's childhood, Irene ran the midwifery ward at the military hospital. She was later fired for providing IUDs to village women desperate for birth control. She turned from nursing to entrepreneurship, buying a small boat and hiring two fishermen. Over time, she grew her small business into a formidable commercial fishing company. Eventually, Kojo's father gave up his engineering job at Sanyo to run the family venture, but Irene was still engaged in the day-to-day activities of the business. She also ensured that her home ran like clockwork. Though she had help from extended family with manual labor, such as washing and cooking, it was still a heavy burden—yet Irene managed to maintain two full-time enterprises, one at her company and the other at home.

With such a strong and multifaceted woman for a mother, why would Kojo expect anything else from the woman he picked to marry? It's no wonder he never seemed to doubt that I could do it all. The real question was, why did I ever want to?

CHAPTER 4

Home Control Disease

Most modern women scoff at the idea that a woman's place is *in* the home. And yet, many women still focus obsessively *on* everything about it—how it's organized, how it's managed, and how the cooking, cleaning, and caretaking get done, right down to the smallest detail. Only one brand of detergent will do. Only organic, 1 percent milk. When it comes to our homes, many women feel a compulsive need to control, to make sure everything is managed in a particular way—our way.

I call this home control disease, or HCD, and I know it very well. Why? Because I suffered from an extreme case of it myself.

Here's a glimpse into it: During the summer of 2007, shortly after Kofi turned one, I had to travel for work the same week that Kojo had to fly to Seattle to handle some family business. Since I couldn't bring a baby along, we agreed that Kofi would go with Kojo. Great! Decision made. Then I proceeded to morph into the micromanaging mom from hell.

I should note that by our son's first birthday, his passport was stamped with four countries. Kofi had gone on many long-distance trips—just never without me. I couldn't imagine Kojo caring for him "properly" for three days on his own. For some reason, I assumed the tasks I handled so naturally would be utterly overwhelming for my husband.

First, I packed their bags, meticulously calculating how many diaper changes lay ahead, so I could include the precise number of wet wipes they would need. I did the same thing for Kofi's food, ensuring that they'd have just the right amount of applesauce and Cheerios for the six-hour flight. I even checked the weather to guarantee the appropriate layers of clothing. Then I typed up and printed two copies of the following "Top Ten Tips for Traveling with Kofi"—one for their checked-in luggage and one for their carry-on bag:

1. Change Kofi's diaper right before boarding in the airport family bathroom so that you only need to change him once on the plane, as the bathroom changing table on the plane is small and awkward to use.
2. During the flight, keep Kofi engaged quietly in your lap by offering him one toy at a time from his grab bag.
3. Once Kofi becomes sleepy and restless on the plane, allow him to fidget in your lap as necessary, but try to avoid allowing him to walk around the plane, as it will then be difficult to get him calm in your lap again.
4. Offer Kofi frequent snacks while traveling so that if he misses a meal, he won't get fussy on you.
5. Milk is fine, but avoid opening juice boxes on the plane since they get messy if he doesn't drink them.
6. Try to find a time each day that Kofi can take at least an hour-long nap. You will both be frustrated if he is overtired.
7. Don't forget to feed Kofi breakfast, lunch, and dinner! Don't use your own hunger to judge when it's time to

eat, as you can go for much longer than he can without food.

8. Remember that Kofi is on eastern standard time. Try to put him to bed as early as possible to compensate for this. Don't bother trying to switch him to Seattle's time zone.

9. Never intentionally wake Kofi when he is sleeping while traveling. His normal sleep schedule will be so disrupted he'll need all the shut-eye he can get.

10. Have fun! He's a really good kid and will self-soothe in almost any situation.

I'd called these my "Top Ten Tips," but they read more like my Ten Commandments—and they show how rigid I was in my views about the "right" way to care for our child. It would have been hard for Kojo to meet my strict standards and expectations, not just about how to travel with Kofi but, frankly, about *anything*. At the time, I'd thought I was being helpful. I thought my efforts made everyone's lives easier. But now I see in this list clear evidence of why I felt so overwhelmed: I was juggling so many balls myself because I didn't trust my husband to hold any of them. *"Don't forget to feed Kofi breakfast, lunch, and dinner"?* Why on earth did I need to tell my husband that?

This kind of behavior is characteristic of women with HCD. As Donald Unger, author of *Men Can: The Changing Image and Reality of Fatherhood in America,* notes, "Many women are emotionally split about what they want. Women have long been dissatisfied that men don't do their share in the domestic sphere. [But when men do take charge], there is often a sharp and reflexive: 'You're not doing that right!' "[1] In one survey, women were so worried their spouses wouldn't complete chores the way the women wanted them, they were more likely to delegate these tasks to their children.[2] At least we have hope that children can learn to do things the right way. Our fear that our spouses won't do things perfectly acts as fuel for our HCD and makes us even more stressed.

The best evidence of my insistence on control in my home was a document I called the Caregiver Log, a sheet of paper on which I requested that every person who took care of my son record the minutest details of his routine. I asked that the times he ate, peed, pooped, and slept be chronicled each day, as well as the volume of food going in and the volume of poop coming out. Our pediatrician had asked us to pay attention to these health indicators when Kofi was a newborn. My continuing obsession with my son's bodily fluids and solids an entire year later was merely evidence that my HCD had hit an all-time high.

Among many other things, the log detailed whether Kofi fed from my breast or the bottle. One day, one of our friends, a newly expecting father, noticed the log on our counter and asked, "If Kofi was nursing, how did you know that he'd ingested exactly four ounces?" To me, the answer was obvious. "I pump like clockwork," I responded. "I know exactly how much milk is in my boobs."

I also had expiration dates running in my head for all the cooked food in the refrigerator. I like fresh meals, which meant there was always a variety of leftovers in the fridge since I'd invariably want to cook something new. Let's say I'd made a meatloaf on Monday, fried chicken on Tuesday, and fajitas on Wednesday. But then, I had a work event on Thursday evening, leaving Kojo home alone. My expectation would be for him to finish the meatloaf *first*, since it had been in the fridge the longest. If I came home and Kojo had eaten the fried chicken and left the meatloaf, I would blow a gasket. "But I really *liked* the chicken," he'd say. To which I'd reply, "So you *don't* like my meatloaf?" He knew not to say anything after that.

Every household task, Kofi-related or otherwise, had to be handled just so. Clothes were folded and put away while still warm from the dryer. Dishes were always in the dishwasher or put away, never given time to rest in the kitchen sink or on the counter. The mail was always opened on the day it came. Junk mail was immediately recycled. Bills and invitations were relegated to their proper place to be dealt with in a timely fashion. Floors were cleaned, mopped, and vacuumed bright and early on Saturday mornings. All the hangers in the closet had to be facing the same direction. Wedding and baby gifts were purchased the minute I knew where the couple was registered. You couldn't call it macaroni and cheese unless it was made from scratch and oven-baked. And don't even get me started on Kofi's bath and bedtime ritual.

I admit that I was an extreme case, but even women who might not be as obsessive as I was about the tidiness and organization of their homes find that once they have a child, they're spending countless hours completing tasks they just don't feel comfortable delegating to their husbands. Whitney, a publishing professional and first-time mom, couldn't care less if the family's laundry stays in the dryer for a week or even if she has to eat dinner off a dirty dish, but she says her family never once left the house or arrived somewhere on time in their daughter's first year. "Why not?" I asked her.

"Well, my husband was always ready to go at the time we'd say we needed to leave, often he'd be sitting by the door with his shoes and coat on, waiting for me. But I was always rushing around packing my daughter's snacks and diapers or changing her outfit and hurrying to get myself ready."

"Why wouldn't your husband get your daughter dressed or pack her snacks?"

"I always had a certain outfit in mind that I'd want her to wear, and I guess I worried he wouldn't pack the right things."

"Doesn't he know what your daughter eats?"

"Of course he does. I guess I should have just let him help pack her up. I always just figured it would be done exactly the way I wanted it to be if I just did it myself."

As this conversation illustrates, most women find at least something that they, often irrationally, feel the need to control—even if that thing isn't a meticulous house or home-cooked meal.

At the time, I associated my HCD with my drive for achievement. I wanted things done perfectly because I aspired to be the best. Some years ago, I was discussing organizational strategy with one of my colleagues, Cindy. I was espousing one of my Tiffany doctrines: to achieve your mission, choose the strategy that you can

execute better than anyone else. "I want us to get crystal clear about
what we can be the best at, and do that," I told Cindy. I'll never forget her response. She said, "Tiffany, it's not everyone's goal to be the
best." I thought about what Cindy said for days but still couldn't make
sense of it. *What kind of person wouldn't want to be the best?*
The fact that I'm still pondering her comment hints at just how deep
my HCD went.

My drive to achieve morphed into a drive for perfection in all
other areas of my life. I wouldn't have been caught dead with chipped
nail polish or wrinkled clothes. Both were signs of sloth in my mind.
My bra and panties had to match, which resulted in countless early-
morning washes and leaving the house in damp underwear. Not only
was I always on time, I couldn't figure out how other people managed to be late. No one under my roof could have visibly dry skin.
Once, at a restaurant, I used the butter for the dinner rolls to get
the ash off of my son's face.

My version of HCD may have been extreme, but all our varying
levels of wanting to control things affects our lives. This truth was
recently depicted in an episode of the hit television sitcom *Black-ish*.
In the show, Rainbow Johnson is a doctor and mother of four who's
thrilled when her husband, Dre, agrees to handle the household
management for a week to give her a much-needed break. Not even
twenty-four hours pass before her HCD kicks in, causing Rainbow to
call the hospital frantically explaining she will be late to a surgery
because she has to deal with an emergency. Dre has gone grocery
shopping and has put all the food in the wrong places in the kitchen,
including a bag of potato chips in the refrigerator. Putting aside
the messages this episode seems to be sending about a man's ability
to effectively complete a household task—messages that implicitly or
explicitly keep women feeling responsible for those tasks—the show
reveals that perfection can be an addiction that results in unhealthy
behavior. Like the fictitious Rainbow, I had discovered that maintaining control of so many details was hard to manage alongside my
career. But how to let go? Power is hard to relinquish, even when it's
power you never asked to have.

Home control disease helps to explain why women who desire and would benefit from their spouses doing more at home often find it hard to actually let them do so. It's fueled in part by a reluctance to abdicate responsibility in the one place female authority is unquestioned. At home, women wield *enormous* power. In the United States, women control 73 percent of household spending.[3] This domination is a recent historical phenomenon, though. Prior to the Industrial Revolution, there was no distinction between public work beyond the home and private work within. Both men and women primarily lived and worked around the homestead.[4] The rise of men heading off to factories necessitated the rise of women's modern domesticity, since someone had to tend to the cooking, cleaning, and children. Now, nearly one hundred years of experience managing the home, tethered to the prevailing belief that women are ordained to do so, has made us bona fide experts. Our ways of doing things have been handed down from generations of women who came before and from the culture at large.

But how did we contract such severe cases of HCD in the first place? Let's start with being born with two X chromosomes. Marian Wright Edelman once said, "You can't be what you can't see." What little girls often see are baby dolls, Easy-Bake ovens, and tea sets. These popular toys ignite our imaginations about our future roles as caregivers, cooks, and hostesses and teach us how to perform them. In researching the development of children's gender identity, Carol Martin and Lisa Dinella found that stereotyped girls' toys encourage children to imitate behavior and learn rules. As girls play with dolls, for example, they get lots of practice mimicking their future caregiving role. On the other hand, stereotyped boys' toys, such as models, encourage children to problem solve, be self-confident and creative, and be independent learners.[5] Parents report purchasing gender-stereotyped toys for their children within months of their birth.[6] So girls' indoctrination to be future home managers begins long before the girl herself is begging her parents to buy the American Girl Bitty Baby in the pink aisle of the toy store.

Over the past thirty years, those aisles have gotten more pink and blue than ever before. In fact, any girl playing with toys from the 1980s until today, which includes most millennials, has received more gendered messaging than girls playing with toys between the 1920s and 1970s.[7] To understand why, I spoke with Elizabeth Sweet, a sociologist and lecturer at the University of California–Davis, whose current research focuses on gender development and children's toys. According to Dr. Sweet, the onset of video gaming in the 1980s meant competition for toy manufacturers, who then engineered gendered marketing segmentation strategies. Basically, if you made one toy but then created a separate boy and girl version, you could sell more of them. "Even though gender attitudes were making progress in the adult world, those advances weren't reflected in children's toys, which became more sexist and more stereotyped," Sweet explains.[8] The result? The gender-neutral brown wooden blocks of the 1930s have been replaced with LEGO's Deep Sea Operation Base for boys and Heartlake Food Market for girls. By playing with these toys, our boys are envisioning themselves exploring the sea, and our girls are imagining themselves selecting broccoli for two dollars a pound. What begins as play when we're children morphs into pressure by the time we're adult women, and the pressure has been mounting.

Martha Stewart is one of the preeminent enablers of HCD. The success of her media empire is driven by the pipe dreams of millions of women striving for homemaking perfection. The allure, also conveyed by bestselling books like *The Life-Changing Magic of Tidying Up* or magazines like *Cooking Light*, is that perfection can be fast and efficient. Once, when hosting a baby shower, I made meat-stuffed phyllo purses, deviled eggs, white chocolate–dipped strawberries, and lemon bars myself, all with "quick and easy" recipes. I spent half the day in the kitchen. I am now certain there is nothing quicker or easier than just ordering platters from your local grocery.

We worry that if things go wrong at home, it will mean we've failed as women, because society tells us that to *be* a successful woman, we need camera-ready kids and a spotless kitchen. At the same time, we're not supposed to openly admit that we feel our success as women is connected to our success at home. That would make us weak, or at least old-fashioned. And we are not weak or old-fashioned. We are empowered, modern women, right?

Take my friend Rebecca, a partner at a major consulting firm in San Francisco. She's a fierce 49ers fan, and on any given day, she and Kojo can be found duking it out over whether Steve Young or Joe Montana was the best quarterback of all time. She is also a powerful executive who manages multimillion-dollar accounts and prides herself on her work ethic, grit, and intuition about client needs. When she and I caught up over mojitos during one of my recent California trips, she appeared to be at the top of her game, but she was conflicted about whether or not she should accept a new role that she assumed would mean spending less time with her kids. When I remarked on how incredible her accomplishments were, seeing as fifty years ago the only job open to women in her field was secretary, she agreed and told me how proud she was to represent a new era. But when it came to her home, she didn't question that she was living in an old one.

That day in particular, she lamented that her kids were eating pizza for dinner while she and I were meeting. "I feel like a terrible mom," she admitted to me. I asked if the evening's dinner plans made her husband feel like a terrible dad. She laughed, "No! He's the one feeding them the pizza!" Mom was having a crisis of conscience over the meal plan, while Dad was speed-dialing Domino's.

Anxiety about our kids scarfing down a few slices isn't really about pizza at all. The real fear for mothers like Rebecca is that if they're not home cooking dinner themselves, it implies that they're not good moms. Being a good mom is the primary role to which women are told to aspire. And their fear of poor performance in that primary role stifles ambition in their role as professionals.

Thus, the pressures associated with a promotion may seem unacceptably high—especially if they coincide with increased demands on the home front. No wonder, then, that a 2013 study from the Pew Research Center "found that mothers are much more likely than fathers to have reduced work hours, take a significant amount of time off, quit a job or, by a small margin, turn down a promotion in order to care for a child or family member."[9] These women know it's nearly impossible to operate at full steam at work and at home. In 2012, researchers Melissa Williams and Serena Chen found that women's power over household decisions reduces the amount of power we're interested in achieving in the workplace.[10] Who would be motivated to run a multimillion-dollar company when she's too exhausted from running her own house? One of the most damaging effects of HCD is that it stunts our career pursuits.

Felicia is a fourth-generation educator who runs a teachers' training program in Minneapolis. When I contacted her by phone to request an interview for this book, she joked that her mother, who was raised on Native American tribal lands, was disappointed with how Felicia manages her home. "I'm so not one with the earth," she quipped. Six times a year, Felicia travels out of state to share her award-winning training model with other school districts. She has built a reputation as a talented and passionate leader who can motivate faculty, administrators, and students alike. But she feels she doesn't have the bandwidth to expand her program any farther. She says she's too busy employing her skills to motivate her six-year-old twin boys and eleven-year-old daughter. When I visited her family's white three-bedroom rambler two months after our phone call, I was most impressed with her sticker incentive program: her kids earn rewards for independently completing household chores and homework and for behavior that reinforces their family's values. I had tried sticker incentives in my own home and failed miserably, so I was fascinated by Felicia's success. The day I was there, her daughter received a sticker for thoughtfully entertaining her younger brothers so that Felicia could meet with me, uninterrupted.

Felicia runs a tight ship, based on a philosophy of regimen and routine. She is convinced that the more everyone in the house knows exactly what to expect, the smoother life under her roof will be, which means the less stressed out she'll feel. She has instituted rules and routines for nearly every aspect of her family's life. There were prescribed steps for meals, for chores, for homework, for entertainment, for bath, and for bedtime. The routine for entering the house is to remove one's shoes, place them in the closet, hang one's coat, and then go to the bathroom and wash hands (this last one was familiar to me; we have it in our house, too). Every item has its place. Every action has its sequence. I suspect Felicia has rules for making new rules. Order is the name of her game.

Whenever Felicia travels, her husband, Ron, a postal worker, pitches in more than usual. When Felicia and I first met, she was preparing for a trip the next day and had already written out extensive instructions. Her bullet points began thus:

- Ryan and Jason have field trip tomorrow. Their lunches are in fridge. Don't forget to put lunches in backpacks.
- There is a new dog walker. Name is Jessie. She'll grab keys from neighbors.
- Casserole in the freezer for dinner. Enough for two nights. Takeout is fine on third night but NO pizza.

I didn't need to read any further. I had written countless lists just like this. I understood the impulse to direct from afar. But I was also learning to spot HCD. Keeping a tight grip on structures and systems is a coping mechanism for beleaguered women. We may have too many things on our plates—but at least we know where everything belongs! If everything *looks* like it is under control, then we can tell ourselves that it is. Never mind that all that energy we put into micromanaging is slowly driving us crazy.

Two days into Felicia's trip, I checked in with Ron. I commented that it must be great to have a wife as organized and prescient as his. Felicia clearly felt it was her responsibility to equip her husband to manage in her absence. She also clearly assumed that her guidance was accomplishing just that. But when I asked Ron, "Do you need all this?" the response he gave might have surprised her.

"Not really," he told me. "She leaves instructions because she wants things done a certain way." And what would have happened if Felicia had left without providing her detailed checklists? "Everything would have worked out," Ron assured me.

I pressed him for specifics: "So you would have packed the lunches? How would you have known about the field trip?"

Ron didn't miss a beat. "A school isn't going to let a child go hungry. Someone would've noticed the boys didn't have lunch. They would have called me. I would have figured out a way to get them some food. No biggie."

If opposites attract, it was no wonder that Felicia and Ron had found one another. He was as cool as a cucumber as he described a scenario that, from what I had witnessed, would have been Felicia's biggest nightmare. Then, he added the real zinger: "The boys would've been fine, but Felicia would've killed me."

———————

As challenging as it is for women to let go at home because of the way we've been socialized, it's doubly hard because we're also creatures of habit. Neuroscientists have conducted studies showing that humans are hardwired to choose the path of least resistance when completing tasks, even when performing on autopilot does not best serve a particular situation.[11] Add to this scientific reality the social reality that women have historically been left out of the public sphere but assigned power in the private, and our compulsion to control our domestic spaces is a no-brainer.[12]

The need to maintain home control at all costs can make it difficult for women to ask for help. I call this the Lone Ranger syndrome, and I've seen its negative effects.

At work, the Lone Ranger syndrome comes from women's faith in a false meritocracy. In school, we are largely rewarded based on our academic performance. We put our heads down, work hard, and achieve great results. Our education is largely a solo endeavor, and individual hard work and persistence pay off. The outcome is a 4.0 grade point average. When we graduate from college and enter the workplace, we employ the same strategy, but it's not as effective in our new environment. I was once coaching a millennial who was distraught at having been passed over for promotion that had gone to a male colleague. "It's not fair," she complained. "I'm the one who pulls all-nighters for clients while he's playing golf with our boss, yet he's the one who gets promoted." Our Lone Ranger syndrome causes us to focus more on our output and less on cultivating the relationships that are just as critical to our career advancement. We go it alone, expecting to be recognized based on our own merits, without asking the right stakeholders to advocate for us.

At home, the Lone Ranger syndrome comes from women's faith in a false efficiency. We believe that whatever we can do better and faster we should just do ourselves. The problem is that we believe we can do everything better and faster, so everything ends up on our list. We can't possibly get it all done, but we still burn ourselves out trying. Because many women have internalized the idea that we should be self-reliant in home-related activities while our husbands act as the breadwinners, asking for help feels like weakness or failure to embody our raison d'être.[13]

In all fairness to women, when we have a lot on our plates, delegating tasks just feels like more work. So we soldier through. But this impulse mutates into a dangerous habit, one that holds us back and keeps us down in other areas of our lives, especially at work. Our domestic to-do lists will never end, and unless we become willing to let something go, we'll never be able to free ourselves from the whirling, twirling madness that I call the life-go-round.

CHAPTER 5

—◆—

Life-Go-Round

In late 2007, as the autumn leaves began to fall, my world really began to spin. I had been a full-time working mom for over a year. On the outside, I pretended to be living my do-it-all fairy tale. I imagined myself as an empowered Alicia Keys–style Superwoman, complete with the S on my chest, leaping back and forth from work to home in a single bound. But on the inside, there were many days where I could barely manage taking one step. I was losing weight, and not in a good way. Plus I felt tired all the time. I wasn't sleepy so much as I was in a state of chronic exhaustion. Kojo was doing well at the bank, and his job was requiring more travel, so he was unavailable to help me out at home (or so I thought). But even when he was home, my general feeling was that he was useless, so it was just better to do it all myself.

One restless night after an insane working-mom day, I called Kojo at 3:00 A.M. I was in New York, but he was in London on business, so I knew he'd be awake. When he asked why I wasn't asleep,

I explained that I couldn't get my list out of my head—the endless tally of all my to-dos, which I couldn't stop running through mentally. Much to my chagrin, Kojo began to laugh. He suggested that if I couldn't sleep because of my list, I should just go and read the Allison Pearson novel *I Don't Know How She Does It*. He had given it to me as a gift months earlier, after I confessed to him that I had fallen asleep during a meeting at work. He knew I loved books. At the time, I had forced a smile and given him a hug to express my gratitude. But I couldn't help thinking, *I can't believe he thinks I have time to read this*. I added it to the stack of books on my nightstand that I aspired to get to. Each night I'd glance at the cover before my head hit the pillow and repeat the title as my punch line to another day.

I thought his idea of reading the book now was ridiculous. Clearly, if I was going to get out of bed at 3:00 A.M., it would be to start checking some tasks off that interminable list, right? But in that moment of exhaustion, something told me to listen to my husband. I made myself a cup of tea, then sat down at the kitchen table and cracked the spine.

In the popular novel, later turned into a movie starring Sarah Jessica Parker, Kate Reddy is a full-time hedge fund manager and powerhouse mom trying to balance work and home. In one scene, she's lying in bed in the middle of the night, mentally shuffling through her "Must Remember" list:

- Adjust work-life balance for a healthier happier existence.
- Get up an hour earlier to maximize time available.
- Spend more time with your children . . .
- Don't take Richard for granted.
- Entertain more, Sunday lunch & so on.
- Relaxing hobby??
- Learn Italian . . .
- Stop canceling stress-busting treatments.
- Start a present drawer like a proper, organized mother.
- Attempt to be size 10. Personal trainer?
- Call friends, hope they remember you.

- Ginseng, oily fish, no wheat.
- Sex?
- New dishwasher.[1]

A bit too familiar, I thought. And I wouldn't have considered it fodder for comedy. But as I continued to read, I started laughing, and a lightbulb clicked in my mind: my struggles were commonplace—so much so that a book satirizing my dilemma had become a national bestseller.

I am hardly the first and far from the only woman to have felt the crushing pressure of simultaneous work and family obligations. Even as the number of married mothers in the labor force has soared from 17 percent in 1948 to more than 70 percent today,[2] the distribution of duties at home has failed to keep pace. Women spend a disproportionate amount of their energy on activities for which they are neither compensated nor publicly recognized, but which take up a great deal of time. In one of my sustainable leadership workshops, I coach women through an exercise where I ask them to write down everything they expect to accomplish in the next twenty-four-hour period. And I mean *every little thing*: working out (or lying in bed thinking about working out), making breakfast, nailing a pitch, prepping to nail the pitch, buying mousetraps, reviewing résumés for a new position, finding a babysitter for Saturday night, packing for a trip, stopping by the bank, getting dressed, applying makeup, deciding what to wear, scheduling parent-teacher conferences—everything until the list is exhausted and they really can't think of anything else. I then instruct them to do the math: calculate the amount of time it should take to complete each item on the list, then add up the total. I have yet to meet a woman who could realistically complete the tasks on her list in fewer than twenty-four hours, and only half the women I meet ever include getting a good night's sleep on their list. The point of the exercise is to show that just making lists and trying to get everything on them completed is not a winning strategy. Trying to do it all guarantees only one result: burnout.

My own to-do list was a prime example. I'd write mine out in the evening to prepare for the next day, and in the fall of 2007, it looked something like this: pick up dry cleaning, iron outfit, put oxtails in Crock-Pot, send thank-you note to last week's dinner party host, chuck expired medicine from bathroom cabinet, take out recycling, review grant proposal, draft holiday appeal, plan Thanksgiving menu, find someone to recaulk tub, call Trinity back. But reality looked very different. Here's how the day would actually go: After getting Kofi up and feeding him breakfast, I'd have just enough time to shake out a dress I'd hope no one would notice was wrinkled and throw the oxtails and some seasoning into the Crock-Pot. I'd end up taking care of the things that were right in front of me and had immediate consequences. Like if I didn't put the oxtails in the Crock-Pot, we wouldn't have dinner that night, and if I didn't pick up the dry cleaning, Kojo wouldn't have a shirt the next day. I might get the phone call to Trinity checked off, but that's only if she called me and I answered my phone. I'd review the grant proposal because someone on my team was waiting for it and there was a deadline. But everything else would be waiting for me when I woke up the next day, along with anything else I needed to add. This is why my to-do list was never ending.

The vast majority of working mothers embark on a similar daily struggle to fulfill their dual responsibilities. Most have no other choice. They are balancing the demands of a full-time career outside the home with the demands of being a full-time boss inside the home. They are sleep deprived because they wake up early and go to bed late.[3] They are stressed because there aren't enough hours in a day to check off all the items on their to-do lists. Their well-being is in jeopardy because the last thing they have time for is working out. And they feel guilty, mostly because they wish they could be more present for their kids. Only 10 percent of mothers who work full-time give themselves the highest ranking for parenting.[4]

Life for these women is a constant merry-go-round—swirling and relentless. As hard as they try, as much as they do, they always feel inadequate. In a 2012 survey commissioned by *Real Simple* magazine and designed by the nonprofit Families and Work Institute, 32 percent of women responded that they often feel that if they did less around the house, they wouldn't be taking care of it properly. During their free time, the majority of these women reported doing tasks such as laundry (79 percent), cleaning (75 percent), cooking (70 percent), and organizing or decluttering (62 percent) because they were stressed about everything that needed to get done.[5] Finding a true balance between work and family seems impossible; we're always worried we're falling short on one front or the other. We feel stuck on a life-go-round that is both dizzying and unsustainable.

The life-go-round is pushing women over the edge. In 2014, researchers at Penn State found that women who juggle work and home were proportionately much more likely to experience higher levels of the stress hormone cortisol than were men.[6] As researchers interviewed the women, they kept hearing about how the end of a workday entailed a return to a whole other demanding job that was waiting for them to complete once they got home.[7]

As a result, women's happiness is declining at rates far greater than that of men's. A National Bureau for Economic Research study suggests that this decrease in women's perceived life satisfaction may reflect "aggregating over their multiple domains," or dual responsibilities in the public and private spheres.[8] But there is worse news: those who report work-family conflicts are more likely to suffer from allergies, migraines, fatigue, mood disorders, anxiety, dependence on drugs or alcohol, hypertension, and cardiovascular and gastrointestinal problems.[9] Similarly, a 2012 study from Harvard and Yale found that women with "high job strain were thirty-eight percent more likely" to experience cardiovascular disease than their peers and to exhibit an increased tendency for smoking, physical inactivity, and diabetes.[10]

Trying to meet impossible expectations will only continue to harm our physical and psychological well-being. Models of working motherhood success—like YouTube's CEO Susan Wojcicki, who's had a successful career while raising five children—and the hard work of professional women's leadership organizations have helped women to see what they can achieve in the workplace, but old cultural norms die hard. The examples we see in our homes, communities, and the media have simultaneously communicated to women that their assuming more responsibility at work does not mitigate their obligations at home. We now have a generation of women who believe that, while they can strive to be anything they want to be, they are still the primary managers of their families and homes. This expectation is a setup for feelings of failure, stress, and guilt. And these feelings come with dangerous health effects. The status quo within our families simply cannot be sustained.

In the fall of 2007, with Kojo working and traveling like crazy and my own career going at full speed, I'd often facetiously announce to my colleagues at the end of a long day, "Bye, guys! I'm off to work now!" I was referring of course to the "second shift" that was waiting for me at home.[11] I tossed it off lightly as if it were a joke, but underneath, the familiar stealth submarine of resentment threatened to surface at any moment. I'd rush home to open the mail, make the rice and veggies to go with the stew, scarf it down while I was feeding Kofi, then start his bedtime ritual. Before Kojo even walked in the door, I'd get agitated in anticipation of the moment when he'd come home, put his hands around my waist, and ask me to fry his kelewele. Then he'd head straight for the blue couch. Fortunately, something else was slowly starting to reveal itself to me: if I couldn't be the perfect worker, wife, mother, and citizen that society demanded of me—and that I, in turn, had demanded of myself—then Kojo would have to pick up the slack.

It wasn't my idea. I was too stressed to originate new solutions to my own problems. It was my college friend Sasha who prompted my lightbulb moment. Sasha was single and without kids, and I still hadn't gotten around to telling her that the worst time to call me

was at 7:30 P.M. on a weeknight. I was loath to be the kind of working mom who didn't have time for her old girlfriends. When her
name appeared on my cell phone at 7:38 one evening, I sighed and
answered. I put Sasha on speakerphone, then took off Kofi's bib and
threw him on my hip so I could carry him and my phone into the
bathroom. Sasha was yelling over the sound of the running bathwater.

"Congratulations, girlfriend!"

"For what?" I was genuinely baffled.

"For being the six-figure woman."

A big smile swept across my face. The week before, I had secured
the largest donation from an individual in my career as a nonprofit
fund-raiser: $125,000. I was so excited about the milestone I had
stayed up for Kojo to get home so I could tell him all about it. He was
the only person I had told, so he obviously spilled the beans. Who
else had he told? Pursed lips replaced my smile. I could feel the
agitation in my throat.

"Did Kojo e-mail you?"

Sasha picked up on the irritation in my voice.

"Well, someone has to. We wouldn't have known if it wasn't for
Kojo. He's like your personal PR agency. All of us appreciate it even
if you don't."

The same person whom I had cast as the villain in my story was
being heralded as a hero in someone else's. That bothered me, and
I became defensive. I dug my heels in and quipped with disgust, "I
can think of the things I need, and a PR agency isn't one of them.
What I would *appreciate* is me not having to do everything around
here."

As soon as I uttered these words, I wanted to hit rewind. For the
first time, my stealth resentment had bled past Kojo. I was firing an
attack on Sasha, who had only called to congratulate me. I immediately felt terrible. Even worse, it wasn't enough for me to believe that
Kojo had done something wrong. For the first time, I was requesting
that someone else conspire with me and affirm that Kojo was the Big
Bad Wolf in my story. Even though I wished I could have taken my
words back, I was confident our girl friendship code required Sa-

sha to take my side. She was supposed to say something like, "He's *still* working those crazy hours? I don't know how you deal with it." Then she was supposed to listen to me complain. Fortunately, Sasha was such a good friend that she refused to take the bait. She knew that I would never speak ill of Kojo unless something was seriously wrong. She was quiet for a moment as my words floated atop the Johnson & Johnson baby wash bubbles. Then she spoke her truth as only a real friend can do:

"Tiffany, I don't know what's going on with you, but I know that Kojo is your biggest fan. If you're overwhelmed, why don't you ask him for help? I know that's not your thing . . . asking for help . . . but it sounds like you need it."

Ouch.

"I have to go" was all I could muster. I was angry with Sasha for saying that to me, but in my heart, I knew she was right.

I couldn't afford to make my spouse the enemy. *I needed his help at home.* It felt like an epiphany—a burst of insight so obvious I was stunned I hadn't thought of it long before. My only hope was to expect less from myself and more from him.

The inspiration to release my resentment toward Kojo once and for all came from an unexpected source—my infatuation with the Obamas. Back then, Barack and Michelle were in the early throes of his first presidential run. Even though I was a Hillary supporter, I admired the Obamas' power, beauty, and adoration of one another. What I most respected was their mutual commitment to improving the lives of others. Their teamwork reminded me that when Kojo and I got married, we'd pledged to change the world together.

To my mind, the Obamas were the perfect role models for our marriage, so I was surprised to read in Barack Obama's book *The Audacity of Hope* that Michelle had struggled with the same resentment I was experiencing. Barack wrote, "[T]he fact was that when children showed up, it was Michelle and not I who was expected to make the necessary adjustments. Sure, I helped, but it was always on my terms, on my schedule." Later he continued, "Michelle's anger toward me seemed barely contained."[12] If a power couple like the Obamas wasn't immune to the strain that meeting society's gender expectations can have on a marriage, certainly Kojo and I could begin to confront our issues.

Except the resentment wasn't *our* issue. It was mine.

I decided that I would play a game with myself to help me manage my resentment. Every time the stealth submarine rose to the surface inside me, preparing for an attack, I would picture Michelle and Barack. For me, their union represented the campaign's promise: hope. Over time, my resentment began to recede as I accepted that the root cause of my unhappiness was not a lazy or irresponsible husband but the expectations I had set for myself. It didn't help that I had never actually spoken aloud my desire to renegotiate the gender roles Kojo and I had reflexively fallen into at the start of our marriage. The ball, I realized, was squarely in my court. And not just in my court but still clutched tightly in my working-mom hands. Managing my resentment was a step in the right direction, but to really turn the ship around, I would have to find a way to let that ball go.

PART TWO

Something's Gotta Give

CHAPTER 6

The Turning Point

In January 2008, I received terrible news that would turn out to be an opportunity for learning how to ask for help in a more effective way. My first clue that something was wrong should have been when Kojo walked through our apartment door at 7:00 P.M. on a Thursday night. He was rarely home before 10:00 P.M. My girlfriend Laura had just buzzed our door as well. She was in New York on business, and I had intended to make dinner for us after I put Kofi to bed.

When Kojo realized our plan, he offered to stay home with Kofi so that Laura and I could go out for dinner instead. "That way you don't have to cook," he said. I was too giddy about my surprise night out with my girlfriend—a precious, rare occurrence for a busy working mother—to wonder why Kojo was home early or why he was volunteering to take care of Kofi. But it all fell into place when I got back and found Kojo in his usual spot on the blue couch, with the television *off*. Instinctively, I curled up next to him and rested my head on his shoulder. It was then he told me they'd shut down the division of his bank. He wouldn't be going back the next day. He'd have to find a new job.

In the months that followed, the entire investment banking industry would collapse, taking our short-term life plans down with them. No longer would we be using Kojo's bonuses to pay off his business school loans, buy a home in New York, or start Kofi's college fund. I was already overwhelmed with trying to be successful at work and managing everything at home; now, I was also the primary breadwinner. I felt more pressure than ever before, and an even greater urgency to redefine my value as a worker, wife, and mother. I knew I couldn't do it all alone.

I thought Kojo's layoff might be an opportune time for us to renegotiate our division of labor at home, but initially things seemed to get worse. I felt bad for Kojo; he had worked extremely hard to transition his career from engineering to banking, and it had turned out to be terrible timing. My sympathy for his situation led me to keep doing the same amount of work at home, giving him time to come to terms with what had happened. I assumed that once his shock and anger cleared, he'd begin to take on more of the housework since his schedule was suddenly more flexible and I was now earning the lion's share of our income. This assumption was misguided.

In explaining the gender gap in household labor, many scholars have proposed an "economistic" hypothesis, arguing that the spouse who makes more money will have the power to get the other person to do more housework.[1] The primary reason why women do more housework, they say, is because men spend more time outside the home earning money and therefore have less time to wash dishes. After all, the marital contract is based on an exchange of income for domestic labor, right? Wrong. As I personally discovered, and as Veronica Jaris Tichenor argues in her book *Earning More and Getting Less,* this economistic theory does not hold out for women. In fact, even in couples where the wife earns more, she still does more housework than her husband.[2] In *The New York Times* reporting of how unemployed people spend their time, 55 percent of women spend most of their time on housework or caring for others while only 23 percent of men do so.[3] Culture and social conditioning has a more powerful influence in our homes than money. I would have to go through more dramatic lengths than earning a paycheck to achieve a different division of household labor.

A little more than a month after Kojo's layoff, the Cleveland Cavaliers were playing the New York Knicks. It was a solid matchup and the star of the night was LeBron James, who the week before had become the youngest player to score 10,000 points in an NBA career. To say that it was an exciting game would be an understatement. But right before halftime, there was a blowout. Not on the court—in our apartment.

That night I had walked home from the train feeling particularly stressed. In order for the White House Project to meet our yearly fund-raising goal, we needed to produce a phenomenal EPIC (Enhancing Perceptions in Culture) Awards, our annual gala that honored innovators who brought positive images of women's leadership to the American public. The previous year's gala had been a smashing success. In 2007, we'd presented Billie Jean King with a Lifetime Achievement Award and honored Liberian activist Leymah Gbowee, who would later win the Nobel Peace Prize. *Glamour* magazine had also won an award for its journalism and publishing, and designer Diane von Furstenburg was among the many notables. Standing under a ninety-four-foot model of a female blue whale at the American Museum of Natural History, PepsiCo's president and CEO, Indra Nooyi, had delivered the keynote remarks on the theme "Add Women, Change History," helping us raise more than $1 million. The 2008 EPIC Awards were scheduled for April 17, just six weeks away, and we were only at 50 percent of our fund-raising goal. As the White House Project's director of development, I had a lot of work to do.

I was walking up the steps to our building, my mind on my to-do list for work, when a violent, piercing cry interrupted my swirling thoughts. It was Kofi. I raced inside, frantically shoving my keys into the two sets of locks. I followed my toddler son's wails to our bathroom, where I found Lucinda cleaning Kofi's nose with a nasal aspirator. Kofi hated that thing, and he was screaming bloody murder to prove it. My heart was still pounding when I turned and noticed Kojo, just sitting there relaxed on the blue couch, completely engrossed in the stupid basketball game. Our son was crying his heart out, and Kojo hadn't even flinched. I called his name, but he was so glued to the TV screen that he didn't pick up on the tone of my voice. I called his name again, and this time he heard me. He turned his head, flashed a smile, and said enthusiastically, "Hey, babe! What's for dinner?"

That's when it happened. That tingling sensation of resentment came rushing through me, forcing its way up to my chest. I inhaled and exhaled deeply to calm myself, but I couldn't contain it. No amount of thinking about Barack and Michelle Obama would help this time. I was experiencing full-blown rage. My fingers curled slowly into clenched fists, and I screamed at the top of my lungs, *"You tell me!"*

There would have been a long dramatic silence except for the roaring crowd of fans and the shot clock jingle emanating from the surround sound. Lucinda scurried past me and put Kofi on Kojo's lap, then ran out of our apartment door with a faint good-bye. I had no idea she could move that quickly.

Both my husband and my almost two-year-old son were just sitting on the couch staring at me. I turned and threw my keys down on the counter, stomping past the Caregiver Log I normally checked religiously, and stormed into our bedroom. I slammed the door behind me and fell onto our bed in tears.

I had yelled at my husband.

For many wives this would be nothing, but for me it was monumental. I had never raised my voice at Kojo. My parents yelled all the time, and they got divorced. Long, long ago—before I had even met Kojo—I had vowed to myself that I'd never be a yeller. Screaming at anyone just is not my style. In fact, my refusal to raise my voice had even become a running joke. Back in our college days,

Kojo and I were once in a heated disagreement (over something we now can't even recall). At the height of our argument, I turned to Kojo and said slowly and coolly, "I think this is a turning point in our relationship." I was going for intimidating and badass when I said it, but Kojo started cracking up. "Is that all you've got?" he managed to get out in between his howls of laughter. I started laughing, too. Ever since then, whenever our disagreements escalated, all one of us would have to do is deliver that line, and the tension would immediately be disarmed. We would both start chuckling.

How had we gone from that to this awful moment?

When I woke up the next morning with swollen eyes, there was a pot of jollof rice on the stove and a Post-it note on the bathroom mirror that read, "This is a turning point."

That day, I felt guilty, hopeless, and uncomfortable—a pulsating headache had twisted down into my shoulders. I knew I should apologize, but my ego wouldn't cooperate. I could feel the pain of the point, but I hadn't yet gotten to the turn. On any previous day, I would have wished that Kojo would get himself out of bed to help me feed Kofi breakfast, get him dressed, and load the Crock-Pot. That morning, I wished desperately that he would remain asleep so that I wouldn't have to summon the words I didn't yet know how to express.

After handing Kofi off to Lucinda, I realized I needed to make a quick outfit change into a cocktail dress and jacket. There was a product launch party for a corporate donor that night, and I'd have to show my face. On my way out of our bedroom after changing, I could hear Kojo's voice. *We should talk later.* I kept moving. I knew my headache would not be cured by a few Advils and one of our talks. We'd need a bigger intervention. Over the next several days, I intentionally avoided bringing up that night. Eventually, time passed, and we never talked about it.

A couple of weeks later I went to Margaret Crenshaw, one of my Sage Mentors, for guidance. "You look awful, hon," she said after I hugged her in the Starbucks where we were meeting. Margaret had retired from a major corporation before hanging her own shingle as a business consultant. She had mentored me during my early days in Seattle and happened to be in New York to see one of her clients. I knew the universe was working in my favor when I reached out to her for advice and she immediately wrote back telling me she was going to be in town. Normally, I would have prepared a set of polished questions to maximize our time together, but on this occasion, all I could do was throw up my feelings all over her between caramel macchiatos.

I explained what was happening at home and how my life-go-round was causing me to alienate the one person who was most in my corner. I knew I needed Kojo's help, but I didn't know how to get it. Up until this point in my life, I'd done a pretty good job of getting whatever I wanted. I'd had a plan for everything, but I didn't have a plan for this. I was so uncharacteristically not together. Margaret confirmed this with her response. "You're all over the place, Tiffany," she said gently. "You've got to slow down and prioritize. You can't do everything. What do you really want?"

Over the next several weeks, I had similar conversations with women who had been around the block more times than I had, and they all repeated some variation of the same theme: get clear about what matters most to you, and the rest will fall into place. I knew what I wanted to fall into place between Kojo and me. I wanted to be able to delegate tasks that were essential to the smooth functioning of our home—and frankly to my own well-being—not with a pinched anxiety that Kojo would never do them right, but with confidence, ease, and ultimately, joy.

But in order to ask for help in a meaningful way, my Sage Mentors told me, I'd have to get clear on what I was requesting of myself *first*.

CHAPTER 7

What Matters Most

I've never been the kind of person that feels the need to reinvent the wheel, so when my Sage Mentors suggested that I seek clarity about what matters most to me, I immediately went off in search of people who I thought had already done it. Books rarely fail me, so I read plenty of them. They included Louise Hay's *You Can Heal Your Life*, *Cooking with Grease* by Donna Brazile, and *The Alchemist* by Paulo Coelho. As I devoured these books, it became increasingly clear to me that my problem wasn't that I was burned out due to exhaustion, stress, or a piled-up list of to-dos. In fact, psychologist Dr. Ayala Malach Pines argues that the root cause of burnout is not that we have too much to do, it's the feeling that the things we do aren't meaningful or don't reflect who we really are.[1]

In *How Remarkable Women Lead*, Joanna Barsh writes about the critical role that meaning plays in the success of women. She explains that those who understand the larger context of what is important to them are more positively motivated at work and less stressed.[2] A recent *Harvard Business Review* study agrees, citing emotional and spiritual needs as key influences on people's engagement and productivity in the workplace.[3] My quest to identify my own overarching purpose involved plenty of self-help books and coaching sessions, but the most pivotal insights came from two simple exercises that anyone can do with little time and no money.

The first was a funeral visualization Stephen Covey made popular in his book *The 7 Habits of Highly Effective People.*[4] I imagined three people—a family member or good friend, a community member, and a work colleague—getting up to eulogize me. I visualized their testimonies about the person I was and the things for which I stood. I imagined them saying things like, "She was a true champion for women and girls," "She believed in me, and she inspired me to believe in myself," and "She understood the power of stories and used them to empower others." And from Kofi: "She was a good mom because she didn't confuse her journey and mine. She guided me but didn't try to live *through* me." I pictured their celebration of my life moving everyone to tears. It felt cheesy as I did it, but boy did it help make my future direction more apparent. I was inspired to live up to these imagined testaments.

The second exercise involved asking a varied group of people, "Tell me about a time when you experienced me at my best." This Reflected Best Self Exercise was developed by researchers at the University of Michigan.[5] I solicited stories from people who knew me at different stages of my life and in different contexts. I adapted the original exercise a bit and printed them all, then circled the words and phrases that kept coming up: *passion, an evangelist, authentic, a powerful voice, determined to win, driven, an old soul*. This second exercise gave me a good window into the strengths and qualities I possessed that had the greatest impact on others.

Although I had struggled in my relationship with my mom during my teen years and young adulthood, by the time Kofi was born, I had reached a level of acceptance with our relationship. Maybe we weren't as close as some of my friends were with their mothers, but I knew my mom could share some stories with me that might be especially helpful as I was trying to get clear on who I really was and what really motivated me. And I was right. When I asked my mom to recall a time when she experienced me at my best, I had thought she would point to an achievement, like when I won Girl of the Year in middle school. Instead, she wrote back, "That day you hit Marcus over the head with a hammer." It was the first time she had mentioned that day since it happened when I was eleven. In retrospect, it was one of the most important days of my life, because it was the day I learned to trust my own voice.

That summer afternoon, I was playing with a group of boys on my block. We were taking turns throwing rocks over the fence into the neighbors' pool. I was wearing a dress, and when the boys hoisted me up to see over the fence, I felt Marcus's hand between my legs. I screamed at the boys to put me down. As fast as my jelly sandals could touch the brown grass, I ran to my father's shed, grabbed the first tool I saw, and swung it as hard as I could. Unfortunately, Marcus didn't duck fast enough, and the hammer swiped the top of his head. Tears were streaming down my face as I ran into my house, past my mom, who was standing at the kitchen sink, and into my room, where I slammed the door. I had never been so angry in my entire eleven years.

The gravity of my actions began to weigh on me minutes later when I heard Marcus's mom yelling at mine at our front door. She was demanding that I come out and apologize. The louder she yelled, the smaller my confidence became. My rage turned into guilt. I feared that I had made a terrible mistake, and the voice of doubt began to taunt me: *You could have really hurt him. What were you thinking? Why did you let them lift you up with a dress on? This was your fault. You're gonna get into big trouble. You're a bad girl.*

I was balled up on my bedroom floor in terror, but then a miracle happened. My mother politely but firmly told Marcus's mom that I was not coming to apologize. "I hope that whatever he did to my daughter he doesn't do to another girl," my mother said calmly. "As far as I'm concerned, Tiffany did him a favor. She is not apologizing." Then she closed the front door and went back into the kitchen.

That was the day I learned that my first instinct was the right one. I learned to trust my inner voice. I learned to stand up for myself. But somehow in the intervening twenty-odd years, I had lost touch with that fierce little girl. I'd grown accustomed to listening to and prioritizing the voices of others instead of prioritizing my own. My mom's recalling of that incident was like my own voice calling out to me from the past, urging me to reclaim my own agenda, my own values—*my life*. Not only had I gained clarity on what mattered most to me, I had learned the importance of valuing what was important to me. Before that, I prioritized what I thought was important to others. I had been loyal to sacrifice as a virtue, even at my own expense.

When I combined the results of the funeral visualization and the Reflected Best Self Exercises, I was left with two considerations I never factored into my day-to-day decision making. The first was my legacy, the imprint I wanted to leave on the planet. The second was my innate gift, particularly my ability to move others. I then added a third consideration: how I wanted to spend my time. When I contemplated all three considerations together—my legacy, my gifts, and my time—what mattered most to me transformed from a distant mirage to a vivid painting. I envisioned a world in which Kojo and I were learning and growing from one another and fully supporting each other in our pursuits, where my son was in touch with his humanity and respected the humanity of others, and where women's talents and voices are fully harnessed for the benefit of all of us.

Although it took me several weeks to do the exercises and reflect on my findings, in the end, they helped me to become crystal clear about what mattered most to me: loving Kojo, raising a conscious global citizen, and advancing women and girls.

Not too long ago, Melanie, a former work colleague who now lives in Chicago, reached out to me for guidance about how she could juggle the new demands that had accompanied a recent promotion. We agreed to hop on Skype. Three years previously, she had made a career transition to retail management, and now, for the first time, she was responsible for her own store. Melanie was a single mom raising an active thirteen-year-old son, Justin, and her mom was battling lung cancer. Melanie learned of her mother's diagnosis before accepting the promotion, and it had been a tough decision. By increasing her responsibility at the store, she would have less time to be a caregiver for her son and mom, yet the increased salary would provide more stability for her family. "I'm already overstretched," she confessed, "but how could I turn down an opportunity like this?" I knew we had to work quickly to come up with a plan before Melanie set herself up for complete burnout. She knew it, too.

When I asked Melanie, "What matters most to you?" she quickly rattled off one-word answers: *Justin, Momma, God, career.* "Of course," I responded. "All those things are important. Let's dig deeper, though. Let me ask you this: What do you *hope for* in relationship to Justin, your mom, God, and your career?" This was a harder question for Melanie to rattle off an answer to. Figuring out what matters most to us is usually not work that can be done over one Skype call.

I suggested to Melanie that over the next several weeks she engage in two exercises, one internal that would give a microphone to her own voice, and the other external, where she'd gather inputs from others, similar to what I had done. To figure out what the internal exercise should be, I asked Melanie to talk about times in her life when she had an aha moment. As she was speaking I noticed a pattern. Many of Melanie's aha moments were related to dreams. She often had vivid dreams and at different points in her life had gotten into the practice of writing them down. That was it! For twenty-one days, Melanie would make sure there was a journal and pen on her nightstand so that she could record her dreams as soon as she woke up. For Melanie's external exercise, she would ask people to share with her the first thing that came to their minds when they thought of her—a word, story, or image that captured the experience they've had with her. I was scheduled to fly to Chicago for a conference so our next meeting would be in person.

One month later, I was sitting across from Melanie in her favorite pizza joint, gooey strings of cheese stretched between my lips and fingers as she rehashed her journey. She had done quite a bit of what-matters-most searching. Reading her dream journal had helped her to discover that she had made many of her past decisions based on fear. As a result, she had unnecessarily closed herself off to wonderful opportunities. She no longer wanted that for herself or for Justin. In reviewing the words, stories, and images from her family and friends about their experiences with her, Melanie noticed that a lot of people appreciated her loyalty and reliability. After a few cups of tea and some wordsmithing, Melanie was confident about what mattered most to her: cultivating fearlessness in Justin, honoring her mother, modeling what it means to "show up," and being open to the voice of God.

I know several people—men and women—who have gone through a process of clarifying and articulating what matters most to them. One of my Levo team members, Maxie, uprooted herself for two months while she sojourned in Bali. Maxie uncovered that what mattered most to her was inspiring others. One of my friends, Josh, spent weeks meditating and asking people to offer reflections on his photography portfolio before getting clear about what mattered most to him: nurturing his daughter's vision for her life and serving as a lens to the soul.

Very few people can clearly and confidently articulate what matters most to them, and it's not because they don't know in their hearts. It's because it's hard to decipher meaning amid all the noise. Some of that noise is imposed upon us: all the cultural messages telling us what *should* matter to us. But it's critical that we take the time and space to discover what *does* matter most for ourselves.

As I got to thinking about what the future would look like for Kojo and me, I saw that the two of us had generally been very clear on what mattered to us as a unit. Early in our marriage, we developed four questions that we asked ourselves to help guide our decision making. The questions weren't written down anywhere, but they had always steered us whenever we arrived at a crossroads, helping us achieve clarity about the direction we wanted our lives to take. Unfortunately, as my life-go-round had ramped up after the birth of our son, this useful tool became a little rusty.

Kojo and I had first made up the four questions on a car ride back in March 1998. Puff Daddy's single "Can't Nobody Hold Me Down" was oozing from the radio, and we were still newlyweds filled with hope and optimism for the future. There was a lot of celebration in the Ghanaian community that day, as it was the country's Independence Day. Kojo and I were returning home from a party and were talking about the perseverance of Kwame Nkrumah, Ghana's first president, who led the liberation movement. Nkrumah once said, "Those who would judge us merely by the heights we have achieved would do well to remember the depths from which we started." Kojo and I were conscious of our families' humble beginnings. His father was born in a tiny village in Ghana and had raised his school fees by selling bread on the side of the road. My father was one of eleven children born into a housing project in Watts, Los Angeles. Though we were raised in different parts of the world, we were instilled with the same values: to recognize the humanity in others, to create our own reality, and that there is no substitute for discipline and hard work. We were also taught that we have a responsibility to make a meaningful impact in our communities. It sounds syrupy and idealistic now, but Kojo and I were truly convinced our union represented diaspora Africa, uniting to advance our people. We knew "the depths from which we started." What was the height we were responsible for achieving, especially given everything our parents had accomplished? We grappled with this question as headlights approached us from the rear, then raced around us on the dark highway.

During Nkrumah's independence speech in 1957, which I was reading aloud from the back of the kelly-green celebration program as Kojo drove, he implored the nation, "We must change our attitudes and our minds. We must realize that from now on we are no longer a colonial but free and independent people."[6] For Kojo and me, this meant that instead of waiting for life to happen to us or for someone to tell us what to do, our marriage would be its own blueprint. I suggested to Kojo that we should create a bigger set of goals for ourselves. Kojo had a different idea.

"No, not goals," he said emphatically. "That's too much pressure. We don't know enough about what will happen in the future."

"So, like, a plan?" I weighed in. "We should create some sort of map?"

"No, we don't know enough for that either. We just need something to help us when times get hard or we're confused or things don't go like we thought they would."

"Okay, well, that's why I like getting advice from other people. Other people always help me figure stuff out."

Kojo was quiet for a moment. I could hear his brain churning.

"Yeah, you're good at that," he concluded. "Why do you find other people so helpful?"

"Because they ask me lots of questions. It makes me think about the situation differently."

"Okay, then it should be a set of questions," Kojo decided. "Let's come up with questions that will guide us."

Not long after I completed the exercises that helped me get clear on what mattered most to me, I started thinking about that car ride so many years ago. I was reading a book called *The Nonprofit Strategy Revolution,* which advocated implementing a strategy screen—a set of criteria that an organization could use to judge if a particular strategy aligned with its identity.[7] In a rapidly changing world, nonprofits need a tool for quick and calculated decision making. The core idea is that a problem-solving strategy should reflect an organization's mission while leveraging its competitive advantage. Each nonprofit has to work collectively with stakeholders to determine the unique set of criteria that will keep them on track.

The Nonprofit Strategy Revolution completely changed my mind-set about how to lead an organization. Unexpectedly, it also illuminated why my earlier partnership with Kojo had been so effective. Before I learned about strategy screens, I thought Kojo and I were a successful couple because we worked hard, had parents who instilled good values in us, and made an earnest effort to be the best people we were capable of being every day. Despite life's setbacks, each of us had grown personally and professionally, and we'd evolved as a unit. We would often thank one another, our families, and the universe for our good fortune. I'm embarrassed to admit that deep down inside I actually thought we were *special*.

My introduction to strategy screens hit me like a ton of bricks—Kojo and I weren't special at all. During that long car ride, we had simply developed a strategy screen, or as I call it now, a Couple's Compass.

Whenever we had a tough decision to make, we'd ask ourselves if the course of action we were considering was aligned with our four questions:

1. Will this advance women and/or sub-Saharan Africa?
2. Is this true to the values our parents instilled in us?
3. Will this put us on a path to financial freedom?
4. Will our descendants be proud of us?

If we could both answer yes to all four questions, then we committed to move forward with that decision, no matter what challenges or sacrifices either of us would have to face. This meant that sometimes we ended up in strenuous situations, like the year Kofi was born, when we decided to move from Boston to New York. My career had been on the verge of taking flight when we agreed to interrupt it, but I took comfort in the fact that Kojo's new job at the investment bank would prepare him to advance the interests of sub-Saharan Africa and put us on a path to financial freedom. We both knew I would soon find a new job, but in the meantime, taking care of our infant son while setting up a new home base for our family was certainly true to the values our parents had instilled. And yes, our descendants would be proud, because we were consistently on track with making a difference to each other and to the world.

I quickly realized that knocking the rust off our Couple's Compass was going to be critical to figuring out how to work better together at home. My life-go-round had become so demanding that I'd become mired in the trees of day-to-day stresses and couldn't always see the forest. I was so busy worrying about the bill I was fighting with our health insurance company, or planning a vacation that never seemed to materialize, that I forgot the end game: leaving a legacy. I knew that if I continued to run myself into the ground, losing sight of our family's larger purpose, Kojo and I would never be able to create a legacy for those who followed us. The Couple's Compass would help us to keep the forest in view, reminding us what mattered most to us as teammates. Once we were both clear on that, everything else was negotiable—who picks up the dry cleaning, who stays home to meet the plumber, who does the meat prep after the Costco runs.

But here's the thing. It is possible for two partners to have a Couple's Compass as an overriding strategy for their decision making, but for each person to be murky about what matters most to them as individuals. It was why my Sage Mentors had counseled me to marry Kojo but to wait to have children. They had enough life experience to know how easily executive women can lose track of what matters most to them, and they wanted me to have more runway without the responsibility of kids to explore my highest calling for myself. Guided by our Couple's Compass, for years Kojo and I had managed well in our joint decision making. Now, for the first time, I achieved clarity about what was most meaningful both professionally and personally to *me*.

CHAPTER 8

---+---

The Law of
Comparative Advantage

I now had clarity about what mattered most to me: loving Kojo, raising conscious global citizens, and advancing women and girls. And Kojo and I reignited our Couple's Compass to tackle life's biggest challenges. We had everything, right? Wrong. I still had to figure out what fairy tales don't ever address: logistics. I had a very long list of things that needed to get done, and I still didn't know how to meaningfully motivate Kojo to pitch in. I was tempted to use his layoff as a springboard, to suggest that since he now had more time during the day, he could help with more things at home. But I was concerned that while that might solve my problem in the short term, as soon as he got a new gig he would just hand everything back over to me; then I'd be right back where I started.

My breakthrough came a few weeks later when I attended a course led by Jerry Hauser at the Management Center in Washington, D.C. The Management Center helps to educate social justice leaders on how to build and run more effective organizations so that they can fully achieve their vision and objectives. I had been sent by my boss to bolster my management skills.

During the course segment on time management, Jerry emphasized the importance of focusing our attention on the areas where we bring the most *value* as managers, instead of on the areas where we might be better than others because of experience alone. For example, as a seasoned nonprofit fund-raiser, I might be better than my staff at drafting annual fund letters, but I brought the most value in face-to-face meetings pitching major donors. No one else on my team could do that. If what mattered most to me was raising money, then my highest and best use was out of the office connecting with people one-on-one. Similarly, if what mattered most to me as a mother was raising conscious global citizens, why was I stressing over organizing Kofi's summer clothes? My highest and best use was reading him a book each night. It was Economics 101—the law of comparative advantage.[1] Put simply, just because you're better at doing something doesn't mean you doing it is the most productive use of your time. It was a lightbulb moment for me.

Sitting there in that training class at the Management Center, a life lesson was dawning on me that far superseded business practices. *What you do is less important than the difference you make.* I could spend my entire life checking off items on my to-do list, and in the end, it would make very little difference. I didn't want my epitaph to read, "She got a lot of stuff done." Instead, I had to figure out how I, and I alone, could make a difference—and this was as true for my homelife as it was for my professional one. Where could I be most useful in order to achieve the things that mattered most? Up until this point, I had always approached my household management by drawing up a huge list of every task that needed to be completed—resole shoes, design photo wall, make a doctor's appointment—and then I would set about systematically trying to check off the boxes. Occasionally I'd delegate, asking Kojo to call the doctor or Lucinda to drop off the shoes, but my HCD made following through on delegation hard because I didn't trust anyone else to match my standards. The only way to avoid a longer doctor's office wait was to secure the first appointment of the day, and the soles had to be rubber. Would Kojo and Lucinda get it right?

Suddenly, sitting in that management course, I realized I had been going about this the wrong way. I had things backward. I should be looking at my list with an eye to the obligations I *couldn't* delegate. Leveraging our highest and best use means employing what we're good at and focusing on the tasks *only we ourselves can do* in order to realize our greatest goals and priorities. If what matters most to me as a parent is raising a conscious global citizen, for example, I am not making myself most useful by scheduling Kofi's dentist appointments. It *is* my highest and best use, however, to frequently talk to him. As a toddler, he won't fully understand everything I'm saying, but it makes a difference if I start the practice now. As he grows older, it's important for me to help him understand his experiences and develop healthy strategies for responding to them that reflect our family values of responsibility, grit, and empathy.

The most powerful outcome of the comparative advantage approach was that it shrank my to-do list dramatically.

Prior to my comparative advantage realization, my to-do list looked like this: *grocery run, schedule preschool tours, pick up dry cleaning, call Uncle Kenny re: surgery, order Lisa's shower gift, marinate chicken, review Seattle flooring estimate, get Kofi umbrella stroller.* All these tasks had to be fit into my day, on top of ten hours at the office and whatever was on my professional to-do list.

Here's what happened to my list when I put each item to the comparative advantage test, asking myself if I was working toward my highest and best use by doing the task in question:

Grocery run: No. I could love Kojo, raise conscious global citizens, and advance women and girls without going grocery shopping.

Schedule preschool tours: No. The environment where Kofi will spend nearly nine hours a day, five days a week will definitely shape him. To raise a conscious global citizen, I definitely need to attend the tours, but I guess someone else could schedule them.

Pick up dry cleaning: No.

Call Uncle Kenny re: surgery: Yes, I need to do this one. It's meaningful for my uncle to hear his niece's voice checking in on him. I want Kofi to know how important family is. Maintaining this relationship is critical. Plus, delegating this task to someone else would be callous.

Order Lisa's shower gift: No. I'll be at the shower. It doesn't matter how the gift arrives at her apartment.

Marinate chicken: No. I'm using a new recipe anyway that anyone can follow.

Review Seattle flooring estimate: No.

Get Kofi umbrella stroller: No.

Out of the eight items on my original to-do list, only one of them was critical for me to complete myself in order to accomplish what mattered most to me. Only one represented my highest and best use. To be clear, the other tasks on the to-do list still needed to be attended to, and I wasn't sure how they would all get done. What was different was my perspective: now I was certain I would not be the one to do them all. Instead of eight things I absolutely had to accomplish to be a good worker, wife, and mom, there was now only one task for me to accomplish and seven that someone else could do. For the queen of domesticity with a bad case of HCD, this change in thinking was revolutionary!

All women have a list of responsibilities they feel they need to fulfill—and too often, our sense of identity is wrapped up in doing them ourselves. As a result, many women try to curate their lives in a way that enables them to get as many things checked off their lists as possible. Maybe they consider working part-time, going into business for themselves, or staying in middle management to avoid additional work demands so that they can keep up with the domestic ones.

The beauty of the comparative advantage approach is that it helps women shorten those lists and keep their eyes and energies focused on what really matters most to them. After that management training course, I decided that there were only three things that absolutely had to be on my to-do list as a mom: carry and birth children, breast-feed them for one year, and engage them in meaningful conversations. (Later, I would add "make scones on weekends" to this list, after my family made a well-negotiated pitch.) Were there other things that needed to happen in order for my home to function? Sure. But from then on, these three were the only tasks I'd feel guilty about if I fell short. For everything else, I could Drop the Ball.

In her recent book *Unfinished Business*, Anne-Marie Slaughter reframes the work-life debate from a tension between women and the workplace to a tension between competition and care in America. Slaughter argues that our core social problem is that we place a premium on competition, as success is largely defined by who wins rather than on care, which is just as important and necessary as a human endeavor. Slaughter is right. If our society valued the work of caregiving—of washing, cooking, organizing, child-rearing, elder care—as much as we valued breadwinning, everyone would benefit. But until our society catches up with Slaughter's vision, what is a woman burned out from the responsibility of breadwinning *and* caregiving supposed to do?

The answer is that she needs to redefine what caregiving means for her and her family. She will have to reject society's unrealistic expectation that she perform breadwinning and caregiving *flawlessly*. She will have to Drop the Ball. That is what the comparative advantage approach can help her to do.

Some of the responsibilities women take on as caregiving duties are not required in order for us to meet our objectives. Take, for example, involvement with a child's school. It is a widely held belief that a parent who volunteers at a child's school or who helps a child with homework is supporting the academic well-being of the child. If ensuring a child's academic achievement matters most to us, we would naturally assume these responsibilities. But the research of Keith Robinson and Angel Harris, authors of *The Broken Compass: Parental Involvement with Children's Education*, proves otherwise.[2] In an article in *The New York Times*, Robinson and Harris write that "most forms of parental involvement, like observing a child's class, contacting a school about a child's behavior, helping to decide a child's high school courses, or helping a child with homework, do not improve student achievement."[3] According to Robinson and Harris, there are three parental activities that have the most influence on our children's success at school: advocating for your children to have specific teachers, talking with your children about the activities they participate in at school, and aspiring for them to attend college. There's nothing wrong with remaining on the school auction committee. But doing so is not our highest and best use if what matters most to us is the academic success of our children.

Getting clear about how we can apply our highest and best use toward achieving what matters most to us allows women to redefine expectations. It helps us to create a filter for our caregiving role. Once we know what *we* need to focus on in order to be successful, we are better positioned to determine what *other people* need to do to better support us. With my newfound clarity about my purpose, and about what constituted my highest and best use, I realized my passive-aggressive approach to getting Kojo to contribute at home was ineffective for both of us.

I was now ready for the next step—asking others to pitch in. The remaining items on my old to-do list fell into three basic categories. First were the tasks I could now laugh about having put on the list in the first place, such as "Marinate chicken." *That chicken will have to be stir-fried with whatever seasoning I throw on it when I get home.*

Second were things that still needed to get done but that I'd have to outsource creatively, like the grocery run, Kofi's new umbrella stroller, scheduling preschool tours, and ordering Lisa's shower gift.

The grocery run and Kofi's stroller I assigned to Lucinda. I had always emphasized that her primary job was to care for Kofi, but before I went back to work, I took care of him full-time and did grocery runs and errands during the middle of the day, and he seemed to do just fine. If I could multitask, so could she. Cross them off the list!

Next up was scheduling the preschool tours. I decided to enlist my neighbor Lynette. She had a toddler the same age as mine; in fact, she was the one who had reminded me to sign up for tours, suggesting we attend them together. I'd ask Lynette to RSVP for me, too, when she went online to register herself.

Then there was Lisa's shower gift. I realized I could just ping my friend Veronica. She was attending the shower, too, and was willing to order a gift on my behalf when she ordered hers. I'd pay her back at the shower.

Finally, I was down to the last category: the tasks for which I'd need Kojo's support. That would be picking up the dry cleaning and reviewing the flooring estimate for our Seattle house. And this time, I was ready to delegate them in a meaningful—not imaginary—way.

This was an important conversation worthy of special attention. I let Kojo know that I had some things on my mind that I wanted to share with him. I scheduled time in advance that would not conflict with any sporting events—or anything else he might have planned. I took a page from Dr. Phil, whose *O* magazine columns offer advice for handling difficult conversations, and I drafted and rehearsed what I wanted to say when I curled up next to him on the blue couch. To fully signal the importance of the conversation, I asked Kojo that the television be off.

This is what I said:

Babe, I've been really overwhelmed lately. I owe you a long-overdue apology for the night I yelled at you. I was very stressed that night, and I'm tired of feeling this way. So I've been doing a lot of thinking about what matters most to me and how I'm spending my time in relation to what I care about. After doing a bunch of exercises, I'm clear that what matters most to me is loving you, helping Kofi to grow into a conscious global citizen, and advancing women and girls. The thing is, I feel like every day I'm spending a lot of my time on little things that don't really amount to my making a big difference in these areas. You have always supported me and pushed me to fulfill my potential, so I wanted to ask you for help. I wrote out the list of some of these things, and I want to know if you can help me with two of them. They'll seem really small to you. In fact, when I tell you what they are, you'll probably wonder why I scheduled time instead of just sending an e-mail. But that's how

important this is to me . . . that you do these two things. One is to
review the flooring estimate that David sent for the house and give
him the go-ahead if you approve. The other thing I need you to do
is to pick up the dry cleaning.

This was a totally new conversation. It wasn't really about the
flooring estimate or the dry cleaning. Even though I was used to
doing things myself, I could have easily just shot Kojo a text asking
him to pick up the dry cleaning or to review the estimate. But by
discussing this request in such a deliberate and thoughtful way, I
was communicating to Kojo that his help was about more than these
two tasks; that by taking these two items off my to-do list, he was
helping me to achieve my purpose. This conversation made clear
to Kojo that this request was about who I was in the world.

More importantly, though, this request was about how Kojo, as
my partner, could be his best self by enabling me to be mine. In
2015, Francesca Gino and her colleagues at Harvard Business School
proved that best-self activation, or reminding people of the moments
when they're at their best, was the most effective tool in inspiring
employees to make substantial improvements in their relationships
and their performance.[4] I spoke to Jooa Julia Lee, one of the researchers, to better understand why. She explained that when we approach
experiences as if they're transactional, like showing up for work
because we're being paid, there is a limit to what we feel we should do
to keep our end of the bargain. If they are paying us to work eight
hours, then we're fine working eight hours, but anything more means
our employer is getting a better deal. On the other hand, when we
approach experiences as if they're relational, like showing up for work
because we're inspired by our company's mission, what we'll do
to achieve the mission is limitless. "Best-self activation allows
people to incorporate their personal identities into their jobs.
Their employer is saying, 'I want your whole self to be involved in
your job, not just your skills.'"[5] Best-self activation works at home,
too. The most important words in my request that would assure
Kojo would follow through were the ones about him: "You have
always supported me and pushed me to fulfill my potential."

After I made my request he responded accordingly. "Of course, babe. I'll do them tomorrow." Then he kissed me on the forehead and pushed the green button on the remote. Kojo is not a man disposed to physical displays of affection. I had even altered our wedding officiator's script to read "You may salute your bride" in case he didn't feel comfortable kissing me publicly (he gave me a hug). So the forehead kiss was a unique and tender gesture.

Finally! I had made the leap from imaginary delegation, when Kojo had no clue what I was asking, to Delegating with Joy. Delegating with Joy is asking someone for help with a higher purpose than the task itself. When we Delegate with Joy, we put the task into a larger, more meaningful context. We're saying to the other person, "I'm asking for your help with [fill in] because you doing so will help me to live my passion and purpose." No one wants to take out the recycling. So if you just ask someone to take out the recycling, that's a win-lose proposition. But anyone who loves you wants you to be your best self. Asking for help with achieving what matters most to you is a win-win. So often when we ask for help we ask with frustration or even contempt for the other person. Sometimes it's painful to ask for help because we feel that by doing so we're being weak. But when we focus on the ultimate outcome, we transition from delegating with resentment to Delegating with Joy.

I was confident that Kojo had heard me not just with his ears but also with his heart. I was nervous, though, when I woke up the next day because Kojo hadn't asked me any questions about his tasks. I'd forwarded him the flooring estimate, but he definitely didn't have the dry-cleaning ticket. I was elated at 10:00 A.M. when he cc'd me on his response to David. Not only had he reviewed the estimate, but he had also posed some important clarifying questions. One task down, one more to go!

Multiple times throughout the day in between my meetings, I wanted to call Kojo to remind him about the dry cleaning, just to make sure he knew what time the place closed. *Don't be a micromanager,* I kept telling myself. *He said he would do it.* The problem was that the cleaners closed at 8:00 P.M., and Kojo had told me he had an interview that afternoon and then drinks with an old colleague afterward. Would he get to the dry cleaners in time?

It occurred to me as I was rushing home to relieve Lucinda that Kojo might have picked up the dry cleaning that morning, after I left for the office. *Ah yes, that's exactly what he did.* I bolted into our apartment and, with Kofi in my arms, opened every closet in the hope of finding a family of neatly pressed shirts, suits, and dresses. But there was nothing. By a quarter to eight, my heartbeat was quickening, and my face was getting flushed. I imagined Kojo at a bar with his friend. This time there was no resentment, nor did my HCD compel me to bundle up Kofi and go grab the clothes myself. I knew that those clothes weren't important in and of themselves, but I was sad because I had hoped that all of the effort I'd put into delegating effectively would work this time. I was trying to keep my chin up when our front-door buzzer rang. *It's Kojo! He can't get his keys because he's carrying the clothes.* I rushed to buzz him in and opened the door. But it wasn't Kojo standing in front of me. It was Martin from the cleaners. I must have looked confused.

"Your husband asked me to deliver."

"You deliver?"

"Yeah."

"Martin, I've been bringing my clothes to you for nearly two years now. How come you never told me you guys deliver?"

"You never asked."

CHAPTER 9

—✦—

On the Precipice of Change

In nearly twenty years of marriage, the most stressful period Kojo and I ever had to navigate was the late spring of 2008. Kojo had been out of work for nearly four months, and he was nearing the end of his unemployment benefits. When we had two incomes, we didn't think twice about hopping in a taxi, but now a canary-yellow sedan with a strip club advertisement atop was a luxury vehicle. Getting a manicure and dry-cleaning any cotton that could be machine washed were also unnecessary extravagances. So was dinner variety. One Sunday, I made a pot of red beans that we ate with rice for the entire week. We were luckier than most families during this time. My income covered half of our day-to-day needs, and we had savings to take care of the rest. But as our savings dwindled, so did my optimism that we'd stay afloat financially. At the same time, even though I was learning to Delegate with Joy, I was still the one primarily responsible for the functioning of our home lives. I was riding my life-go-round, and it seemed to be going as fast as ever.

Growing up with hardworking parents had inspired me to adopt the motto "When the going gets tough, the tough work harder." So to support my family, that's exactly what I did. I poured myself into my work, both at home and in the office. At the office, my dedication was paying dividends. One of the deals I helped broker was turning out to be a landmark initiative called Women Rule, a partnership between the White House Project, *O* magazine, and American Express. Women around the country had submitted their ideas about how they envisioned themselves changing the world. We selected eighty of the most impressive and flew the winners to New York City for a three-day training during which they developed blueprints to implement their ideas and dreams. There was an eight-page Women Rule spread in *O*, and several of the social entrepreneurs went on to execute their goals in big ways. The initiative's outcomes exceeded our dreams. Soon afterward, I was promoted from director to vice president at the White House Project, a step up that was accompanied by a raise, which my family needed more than ever.

The Women Rule endeavor had been a convenient distraction from mounting tensions at home. In the process of employing my "When the going gets tough, the tough work harder" motto, a chasm had developed between Kojo and me. The divide was mainly due to my nagging and the alienating messages I was sending him. I didn't necessarily say these messages aloud, but I didn't have to. My actions screamed louder.

My first message addressed how we managed our networks. Kojo knew lots of people from graduate school and past jobs, but he seemed to spend little time cultivating relationships with them. Meanwhile, I spent a lot of time cultivating my own relationships. I prized having a group of people who could help me achieve clarity through their guidance and encouragement, and I relied on their expertise to help me problem solve. My network had also made my professional transitions seamless. Unlike many of my colleagues, I didn't have parents who could leverage their social or economic capital on my behalf. Nor did I have an Ivy League brand on my résumé. But I *did* have my network. Whenever someone opened a door for me, I raced through it. As a result, I had never needed to apply for a job. As soon as I was ready to make a career move, someone in my network inevitably steered me to the next opportunity. That's how I'd landed my job at the White House Project: When I moved to New York, one of my colleagues, Laurisa Sellers, told me to go find the project's leader. "Tell Marie I sent you," Laurisa had instructed.

Kojo's view of networking was different from mine. One of his most compelling arguments for why we needed to uproot ourselves from our happy life in Seattle and invest nearly $200,000 was so that he could attend a top business school where he would, in addition to a degree, acquire a professional network among the school's alumni. But after five months of his being unemployed, I realized that it was impossible to simply *buy* a network, tapping into it when you needed it. The most powerful networks are nurtured over time.

While Kojo's list seemed to sit idle, I began doubling my networking efforts to include professionals in finance—his field. To support Kojo in his job search, I attended more coffees and events so I could meet more people on his behalf. But I could only do so much. Many of the people I was meeting were piecing together careers that had also been decimated by the financial crisis, so they could only refer me to others. Network cultivation is like growing a garden; it takes time to bear fruit. Unfortunately, we didn't have time. My message to Kojo: *I'm compensating for what you should have already built.* In response, he no longer asked me for leads. We stopped operating as a team, which is the last thing we should have been doing when our networks might have intersected.

My second divisive message pivoted around the desired outcome of his job search. Kojo wanted a job that, well, made him *happy*. With his newfound time and freedom, he had taken himself through some of the same growth exercises that I had done in order to discover what mattered most to him. For him, the ideal result of the job search would be finding a role that fueled his passion for furthering sub-Saharan Africa and maximized his experience in telecommunications, engineering, and finance. He had also decided that, since there were so few traditional investment banking jobs available, he would start pursuing his longer-term goal of joining a private equity firm.

To me, this was like thinking, *Since there are no sales jobs left at Old Navy, I'll just go get one at Brooks Brothers*. I was totally on the same page in the beginning. I supported his hunt for the ideal job as well as his simultaneous focus on the private equity sector. But after a few months of pursuing both options with no results, I felt that his goal should simply be to find a well-paying job that didn't compromise his integrity. I began operating from a "beggars can't be choosers" mind-set. Kojo's mind-set was more "shoot for the moon, because even if you miss you'll land among the stars." I didn't want to be the kind of wife who dashed my husband's dreams, but I pushed for a more pragmatic approach. After all, we had a family to support. I wanted him to be happy, but it seemed an impractical splurge when our bank account was dwindling. My subconscious message to Kojo: *You're prioritizing your happiness over your family's livelihood*. His response was to stop talking to me about his search.

My third alienating message to Kojo was about housework. In the beginning of his job search, I was happy to carry the same share of the responsibilities at home as I had when we were both employed so that he could focus full-time on his professional goals. The dry-cleaning incident had taught me that I could effectively Delegate with Joy, but I was still doing more than my husband around the house. This state of affairs had now outworn its welcome.

Unlike when I was embarking on a job search and still taking care of Kofi in 2006, we now had Lucinda caring for our son during the day. And I was the one primarily managing her from the office, even though Kojo was at home. After four months of handing Kofi off to Lucinda in the morning and dashing to the office before Kojo even woke up, I felt the situation was unfair. And even though Kojo was doing more than he had done before his layoff, it was getting harder to Delegate with Joy. My old resentment began to surface. I tried hard not to compare the two of us, but then I'd come home at the end of the day to a pile of dishes and think, *If I were unemployed and didn't have to take care of Kofi, not only would I have a job by now, but this place would be spotless!* Even with my raise, we were going to have to let Lucinda go if circumstances didn't change soon. We were cutting fiscal corners every way we could, but no amount of Fine Fare sale coupons was going to reduce our expense column the way her pay would. The prospect of losing Lucinda terrified me because my expectations of Kojo were still so low. I couldn't imagine him running the house and caring for our son the way that Lucinda or I could. My message to Kojo: *You can't manage details.*

All of my indirect messages had far more power than I realized.

Claude Steele, a social psychologist, has studied how negative messages rooted in stereotype can trigger poor performance. In his 2011 book *Whistling Vivaldi,* Steele describes an experiment in which a group of Asian women are asked to complete a math exam.[1] Many of us are familiar with the two divergent stereotypes at play in this experiment: Asians are often assumed to be good at math, whereas women are often assumed be bad (or worse than men) at the subject. Could reminding Asian women about either of these identities affect their performance on a math test? Turns out, the answer is yes. When Asian women were provided with instructions before the test that included a reminder they were Asian, thus reinforcing the positive association with high math performance, they performed better. When provided with instructions that emphasized their gender, thus reinforcing the negative association with low math performance, they performed worse. The cultural codes within these messages had an immense impact on the individuals' subconscious belief systems and thus on their actual performance.

In the same way, what women believe the men in their lives can and can't do—and the messages we send to them about our beliefs—influences their behavior. If we don't have or don't demonstrate faith in our spouses' abilities, the chances that they will confirm our doubts is very high, as is the likelihood that they will resent us for doubting them. That's exactly what was happening with Kojo and me. The less I believed Kojo could effectively manage our home, the less motivated he was to do so.

By late April, my overwhelming feeling that Kojo wasn't carrying his share of the job hunting and household load was crushing—for both of us. As resentment on my end mounted, Kojo interpreted all my messages to mean one thing: *She doesn't believe in me.* At the time, I didn't see the connection between the messages I was sending my husband and his actions at home. But I did notice the result: the dishes, laundry, and mail piled up more than they ever had before. We were also growing emotionally and physically distant. We used to talk all the time, but at this point, we had stopped even asking each other "How was your day?" And our sex life was virtually nonexistent.

Our only respite was celebrating Kofi's second birthday. I splurged on buttermilk, cocoa powder, cream cheese, and two bottles of red food coloring to make a red velvet cake. We were happy that night. It's funny how we think we want something, but then as soon as we get it, we realize that it's not what we needed. That happened to me when, right after we helped Kofi blow out his candles, Kojo told me that after giving it much thought, he had decided to take whatever opportunity next came along. He'd given up the moon, he said, and would settle for whatever came across his path. He admitted the job search was harder than he had originally anticipated, and he thanked me for working so hard. I appreciated what he was saying, but it also broke my heart.

I told Kojo it was time to lay off Lucinda, which would buy us some time financially so he could continue to pursue what mattered most to him. Plus, Kojo and Kofi would have fun spending more time together. What happened next startled me: Kojo seemed genuinely excited. For the first time, it hit me that my husband really *wanted* to take care of his son, but he had never suggested it because of my insistence that we needed Lucinda and because I had never communicated to him that I thought he could do a good job. We decided to tell her at the end of the week.

But when Friday came around, I got some news that I knew would put a dent in our plans. It took everything I had to practice restraint and wait until the end of the day to tell Kojo. The information would be better received in person. I sent him a text message on my way home. *Have something to share. Let's talk to Lucinda next week.* He immediately texted me back. *Okay, me too!* I took his exclamation point to mean he had good news. When I arrived home, I reviewed the Caregiver Log, then took Kofi from Lucinda so she could head out. As soon as the door was closed behind her, I turned to Kojo.

"Do you want me to go first, or do you want to go first?" I asked.

"You first."

"I'm pregnant."

"Really?" He was already getting up from his spot on the blue couch. I put Kofi down on the floor. Kojo kissed me on the forehead. Then he held me tight and said, "Well, all right! My boys can still swim!"

"Okay, your turn," I said, laughing.

"I got a job offer."

"I knew it!" I screamed. I was giddy.

"There's more," he said. "It's not ideal. Sit down."

I picked up Kofi and held him in my lap. Kojo explained he had landed his dream gig—a position with a private equity firm that invested in Africa—and that he would be a key member of a new team. But there was a catch. The firm was based in Dubai. If Kojo accepted the offer, he'd have to move to Dubai full-time.

This prospect presented complications to say the least. I knew there was no way in hell I was going to give up my awesome job to move to a country where my knee-length skirt would be considered indecent exposure. In my heart, I already knew Kojo would go and I would stay and that the distance would be hard. But the distance would be our choice. I immediately thought of Lucinda, who had to leave her children in Barbados when she first immigrated to the United States. I thought of military families who were so often separated by long deployments that they had no control over. This would be complicated. But in the moment, my jubilation for him and our expanding family trumped diving into details.

"We'll figure it out" was all I said, and I meant it.

Kojo put Kofi to bed. And then we did what any couple does who has just learned that they have a baby on the way and a financially secure future: we had great sex.

PART THREE

✦

Drop the Ball

CHAPTER 10

Go Ahead, Drop the Ball

With a new baby on the way and Kojo about to be based overseas, we got to work on our fairy-tale logistics. We enrolled Kofi in a full-time day-care program (the cost dropped significantly once a child turned two) and gave Lucinda notice, but not before sending e-mails and making phone calls enough to find her another job. Since her new family didn't need her immediately, she stayed with us for two more months to support our transition. There is a large expatriate community in Dubai, and we relied on our contacts to help find Kojo an apartment and sort out his paperwork. We upgraded our international calling plan and scheduled a full maintenance for our car. I thought the latter expense was unnecessary since we mostly rode the subway. Plus the car was in great condition—it was seven years old and had only fifty thousand miles. But Kojo insisted. He didn't want to worry about his pregnant wife and two-year-old son driving in an "unreliable" vehicle. I thought he was being irrational. Of the gazillion details we were managing, though, there was one that we overlooked. It was the detail that would change everything.

Imagine three months of unopened snail mail forming a mound on your kitchen counter. Every time you walk by, it calls your name, but you ignore its pleas and continue to go about your life as if it's not growing larger and more plaintive each day. This was my situation during the summer of 2008.

The night before Kojo and I each made our big announcements, we had agreed that Kojo would assume the task of managing our mail; it was one small thing he could do to help free up my time. Ball, dropped. The next day, he grabbed the envelopes from the mailbox and put them on the counter, I'm sure with every intention of opening them later. But later never came. Each day he would bring the mail in and add it to the pile on the counter. Each day I'd resist the urge to mention that pile because I had Delegated with Joy and I didn't want to micromanage. I willed myself to believe that Kojo had a sound strategy in mind, maybe he'd sort through a critical mass of mail in one shot.

This accumulation continued for four weeks. It wasn't long before the mail became easy to ignore; we had more pressing matters on our hands. Kojo's first stint abroad was supposed to last one month but turned into two. In his absence, I chose to let the pile of mail grow. I wasn't intentionally trying to prove a point, but the sudden transition from having an unemployed husband at home to one living on the other side of the world while I was managing a full-time job, a two-year-old, and morning sickness made the mail seem relatively trivial. Besides, when I thought about what mattered most to me and factored in my highest and best use toward achieving it, I just couldn't justify spending the hours it would take to sort through the mail; I knew that it would not be a good use of the precious little time I had.

For the first month, my home control disease called my comparative advantage strategy into question nearly every day. A tiny voice in my head would taunt me: *Tiffany, you're so irresponsible. That pink envelope is probably a birthday party invitation, and who-*

ever doesn't hear from you is going to think you're the rudest person on the planet. That envelope with the bold letters is probably a notice about that parking ticket you got a while back. If you don't open that envelope, they're going to come and arrest you, and it will ruin your family's life and your entire career. You'd better hope that no one drops by your place unexpectedly. You'll have to have an entire conversation with them outside on the stoop because there's no way that you could let people know that you've let the mail pile up like this. You're just making your life more difficult because Kojo is not going to sort through all this mail. You might as well make your life easier and just do it yourself.

Some days my HCD got so loud that I was tempted to open an envelope. I'd blast Rihanna's "Don't Stop the Music" while vacuuming to drown out the incessant voice in my head.

Then, over time, something amazing began to happen. The larger the pile became, the less responsibility I felt for it. Instead of making me feel terrible, my HCD started justifying my actions. *Girl, that pile is so big it couldn't possibly be yours because you'd never have let it get to this point.* Plus none of my worst fears materialized. I wasn't getting evil looks or angry messages for missing anyone's party. No one arrived at my door to read me my Miranda rights. In fact, one evening, a neighborhood mom stopped by to borrow my baby food grinder, and I had to let her into our apartment because I was in the middle of giving Kofi a bath. I was just about to apologize for the mess when her face lit up. "Oh, my God! Is that your mail? And all this time I've been feeling horrible about myself, wondering how you do it all because you're so goddamn perfect. No offense, but you just made my day!" I was so embarrassed, but she was so happy. The world hadn't fallen apart, and my anxiety about the mail piling up began to wane.

One evening, as Lucinda was handing Kofi off to me, she offered to sort it.

"The mail is getting a little out of hand, don't you think?" she said.

"What mail? I don't know what you're talking about," I responded.

I could barely get the words out of my mouth without cracking up. The pile was just that ridiculous. I told Lucinda it was such a big job at this point that I'd just leave it for Kojo, who was due to return home any day. I also knew that Kojo is a private person, and he wouldn't have wanted anyone else going through our mail. It sounds crazy, but it felt liberating for me to get to a point where I wasn't obsessing about it—at all.

Months before, I had learned how to Delegate with Joy—to put my ask into a positive context that would motivate Kojo to follow through—but at the end of the day, I still felt responsible for making sure things got done. I still hadn't released the expectation that it was my job, until now. Once I had adopted the mind-set that it wasn't my responsibility to sort the mail, I no longer felt the omnipresent pressure to do so. I had gotten the first taste of what it felt like to truly Drop the Ball.

When Kojo returned to find three months of mail waiting for him on the kitchen counter, he seemed a little stressed.

"That's a lot of mail," he said.

"I know," I responded cheerfully. "I've been so busy while you've been gone, but I knew you'd deal with it like you said you would."

In that moment, our mail management finally role switched.

It hadn't happened when he'd agreed to take responsibility for the mail three months earlier. Rather, it happened when, for the first time, he really *saw* the mail, and when he, too, felt the desire for it to disappear. This situation could only have occurred because I had grown totally comfortable with the pile—and exercised a little patience (okay, a lot of patience).

For the next two days, the loud grind of our paper shredder filled the apartment as Kojo opened each and every envelope that had stacked up. All that unopened mail did have consequences: unpaid bills, more than one missed birthday party, and an unpaid parking ticket that had gone to collections. After going through all the mail, Kojo spent the rest of the week dealing with the effects. To this day, the mail in our home can still pile up, but never for as long a period as it did that summer.

The mail event was a watershed moment for us because it was the first time I learned that Kojo had a threshold for disarray at home—his tolerance was just way higher than mine. I also learned that even after I Delegated with Joy, and even after Kojo accepted, the task hadn't really been handed off. This was not a onetime occurrence. I came to expect that, more often than not, Kojo was going to drop the ball, but under no circumstances should I pick it up, except in an emergency. Nothing in those envelopes was an emergency. In a life-or-death situation, no one would be notifying me about something vitally important via snail mail. I just had to trust that in time, Kojo would see the ball lying there and retrieve it.

———

Don't get me wrong: not picking up the ball takes fortitude, especially in the beginning. I'm certain that when social reformer and writer Frederick Douglass said, "Without struggle there is no progress," he didn't have three months' worth of unopened mail in mind, but that might be what we will have to endure in order to end our life-go-rounds. The alternative is infinitely more frustrating, as so many women know. I was recently at a conference with a group of high-powered women. One was a U.S. ambassador. After discussing world conflicts, we ventured into the familiar terrain of household management and the roles of our husbands. The ambassador weighed in first. "When I see a sock on the stairs, I bend down and pick it up. He walks right by it. He doesn't even see it. So basically I end up doing all of the work because I'm picking up the proverbial socks."

Then another woman chimed in. "My husband sees the sock, but he still walks by because he knows that I'm going to pick it up." I posed the question, "Well, what would happen if you left the sock there? If you walked by it just like he did?" Another woman: "More socks would pile up. Endless socks! I could never let it get to that point. And even if I could, he knows I'm going to pick them up eventually, so he's never going to do it." Turns out there is real-world research to back up her conclusion.

What the men in these women's lives all counted on was their wives' greater investment in the communal space of the family. Simply put, men believe women care more about socks on stairs, and so they aren't incentivized to pick them up. In 2013, economist Irene van Staveren enlisted men and women to play a game that gauged their beliefs about which gender is more benevolent. Participants were each given the same amount of money—let's say ten dollars—and told that whatever amount they collectively contributed to a group pot would be doubled by the researchers and divided among them equally. Each of them could keep whatever amount they withheld from the collective pot. Obviously, it was in everyone's best interest to put all of the money into the collective pot, to act more communally. That would double the winnings for everyone. But no one wanted to be hoodwinked by contributing all their money, only to have it doubled and shared with their less benevolent colleagues who'd come out on top because they kept some of theirs. Interestingly, men generally assumed women would give more to the collective pot; they believed women were more stereotypically communal.[1]

The truth is that women might indeed give more to the communal pot, but the result is that we're also more resentful, tense, stressed, and silent in the process.

What I learned from Dropping the Ball on the mail was that I had to become less communally minded to give Kojo an opportunity to be *more* communally minded. Letting the mail pile up was also the only way to build my credibility. In one survey, 30 percent of men were so certain that the women they lived with would flake on their insistence that the guy do more housework, the men intentionally completed tasks poorly to ensure the frustrated women would just do it themselves the next time. It worked. A quarter of the men who intentionally did a poor job were never asked to pitch in again, and 64 percent were only occasionally asked to help.[2] Their brilliant strategy reminds me of one of my favorite Shel Silverstein poems:

If you have to dry the dishes
(Such an awful boring chore)
If you have to dry the dishes

('Stead of going to the store)
If you have to dry the dishes
And you drop one on the floor
Maybe they won't let you
Dry the dishes anymore

I wanted Kojo to understand that when I said I was passing something off to him I truly meant it, and I trusted that he'd get to it eventually.

Patience is essential to ensuring that once a task is Delegated with Joy, it stays that way. Ripping open all those envelopes was tempting for me in the short term, but patience was key to ensuring that Kojo took over the mail for the long term. Practicing patience can be challenging in our hurried "just do it" culture. We've become wired for instant gratification, and in this day and age "our expectation of 'instant' has become faster," notes academic Narayan Janakiraman.[3] In 2011, Janakiraman conducted a study called the Psychology of Decisions to Abandon Waits for Service, which examined consumers' decisions to walk away from service lines after certain durations of wait time.[4] Janakiraman hypothesized that two opposing psychological forces would influence the length of time people were willing to wait in a line. On one shoulder was the voice of "waiting disutility," or the urge to abandon the wait because of the time they perceived they were wasting. On the other shoulder was the voice of "completion commitment," or the urge to continue waiting to gain the reward of the time already invested. Janakiraman found that the average person abandoned the line during the middle of the wait due to these opposing forces.

To Drop the Ball at home, however, our "completion commitment" voice must be louder. Unlike Janakiraman's test subjects, we must stay in the line. Patience is more than a virtue; it's a powerful strategy. Allowing tasks to sit uncompleted reinforces what needs to be done and by whom. The mere passing of time has an amazing way of getting others to contribute, and not just at home. How often have we been in a classroom with men who dominated the discussion with half-formed ideas because they raised their hands before they even thought about what they would say? This dynamic created such a gender disparity at Harvard Business School that professors were encouraged to have students submit questions and comments in a box that the professor would draw from randomly. Women at home are often like those overeager boys in the classroom, raising our hands before being thoughtful about the outcome we're trying to achieve. One of the simplest things an educator can do to create a more inclusive classroom is to wait longer before calling on students.[5] Similarly, one thing women can do to create an inclusive workload at home is to wait longer before undertaking tasks.

The title of the Dan Hicks song "How Can I Miss You When You Won't Go Away?" can be adapted to underscore the power of patience: "How Can I Wash the Clothes if They're Always Clean?" In other words, expecting less of ourselves and more from our partners requires that we not only release a task to the other person, but we also resist doing it ourselves, even when it doesn't get done.

CHAPTER 11

---•---

Clarify Who Does What

By the time Kojo had returned from his first two months in Dubai, we had both adjusted to the fact that having him work overseas would be our new lifestyle. After the mail incident, I'd experienced an exhilarating new freedom from worrying about every little thing. I had already gotten a taste of what it would be like for him to be more engaged in managing our home—and I liked the flavor. I wasn't going back. With Kojo scheduled to return to Dubai in five days, we needed a new system, one that would enable him to participate in running our household in a more organized and on-going way.

One afternoon, I was in a project launch meeting at work. I was using a whiteboard to lead a brainstorm of all of the tasks that needed to be accomplished to meet our goal. After we had exhausted the list, I began assigning roles to people. It suddenly occurred to me that women who are successful managers in the workplace abandon their best professional practices at home. In fact, at home, women often do the *opposite* of what makes us such effective leaders in the office.

Here's a big one: Good managers set expectations up front. They communicate the vision, then allow their teams to create and execute their own plans to get there.[1] Effective managers know that when people are clear about their roles and responsibilities at the outset, they can more efficiently accomplish their goals. At home, however, we assume our spouses understand our vision, and then we wait until after they've screwed up to tell them that they completed the job off spec. I could appreciate that this order of events would be demotivating to the individual who put forth a well-intentioned effort to deliver.

That's when it hit me: *Why don't I try this whiteboard idea at home?*

That night I sat cross-legged in my bed with my laptop and opened a new Excel spreadsheet. I populated the first column with every task I could think of that was required to manage our home. It was the first time I got the entire list out of my head and onto a document. I tried hard to remember the things that Kojo did that I didn't; I wanted the list to be as exhaustive as possible. Here's what appeared in that first column:

Vacuum/sweep all floors
Dust living area, including electronics and windowsill
Mop/scrub kitchen floor
Clean kitchen sink
Clean inside of toilets
Scrub bathtub and shower wall tiles
Clean bathroom mirrors
Clean bathroom sinks and counter
Wash bathroom rugs
Dust bedrooms
Change bed linens
Wipe kitchen counters and table
Vacuum carpet under high chair after meals

Clean top of stove
Straighten Kofi's bedroom
Wash, dry, fold, and put away Kofi's clothes
Wash, dry, fold, and put away adult clothes
Morning: unload dishwasher
Evening: load dishwasher and wash pots
Garbage and recycling takeout
Grocery store runs
Costco runs
Sunday food prep
Dinner cooking
Pack lunches
Morning breakfast
Pay bills
Monitor cash flow
Budgeting
File taxes
Sort mail
Clothing and sundries inventory
Liaison with day care
Coordinate babysitters
Haircuts
Kofi's doctor appointments
Nightly bath
Alternate car parking
Car maintenance
Car washes
Manage Seattle house
Get gifts for friends and family
Manage family calendar
Respond to family event invites

Next, I made three additional columns. At the top of the first one, I typed "Tiffany." Then I deleted my name and typed *Kojo*. I was done being the default primary manager of our home. From now on, Kojo's column would always be first. At the top of the next column I typed *Tiffany*. Finally, at the top of the third column, I typed *No one*. Little did I realize this last column would turn out to be the most important.

Next, I started populating the cells in my column with *X*s next to the tasks I currently performed. I got halfway through typing a lot of *X*s before I realized that presenting my husband with a list of household management duties that made it obvious how much more I did was not a winning strategy. I would have never done that to my team at work. *The cells should be completely blank when I show this to Kojo,* I thought. The point of the exercise was for us to work together to figure this out, as a team.

I emerged from our bedroom carrying my laptop and curled up next to Kojo on the blue couch. I sat my laptop on one of the cushions, right next to his remote. He put his arm around me. By the time Brian Williams was wrapping up his "Making a Difference" segment of the nightly news, I had my ultimate Delegating-with-Joy speech ready to go:

Hey, babe, I have an idea. I think you'll like it. Wanna hear?
(Wait for yes.)
You know all that time you spent dealing with the mail? I thought of a way for both of us to not be so overwhelmed by stuff like that. We know what matters most to us, and it shouldn't involve being stressed about chores. You'll be headed back to Dubai in a few days, and I was thinking that before you leave, we could come up with a plan to ensure we both know who's on first when it comes to household stuff. Then we can manage our areas in whatever way works for each of us. No more stepping on each other's toes.

Kojo was in at the word *mail*.

I put my computer on my lap, opened it, and showed Kojo the list. He agreed it was a great start but said I was missing stuff. I couldn't imagine what he could be talking about given that I was the authority on managing our home, but I decided I should just indulge him.

"Okay, what's missing?" I asked.

"Well, to start, who replaces the Brita water filter in the fridge?" I couldn't help smirking. *Seriously? He just had to find this one little thing he does?* But this exercise was important, and I could tell he was engaged, so I decided to play along.

"Sorry, hon. I didn't think of that." I added a new row to the excel sheet and typed *Replace Brita filter*.

Kojo continued. "And who buys all our plane tickets for our personal travel and keeps track of our miles and makes sure that we're using our miles when it's more cost efficient?" Okay, he had some points on this one (pun intended). I couldn't tell you what my frequent flyer numbers were, and we both had them for multiple airlines. I created a new row and typed, *Book family airfare*. Kojo let out a one-breath chuckle. He took my computer off of my lap and set it gently on his lap. Then he deleted *Book family airfare* and typed *Family Travel Coordinator*. He looked at me.

"Babe, when we get to where we're going, who has already booked the car rental and the hotel and found the best deal?"

"Okay, fine," I said. "You do that." Now the man was on a roll. He added a new row and typed *Botanist*.

"What?" I exclaimed incredulously. He looked at me again.

"The last time you watered a plant was in 1996 before we were even married. It was a cactus, and it died. I've been taking care of everything that's green and grows since."

"You've never taken care of the mold that grows on old food you leave in the fridge," I retorted.

"You've never taken care of anything that breaks around here."

"You never even notice when things break!"

"That's true, but when you notice that they break, you tell me to fix them and I do, or I have to track down Lionel. So who's doing the real work on that one?" It was a LeBron James slam dunk. Especially because it took me a moment to realize that Lionel was our super. I hadn't even known his name. I sat there quietly on the couch and watched as Kojo added several new rows:

Chief Technology Officer ("When have you ever programmed your phone or laptop?")

Investments Manager ("Do you know how much money is in your retirement account?")

Math Teacher ("You read and talk to Kofi, but who drills him on his math puzzles? And by the way, those take time to find and download from the Internet.")

"But this isn't fair," I protested. "This isn't the stuff that you've ever done day in and day out."

He looked at me again, then added another row and typed *Kofi Night Nurse.*

"Oh, c'mon," I said, exasperated. "Kofi sleeps through the night."

"No, *you* sleep through the night, and it's because of me." My mind immediately flashed to all the cocktail parties where I casually mentioned what an awesome sleeper my son was.

"Well, how come you never told me that Kofi is up at night?"

"And give you another thing to worry about unnecessarily? No way."

It was the fourth quarter with seconds left on the clock, and I was behind by double digits. I attempted a Hail Mary. "The list was supposed to be a set of to-dos, with action verbs, not job titles," I said. My husband only laughed and kept going.

This was how Kojo and I populated, together, our first official Management Excel List, and it was the dawn of a new era. If you had asked me before this exercise what percentage of household and child-rearing work my husband did, I would have smiled and said, "Oh, he's fantastic," but in my head, I would have been rolling my eyes and thinking, *Five percent on a good day.* After I tallied all the items I had added that I knew Kojo did, then combined it with his new rows, it was more like 30 percent, a staggeringly high number given my belief that he did hardly anything around the house. Talk about an eye-opener.

We quickly started calling the Management Excel List our MEL.

Over time, MEL would prove to be our most useful tool for negotiating and tracking our household responsibilities. In the beginning, we mostly divided tasks by location: *Does this task require you to be there in person, or can it be done virtually?* Since Kojo spent the majority of his time overseas, he was assigned any task that could be done using technology or that only required his physical presence intermittently, such as car maintenance and Kofi's regular doctors' appointments. Later, we would use factors other than geography to renegotiate MEL, like our work schedules, talents, and interests.

The most revealing part of our MEL exercise was deciding which Xs should go in the *No one* column. This column represented our acknowledgment that there was more to running our household than both of us could ever accomplish. We would stop making assumptions about what the other person was doing—or should be doing—and we would not blame each other for what didn't get done. We mutually agreed that some things just wouldn't happen, and we'd be okay with that. For three months, the car would be dirty, the living room would be dusty, and our clothes would never be folded. I'd grab clean socks and underwear from the laundry basket instead of drawers. If anyone asked us if there was anything they could do to help us out, we'd have a list ready, but for now, Kojo and I would ignore those items and revisit them in three months when he returned.

Dropping the Ball is not a static, onetime occurrence; the details evolve over time. MEL has given us a consistent, flexible mechanism to renegotiate our expectations of one another. Who does what has fluctuated throughout our partnership depending on practicality, priorities, and the ebb and flow of our careers. For most years, I did school drop-offs because I was the parent who was stateside, but during one of Kojo's job transitions, his international schedule was reduced dramatically, so we retooled MEL, and for a year, he did daily drop-offs. Kojo also did a lot more cooking when he was in the States than he had done in the past, mostly because he enjoys traditional Ghanaian food that he's gifted at preparing. But when he became consumed with launching a new fund, I took over more of the cooking. Similarly, when I was in the midst of one of the biggest transitions of my career, Kojo took MEL, put Xs under his name in every row, and said, "I'll take care of everything until you get through this." It was incredible!

By removing the tension that stems from misaligned expectations that are never fully discussed, a MEL can help any couple with busy schedules better navigate the domestic sphere. As Jessica De-Groot, founder and president of Third Path Institute, notes, "Couples that practice shared care do so intentionally. They come together as a couple to imagine what they each want."[2] Understanding and appreciating our spouses' particular interests and differences are important to establishing teamwork. Valuing how someone else operates, versus just complaining about it, helps us to adjust our expectations as well as our own behavior for the good of the partnership.

My friend Brian and his partner, Mark, are a case in point. I've known Brian for several years, and the very first time we met, I was impressed with how organized he seemed. Brian is a record executive whose life-go-round includes raising a ten-year-old son and thirteen-year-old daughter and coordinating hospice for his terminally ill father. The latter was particularly painful, as his relationship with his father had been strained ever since Brian came out to his family. Brian's partner, Mark, a software developer, was there for him emotionally but fell short when it came to getting things accomplished at home.

Despite working long hours, Brian was clearly the primary caregiver of the kids and took the lead in managing their household. He was the parent who attended the PTA meetings, signed the kids up for sports, and even combed and braided his daughter's long, curly hair. When Brian and Mark hosted a dinner party, it was Brian who greeted guests at the front door and who kept everyone's wineglasses full throughout the evening. If I was once the queen of domesticity, Brian was the king.

Unlike with me, however, societal norms or cultural expectations weren't driving Brian into HCD overdrive. He was fueled by a different pressure: the kids were his from a previous relationship. Mark happily inherited the kids when he and Brian got together, but Mark had always been single with no children. Brian told me that in his first relationship, they contributed equally to the household, but when he and his ex split, Brian took sole custody of the kids. Now that he was with Mark, he had de facto responsibility when it came to managing the home ship. He also wondered if it was even fair to ask Mark to pitch in. "I know how it ended up like this," he lamented to me once, "but I don't know how to get Mark to do more." All I could do was let out a sigh and shake my head with empathy. *Ooh wee. I know the feeling.*

Months later, I met up with Brian at my favorite Harlem wine bar and was riveted by his update. Over glasses of Manuel Manzaneque, he shared with me how he had leveraged one of his and Mark's differences to secure more help at home. Unlike Brian, Mark is very competitive, so much so that he wasn't motivated to assume household tasks that he thought Brian was better at performing. One Saturday morning, however, Brian needed to check on his father, so Mark watched the kids. He made them pancakes, which the kids loved. More notably, the kids told Mark that his pancakes were *better* than Brian's. That was all it took. Mark became a pancake-making machine. In addition, when it became clear that Brian was useless at science exhibits, Mark jumped at the opportunity to help Brian's daughter with her science fair project. For Brian, the pancake and science-fair episodes were aha moments: "Knowing that Mark is motivated to do the things he's especially good at has allowed me to take a step back," Brian said gratefully. Figuring out Mark's unique motivations helped Brian know which balls he could drop. The moral of the story: instead of seeing differences as a pain point—"If only he were more like me"—we can use them to initiate critical conversations about our spouses' desires and motivations and to discover new opportunities for partnership support.

In approaching these conversations, we can learn a lot from our gay brothers and sisters. Research conducted in 2015 by the Families and Work Institute, in partnership with PwC, found that same-sex couples negotiate home management much more effectively than heterosexual couples do.[3] Why? Because most straight couples operate by default along gender norms—as Kojo and I also did before we created MEL—whereas same-sex couples who both work outside the home are more likely to divide responsibilities using criteria like skills, talents, and interests. As a result, each person is more in alignment with his or her highest and best use.

When a couple begins to operate from this mind-set, creating a MEL and codifying who has responsibility for what becomes a simple exercise. A delightful side effect of MEL is that it gives us a third party to blame when balls do drop on either side so that we don't take life's little mishaps too seriously. Whenever something comes up that we had forgotten to list in MEL, and therefore it never got done, Kojo and I will look at one another and say—only half jokingly—"I guess we need to have a meeting with MEL, huh? He's slipping!"

CHAPTER 12

 ⊹

Believe in Team

By the fall of 2008, with Kojo once again in Dubai, we had hit a rhythm in the joint management of our household, and I was beginning to feel the positive impact of Kojo's contribution on other areas of my life. MEL, our system of charting who was responsible for which household task, was working. We were clear about our expectations of each other and knew exactly what each of us was supposed to do to keep our home ticking. We had become All-In Partners: two people working full-time outside the home and co-managing caregiving within the home. What was most incredible was that we had achieved All-In Partnership with Kojo living across an entire ocean.

The reality of our new household division of labor was erasing my old story line about my husband being useless on the home front. I saw now that a good portion of my resentment of Kojo was misplaced. He had never been a bad husband. To the contrary, he had been trying to be a good one—by living up to the cultural expectations that he be the breadwinner and provider. In her essay "The Politics of Resentment," psychologist Marlia E. Banning notes that because resentment is "fundamentally premised on the *displacement* of the ability to speak about or act directly on the original injustice, it results in a shift of negatively loaded emotion to other human targets."[1] I had been treating Kojo as my adversary, when in fact we shared a common enemy: the cultural standards that had made me feel like I had to do it all, combined with workplace structures and values that are still designed for the ideal male worker.

The truth is, just because our partners leave dishes in the sink for us to wash doesn't mean they're jerks or Neanderthals. Throughout their lives, they've been internalizing the very same messages about gender roles that we have. Research conducted in 2014 by Robin Ely and her colleagues at Harvard Business School highlights the result of men's social conditioning when it comes to gender roles. Upon graduating from business school, 60 percent of gen X and baby boomer men said they expected their careers would take priority over their spouses'.[2] That indicates that the majority of men expect that their current or future wives will be managing their homes, whether the women worked full-time or not. In fact, when a man thinks otherwise, it makes headlines. When Max Schireson happily stepped down as CEO of the software company MongoDB to spend more time with his family, it was an anomalous move. So was his view that his wife, a doctor and professor, should not have to bear the brunt of the responsibility of homemaking. "I am forever in her debt for finding a way to keep the family working despite my crazy travel schedule," he wrote in a blog post announcing his decision. "I should not continue abusing that patience."[3]

Most men are no Max Schireson. Indeed, even at the office, many men expect their female colleagues to do "women's work." Author and law professor Joan Williams describes this state of affairs as "office housework," with women saddled with undervalued assignments such as party planning or diversity/inclusion committees, roles that invariably pull them away from more competitive, career-advancing opportunities.[4]

But as the notion that housework is woman's work was being up-rooted in our home, my old resentment was melting away. Because I was the one who had been more motivated to change the previous dynamic of our relationship, it made sense that I was leading the effort, but there was no longer any doubt that we were a team. And just in time, too, because the little acrobat inside me was making his or her presence known, and we both understood that a new baby would add a whole new set of tasks to our household management routine.

--+--

In November, when I expressed my anxiety that Kojo might miss the birth of our second child because he was in Dubai, my ob-gyn suggested I simply schedule an induction for a week before my due date. I had no idea people did this! You mean I could control the timing of the birth of my child? This was music to the ears of a woman with HCD (even if I was in recovery); I signed up on the spot.

My pregnancy had been healthy and uneventful up to this point, so when I told Kojo about my brilliant plan, he insisted that scheduling an induction wasn't a good idea. He asked me not to do it, and he made me a promise: "I won't miss the birth. Trust me." I didn't know how he could promise such a thing when the flight from Dubai to New York took at least fourteen hours, and most babies come whenever they want. Still, I canceled the induction, thinking wryly that it might be my ultimate exercise in Dropping the Ball. What's even more incredible is that I wasn't even stressed about it—until we closed in on my February 26 due date.

Like many ambitious women, my plan was to work right up until the baby came, which meant I found myself at the end of February hustling to follow up with donors before I went missing for three months. During one of my final phone calls, I put the foundation program officer on hold twice while I breathed through minor contractions. I decided that would be my last call.

I started to panic. *Will Kojo make it in time?*

I glanced over at the tight rosebuds that had arrived earlier that

day with a note that read "I'll be there." But Kojo's flight wasn't scheduled to depart Dubai for three more days. I got down on all fours in
my office and assumed the yoga cat pose to relieve the pain of my
contractions and my growing anxiety. Sure, there were times when
Kojo hadn't done what he said he was going to, but he had never
broken an actual promise. I thought about the last time he had given
me his solemn word, which had been exactly one year before.

—◆—

Around Valentine's Day in 2008, I was still in the early stages of figuring out how to Delegate with Joy when I was invited to serve on
the board of Harlem4Kids, a nonprofit committed to providing
weekly music and literacy programming to babies and toddlers in
Harlem.

I was madly in love with Harlem4Kids. When we first moved to
New York, our son was two months old, and a neighbor had suggested Kofi and I attend their Saturday program so I could meet
other new moms. The friendships I formed there became enduring
bonds, and the Harlem4Kids community is still an important part
of my support system. I got advice and resources through the group's
LISTSERV, and each week Kofi got a fun and stimulating experience at story time.

Needless to say, I was humbled when I was asked to join the
board. I felt that my background in nonprofit fund-raising and administration could be useful in helping the organization achieve its
goals. More importantly, serving on the Harlem4Kids board would
allow me to fulfill two of my highest priorities: advancing women
and girls and raising my children to be conscious global citizens.
Since most of the babies and toddlers were brought in to the weekly
story times by their mothers, supporting Harlem4Kids was a good
way to help women build the networks they needed to thrive. In addition, I had already decided that my teaching method for raising
conscious global citizens would be through modeling—I wanted my
behavior to demonstrate my values to my children. By serving on a

nonprofit board, my son would observe me engaging in my community, not just talking about it.

My parents had taught me how important it is to contribute to our communities, but up until that point, I did not feel as if I was contributing to Harlem. I went to work, went to networking events in the evening, and took care of managing my home. My life-go-round had been spinning too quickly for meaningful civic engagement to hop on for the ride. In Seattle and Boston, I had been active in the alumnae chapters of my sorority, Delta Sigma Theta, which has a rich history of community service. But when I had a baby and moved to New York, the chapter meetings I had once religiously attended became nearly impossible. I was already feeling guilty that I wasn't an active Delta.

Luckily, the makeup and culture of the Harlem4Kids board removed some of the barriers that had made it difficult for me to be involved in my community. Every member of the board was a working mom with young children who were either in the program or who had attended it previously. They all understood the demands of balancing work and home and trying to integrate volunteerism. As a result, the board's schedule made it easy to participate. Meetings were held monthly on Sundays in the board chair's home in my neighborhood. The agenda was the only formal part of the meeting. Even the attire was informal—we could show up in yoga pants and T-shirts if we needed to. But the winningest aspect was that I was welcome to bring Kofi if I didn't have child care.

The board was a perfect fit, but there was a catch: Sundays were my food-prep days. Because I had limited time to cook Monday through Friday, the best way to ensure healthy meals for my family was to plan the week's meals in advance. I'd do the grocery shopping, chopping, and most of the cooking, and then divide the meals into portions and store them in the fridge for the week. That way we'd only have to boil a pot of rice or some broccoli each evening. I did not believe in takeout, mostly because I found it insanely expensive. Also, by cooking my own food, I knew the ingredients that went in and that it would taste good. My obsession with low-cost, nutritious meals meant that I lived in New York City for three years before ordering takeout for the first time—a fact that most New Yorkers find hard to believe. Just thinking about the impact that the Harlem4Kids board meetings would have on my food-prep Sundays was enough to make me consider declining the invitation.

Why, you might ask, couldn't I just drop the food-prep ball in Kojo's lap? He was already helping with household chores like laundry or following up with the flooring estimate, but prepping food and figuring out meals for an entire week—this was not a task I thought he could handle. My biggest hurdle to passing the food-prep ball to Kojo was that I had assumed he was incapable of doing anything in advance. Unfair? Maybe. But history was my guide. It was not uncommon for us to have a formal gala event on our calendar for months, yet Kojo would wait until it was time to get dressed to ask, "What should I wear?" Meanwhile, I'd picked out my outfit a week in advance and ensured it was hanging cleaned and pressed in the closet!

To my mind, Kojo was great when it came to handling small or regularly occurring tasks. But the idea of him planning and prepping an entire week of meals was just too far-fetched. Because I had convinced myself he couldn't handle it, it didn't even occur to me to ask.

A few days after I received the board invitation, Kojo and I went on a belated Valentine's Day date; a work event had prevented us from celebrating on the actual night. It wasn't fancy (he was still unemployed at the time), but we enjoyed a much-needed evening out at our neighborhood Caribbean dive. Dates were a rare time for us to catch up on the details of our lives, and on this particular evening, Kojo updated me on his job search, and I shared the latest happenings at my office. By the time we got to the sorrel-and-lemon pound cake, I mentioned the Harlem4Kids board invitation. Kojo expressed surprise that this was the first time he was hearing about it: "Why were you holding out on me? That's cool, babe. Proud of you."

He assumed I had accepted. I quickly explained that I wasn't going to do it. There was no way I could fit it in with Sunday being my food-prep day.

Kojo was baffled.

"But you love Harlem4Kids," he said. "Plus board service looks good on your résumé. You can't say no. Why don't I just do the food-prep on Sunday? No biggie."

I chuckled. He seemed offended.

"What? You don't think I can do it?"

"Well, that would require you thinking in advance about what we're going to eat, getting all the ingredients, and prepping them so they're ready for each night. It requires a lot of, well, *planning*."

I delivered these remarks with lighthearted skepticism. I hadn't anticipated that Kojo would channel his machismo to take on the challenge.

"Let's make a deal," he replied. "You say yes to the Harlem4Kids board, and I'll prep the food on the Sundays of your meetings. *I promise*."

I reluctantly agreed but silently predicted it would be a disaster. I had just signed myself up for more work—the board meeting and the food prep—since I couldn't imagine Kojo actually following through.

Three weeks later, when I walked into our apartment after my first board meeting, my expectations were initially confirmed. There was Kojo, sitting in his usual location on the blue couch. The kitchen was spotless, which I took to mean he hadn't set foot in it. But then the lingering aroma of ginger, peppers, garlic, and onions simmering with fresh tomatoes reached me. I made a beeline for the refrigerator and pulled the door open, as if surprising a thief inside.

Nada.

"Check the freezer," Kojo called, his voice smug. I smiled. Inside the freezer were seven perfectly portioned and stacked plastic containers of chicken stew.

"So we're going to eat the same thing every night?"

"Yep!" he replied enthusiastically.

It wasn't the way I would have done it, but he had exceeded my expectations. I flashed back to Kojo's response to my board invitation. His words to me then seemed appropriate for this moment, too. I curled up next to him on the blue couch and whispered in his ear.

"Why were you holding out on me? That's cool, babe. Proud of you."

———

Kojo had kept his promise then, and he would keep it now. Somehow, he and our baby colluded to give Kojo plenty of time to make it back from Dubai. He arrived in New York a month after Barack Obama's presidential inauguration and two weeks before our baby was born on March 4, 2009. For both of my children, I had requested that the doctor not share the sex of the baby with me. As difficult as not knowing was, I did it to protect my children from my own meddling. If I knew their sexes, I'd immediately start planning too much of their lives before they'd even gotten a chance to take their first breath. I considered the nine-month wait my first act of motherly sacrifice. All that being said, I had a gut feeling that I'd have another boy, so when Kojo announced in the delivery room that we had a girl, I panicked again.

"But I don't know how to cornrow!" I wailed, before I had even laid eyes on her.

All I could see was my mother beaming with pride when strangers at the supermarket would comment on how beautiful her girls' hair was. So I would learn. Our daughter's hair would be beautiful, too.

Her first name would be Ekua, the traditional Ghanaian name given to a girl born on a Wednesday. I asked Kojo if we could break the father naming tradition so that I could select her middle name. He agreed in a heartbeat.

I chose Amala, which means *hope*.

CHAPTER 13

Recruit a Village

During the year that Kojo was in Dubai, there was a reason other than MEL to account for my relative well-being: Toyia Taylor. Toyia was the friend who had invited me to the fateful seventies Halloween party when we were in college, the one where Kojo had first noticed me. She moved to New York several years before Kojo and I did, and she was Kofi's godmother. Toyia was one of several people in our lives who questioned our decision to live on separate continents, but she loved us nonetheless and stepped up when we were in need. Toyia's way of being helpful was unique and incredible: despite her own busy life as an artist and educator, she vacated her rent-controlled apartment in Brooklyn to move in with us while Kojo was gone. She lived with us for an entire year. In order to make room, we gave Toyia Kofi's room and moved Kofi into my bedroom (Ekua joined Kofi and me after she arrived). It was a tight squeeze, but Toyia's presence proved vital. She even got her own dedicated MEL column. She was a phenomenal cleaner and a great cook, and she could stay with Kofi when I had to work late or travel.

Toyia wasn't the only person who chipped in to help. My extraordinary mother-in-law, Irene, would fly in from Ghana for weeks at a time, often without much notice. And more than once, Kojo's guy friends took me on weekend Costco runs. My friend and neighbor Michelle also helped me organize all of Kofi's old clothes in anticipation of the new baby, and I finally got to know our super, Lionel, on a first-name basis. Even our apartment landlord, who lived in California, would keep me notified of building news and pitch in to coordinate repairs if neither Lionel nor Kojo was available.

Whenever people asked me how I was able to manage my job, two kids, and our household with Kojo in Dubai, I would often give credit to these individuals. The usual response would be, "That's wonderful. You guys are so fortunate." But the level of support Kojo and I received was less about luck or fortune and more about dire necessity, since so much of what people helped us with—cleaning, child care, cooking, home repairs, and shopping—were tasks that later in our careers we hoped we would earn enough to be able to outsource. But in those years, we weren't yet at a level where we could afford to hire people to cover these tasks, and so the help we received from our circle was not only crucial but also deeply appreciated.

There is no denying the simple truth that for dual earners with high incomes, the life-go-round is a bit less taxing. In 2013 and 2014, Laura Vanderkam asked over one hundred mothers who earned at least six figures to log how they spent their time for a week.[1] Counter to the conventional narrative, she found that women with high-powered jobs are better able to achieve a work-life balance because they can afford to outsource labor. These women also enjoy a level of autonomy in their positions that allows them to be flexible with their time when necessary.

The challenge is that in order to get to one of these high-powered jobs, we have to go through a period of being middle managers without the privileges that a higher salary and autonomy at work provide. This is the time when an All-In Partnership is essential, but so is having a village that will step up to support our success. It's important for couples to understand that cultivating a village of people who are willing to carry the ball for us requires intentional action on our part: we have to ask for help and make our needs known. Once we do, we may find that support comes to us from surprising sources.

———

Cecile and Rhonda were two women who approached me after I spoke at a women's conference. During my keynote, I quoted Madeleine Albright, who once said, "There's a special place in hell for women who don't help other women." Cecile and Rhonda couldn't have agreed more and rushed up to tell me their story.

They had been saying "Let's have lunch" for six months after they first met one another at their church. They were both full-time working single moms with one son each, and it was tough to get their busy calendars to align. When they finally made it happen, they couldn't believe it had taken them so long. As they shared their stories over Subway chicken chopped salads, they realized they had a lot in common, from their ability to recall every episode of *Sex and the City* to their girlhood dreams of being fashion designers. Cecile was now a nurse, and Rhonda was the program manager for a transitional housing shelter. They were both divorced. Neither regretted her decision to leave a dysfunctional marriage, but they did lament the challenges of raising their sons alone. The day they first had lunch, Cecile was particularly stressed. She didn't want to move her twelve-year-old son, Malik, from the home he had grown up in, but without her ex-husband's income, she was struggling to make the mortgage payments on her nurse's salary. Meanwhile, Rhonda was thinking about moving out of her apartment in order to find one closer to her eleven-year-old son Justin's school. She wanted him to be able to walk home without her needing to hire a babysitter.

"Where does Justin go to school?" Cecile asked.

"Hamilton."

Cecile's mouth dropped open. "That's seven blocks away from my house."

For two women of faith, this was not a coincidence. That Subway lunch two years ago cemented their friendship and was the beginning of their All-In Partnership. Rhonda and Justin moved into the four-bedroom house with Cecile and Malik, and the arrangement worked so well that they considered starting a movement for single-mom roommates. Both family units lead separate lives, but the women share resources like housing expenses, cooking, and child care, and everyone thrives. So much so that whenever Cecile or Rhonda goes on a date, the other will jokingly chide, "Have fun, but don't lose your mind and marry him!"

As Cecile and Rhonda demonstrate, not every All-In Partnership is a married one, and a village can be created in unconventional ways. Especially for single women, enlisting people who can help shoulder the load is critical to ending their life-go-rounds. In fact, one of the sublime benefits of Dropping the Ball is the village of support that we inevitably build once we do so. A village is an inner circle of people who volunteer or are recruited to support a family's success. Their contribution might be so vital that they are awarded their own MEL column, and sometimes even a bedroom in your home. For Kojo and me, our village has become indispensable, because even with both of us pitching in to manage a household, there is still no way to cover every detail that needs our attention.

Our village has included five groups of people:

The first group is *Family Members*—people who are so invested in our success that we don't feel we're imposing on them when we ask for help. We are confident that their driving motivator is their love for us, and we cherish them and feel love toward them in return. To be clear, not every member of our biological family fits this category. Furthermore, not every person we consider as family is our biological relative. Our family includes my sorority line sisters, our children's godparents, and members of the church that helped raise me. Some might refer to these people as close friends or family friends, but we think of them simply as family. Some people live near enough to their family of origin that they can be an amazing resource. But given that as of 2013 only 29 percent[2] of couples prioritize living in proximity to their biological parents and extended kin, redefining family in a way that works for us is essential.

The second group of village members is our *Neighbors*. If a couple happens to live in the community where one or both of them grew up, this group may be ready and waiting. Many of us have moved away from home, however, which means these village members might need some recruitment to understand their role. I actually needed to do this with one of our new neighbors when Kofi was six. The neighbor had corrected Kofi for calling him "Mr. Harding," telling Kofi to just call him by his first name. Kojo and I liked this man a lot and felt that he had our family's best interests at heart. So I knocked on his door a few hours later. After saying hello and thanking him for being such a good neighbor, I told him there was a way he could help our family. "Could you please insist that Kofi address you as 'Mr. Harding'?" I asked. "That is a signal to him that you're someone in this community to whom he is accountable. I won't always be around, and neither will his dad. We have to know that other people are looking out for him. And he needs to know that you're looking out for him, too. Calling you 'Mr. Harding' reminds him that you're someone he needs to listen to and respect should you need to correct him or give him encouragement. Are you willing to be there for our family in that way?"

Mr. Harding immediately agreed and said he felt humbled to be assigned this role. He had always been a friendly neighbor, but after that conversation, he leaped to lend a hand whenever he could. Once, I had dragged the kids' bikes out of our storage unit only to discover on the sidewalk that the tires were flat. I couldn't carry both bikes to the bike shop while holding my kids' hands, so I told them we'd have to ride the bikes another day. They were having a double meltdown on the sidewalk when Mr. Harding came to the rescue, carrying the bikes to the shop so we could fill the tires. I thanked him for being such a vital member of our village.

The third group of our village is comprised of *Nonpaid Working Moms*. Often known as stay-at-home moms, the truth is, these women do not stay at home. They spend a great deal of time outside the house shuttling kids around, and they do every bit as much overall labor as women who work professionally—they just aren't paid for their efforts. The mommy wars are so over, because we all need each other. These are the people in our village who we can text under the table when our meeting is running over and ask them to grab our kids when they pick up their own. They give us tips on which teacher's class we should lobby to get our kids into, and they are critical during medical emergencies, staying with a child who has the flu on a morning when you have a presentation you just can't reschedule.

Nonpaid working moms also seem to know a lot about early childhood development. I can't imagine they have more time to read books than professional working mothers, so maybe it's because they spend more time with their kids than we do. Either way they are a golden resource. Here is a recent exchange I had with one of them after not seeing my kids for three days because I was juggling work commitments and a deadline for this book:

On Sunday at 7:46 AM, <Cheryl> wrote:

> *yesterday with kids was a great day!*
>
> *swim*
>
> *art making*
>
> *play*
>
> *art viewing*
>
> *relay races with other kids in central park. . . .*
>
> *back home to roller skate around the house . . . in old school roller skates . . .*
>
> *chicken fingers, fries and a movie.*
>
> *i love that ekua just goes with it here . . . she plays with all and makes herself at home*

*love both your kids so much. . . . like family to us—they were
a joy to have for all of us.*

lucy attacked kofi and told her how much she loved him!

On Sunday at 9:38 AM, <Tiffany> wrote:

*I cried when I read this message. I was up till 3 working on
a project last night. This after spending the past 48 hours in
Baltimore speaking at a conference. On the train rides I
was frantically writing script for a new series of career development videos Levo is producing. We shoot tomorrow.
And after being so happy over finishing the first draft of my
book I just got word from one of my readers that an entire
section doesn't work. I really need to rewrite 3 chapters
before I hand it in to my editor and hadn't factored that
into my deadline. Saying that I'm stressed would be an
understatement.*

*Most of the time I feel that I'm on track in being an awesome
partner, mother and global citizen. But yesterday the guilt
began to sink into my consciousness mostly because I hadn't
connected with the kids. I read your email and felt an immense burst of gratitude. Here I had been imaging their broken hearts over me moving at lightning speed when, in fact,
they were having a blast yesterday! And in wonderful
hands. THANK YOU.*

On Sunday at 9:48 AM, <Cheryl> wrote:

*you are a rockstar . . . i love partnering with rockstar
moms . . . like you, susie, amy . . .*

i am not sure i am a role model but you are . . .

*and my kids are soooo much happier with their friends
around.*

it does take a village as kojo might say . . . and we need your family in it

i am sure they love you but don't think you were painfully missed!

My nonpaid working mom village members have helped me avert countless crises, and I could never repay them. But I do my best to support their civic endeavors, as they're often on nonprofit boards, and we frequently host sleepovers to try to give them a break. One of them let me know recently that she was looking for an opportunity to reenter the workforce. She asked if I might know someone in marketing whom she could talk to. She delivered the question as if she were asking me for a very big favor. "Are you kidding me?" I said. "Of course!" Everything these women do for me enables me to advance my career and keep my connections current. My Rolodex is their Rolodex. I fired off a series of e-mails on my friend's behalf that very day.

The fourth group in our village is the *Babysitters*. These are the only paid village members. Kojo and I quickly figured out that it is best to have several of them on call and to draw from a diverse group, because we often need a babysitter at the last minute. College students are great, but we've had the most success with actors and musicians who babysit as a side job. One of our babysitters was in between Broadway shows and had just finished up a stint as Mary Poppins. She taught Kofi and Ekua all the songs. It was magical. There are now platforms like Care.com and UrbanSitter.com for anyone who doesn't have a handy supply of real live Mary Poppinses to rely on. We've used these solutions to find babysitters as well. Over the years, we've developed a few cardinal rules of working with babysitters to ensure they're full-fledged village members:

1. Whenever we pay sitters, we include a handwritten note of gratitude that acknowledges them as village members. It can be two lines. Really.

2. We ensure our sitters get home okay. We pay for their train or cab fare, and if it's late at night, we use Uber to call them a car or we drop them off ourselves. If they're walking, we ask them to text us when they get home so we know they got there safely.

3. We respect the referral relationship. If they ever refer us to another sitter, we are careful to always give them first right of refusal on future jobs.

4. We feed them. We let them know they are welcome to eat whatever is in our kitchen. And if their dietary requirements are different from ours, we order from a takeout restaurant that meets their needs.

5. We invest in their leadership journey above all else. This means if we know of a job lead that's in alignment with their passions (remember, babysitting is their side job), we make the connection. We've lost some really awesome regular babysitters this way, but they are still loyal members of our village because of it.

The fifth group that should be part of any village is the *Specialists*—friends and associates with expertise that allows you to shortcut household management tasks and solve issues. For example, it's helpful to have a village member who is a mechanic or who knows a lot about cars. It's also been beneficial to have ongoing relationships with a pediatrician and other types of physicians, an attorney, and a travel agent—but not as their clients. These specialists might be fellow parents at our kids' schools, people we meet at work or social events, referrals from friends, or former college classmates with whom we kept in touch. For a long time, Kojo and I couldn't afford to be paying clients to many of the specialists in our village, and because we weren't their clients, we were careful not to take up too much of their time. The primary question we ask our specialists is "What would you do if . . . ?" or "If you were looking for X, how would you quickly find it?" Our basic assumption is that our specialists know way more than we do in their areas of expertise, so the most direct path to success is doing what they would do. My sister once told me, "Tiffany, you're so boring. You never want to learn a lesson for yourself." My response?

Why should I waste time trying to learn something from the beginning when other people can share their hard-won knowledge with me?

It's important to note that specialists don't always have to be professionally affiliated; some offer expertise in personal matters. For example, two of our most treasured specialists are a couple who have been married for nearly fifty years. We have tremendous respect for them individually and as a unit, and they have given us invaluable relationship insight.

As busy professionals, Kojo and I have often had to rely on the grace and benevolence of our village. One week, for example, we couldn't avoid traveling simultaneously. I was scheduled to present at the inaugural MAKERS conference in California, and Kojo had to be in Lagos. We try to ensure that one of us is home with the kids each night, but on this occasion, the confluence of trips was unavoidable. On the last day of the conference, a snowstorm descended on New York, and all flights in were canceled. It was my worst nightmare. We had carefully timed the trips so that our kids would have only one evening without either parent. I had arranged for our regular sitter to spend the night with the kids and to take them to school the next morning, but she had another job to go to after she dropped them off at school, and technically, there wasn't anyone to do a kid pickup should someone get hurt or sick during the day. I knew, of course, that I could call on one of the nonpaid working moms in my circle, but I prayed to God that I wouldn't have to, trusting that I'd be home in time to do the after-school pickup myself.

My anxiety level skyrocketed as soon as I learned of the snowstorm, and I immediately sent an e-mail to the village members I had notified that we'd be out of town, in case of just such an emergency. They all weighed in at once to say Kofi and Ekua could stay with them. In the end, Cheryl, one of the nonpaid working moms, picked up my children from school and brought them to her house for an impromptu slumber party with her kids. My children were in such good hands. I should confess that, once upon a time, the HCD mom in me would have been obsessing about my daughter's tight curly hair looking crazy at school the next day because the white mom wouldn't know how to comb it; or the fact that my son would miss his after-school tutoring lesson because it would be too much trouble for my friend to take him with all the children she now had to wrangle; nor would my kids be able to wear their own clothes; and of course I couldn't be confident that all their homework had been completed—but that was *then*.

Now, instead of spending the rest of my trip freaking out about details over which I had no control, I could appreciate the positive side of my extraordinary circumstance: I had twenty-four hours with nothing to do and no one to take care of, and I was stranded at a five-star resort. Before reaching out to my village, I had been so stressed about the flight delays and beating myself up for being such an irresponsible parent that I hadn't even looked up to see the amazing view. The ocean was spectacular. I scheduled a massage and afterward sat for hours in the spa, just daydreaming. It reminded me of my girlhood, when I would spend an entire afternoon on a Strawberry Shortcake blanket in my backyard, writing one poem, only interrupted by my mother calling me in for dinner. After my time at the spa, I spent the evening sitting for hours next to a fire, laughing with my dear friend Jennifer over a bottle of wine and countless courses of delicious food.

The next morning, I went for an invigorating run along the beach. The waves teased me. With every few strides, the Pacific Ocean came to greet me, then it playfully retreated. I breathed in. I pushed it out. Everything was clear. After my run, I practiced yoga against a backdrop of the most magnificent sunrise. I arrived back in New York a better wife and mother, harnessing another level of appreciation about what it means to Drop the Ball.

PART FOUR

All-In Partners

CHAPTER 14

＋

Done Is Another
Person's Perfect

I hate my kitchen faucet. It looks like it's from the seventies, and not in a cool retro way. And yet, I love that ugly faucet, too. It reminds me every day how far I've come and how much I've gained by flushing my HCD down the drain.

Let me explain.

One morning as I was scrambling to pack lunch boxes, which I had almost forgotten to do because I was up until 2:00 A.M. the night before prepping for a big meeting (for which I was about to be late), I noticed the faucet was leaking. I knew I wouldn't be able to deal with it for at least a couple of weeks, so once the lunch boxes were packed, I sent Kojo a text: *Kitchen faucet leaking. Please fix.*

I didn't think twice about the fact that Kojo was in Dubai. We had created our MEL, so I knew he would find a way to handle it. And handle it he did. When I arrived home that night, there was a shiny new and woefully unfashionable faucet staring back at me. Ugh. I'd been envisioning something classy and sleek—something

Gwyneth Paltrow would approve of. I immediately began mentally rearranging my schedule so I could find the time to swap out the faucet the next day.

Then sanity prevailed. The whole reason I'd texted Kojo was because I'd had too much on my plate to deal with the sink myself. And there was an *X* in his column next to *Facility Maintenance Director*. How lucky I was to have a spouse who, even across the Atlantic Ocean, had managed to get a leaky faucet fixed in fewer than twelve hours in response to my five-word request. An ugly faucet was a small price to pay for an infinitely improved quality of life.

In every home, there are leaky faucets—real and metaphorical. Women must trust other people to tackle the problems, even if they do it differently from how we would. It's time to take a page from Princess Elsa of *Frozen* and simply let it go. If we can do that, we're likely to discover the kind of innovation that can transform our lives on the home front for good.

The insight I gained from delegating the task of fixing the leaky faucet to Kojo was an important one because for so long, most of the learning about how to manage our home had involved a transfer of knowledge from me to Kojo. Rarely was it the other way around. Just as the workplace is a male-dominated environment, our household was a female-dominated environment, even more so given my HCD. And with no human resource staff at home to draw attention to this inequity, Kojo had often experienced worse than an ultimatum. It was just *my way;* the highway wasn't even an option. But once I began relying more on his help—and really letting him do things his way—I benefited in new and unexpected ways. Take, for example, Kojo's having the dry cleaning delivered. For two years, I had been rushing around to pick up the dry cleaning, while in one day, Kojo figured out that it could be delivered according to a schedule that worked for our family. I had never even thought to ask! Every time I learned something new from Kojo that altered my behavior at home, it shook up our status quo. Each of these disruptions served as a reminder that diversity, when leveraged to solve problems in new ways, is a magnificent thing.

I stumbled upon another example of Kojo's innovation at home when, for the first time, he needed to find a babysitter. I was just returning from a business trip, my flight pulling up to the gate when he called to request that I forward him the names and cell numbers of all our babysitters. Because both of us traveled so much, I had assembled a healthy roster of them to fill in when we needed child care during the evenings and weekends. I was curious to know why Kojo was suddenly so eager to find a sitter, since this task usually fell to me. He explained that a client of his was in town unexpectedly, and he needed me to attend a dinner with him that night. Given that I had just arrived back in New York, I wasn't thrilled at the prospect of having to put on a cinching black dress and smile pretty to help him close a deal. Kojo knew I would much rather stay at home with our kids, whom I hadn't seen in two days. His strategy was to soften his request by volunteering to find the sitter.

"That's going to be impossible on such short notice," I told him with certainty as I reached up to grab my carry-on from the overhead bin.

Whenever I received last-minute invitations for evening work events, I usually just declined because I knew it would take me at least an entire day to find a sitter, and there wasn't enough time. But thirty minutes after I got off the phone with Kojo, he texted me the name of the sitter who would be watching our kids that night.

Over time, Kojo learned that it was easier to extract a yes from me for evening events if he volunteered to find the sitter. And over time, I observed that his ability to find a sitter within thirty minutes was not a fluke. One day, I finally asked him how he was always able to find a sitter so fast. I couldn't understand how it took him less than an hour to complete a task that usually took me close to two days. My method of finding a sitter was to send an e-mail or text days in advance to the person who I thought would be the best fit based on her work or school schedule and her place in our babysitter rotation. Then I would wait to hear back. If the potential sitter could do the job, I would book her. If she couldn't, I'd move on to

the next sitter on my list. To my mind, this was the most consider-
ate and fair way of booking the sitters.

When Kojo described *his* hiring strategy I was speechless. Whenever he had a babysitting request, he would draft a text and send it to
all the babysitters simultaneously and openly. That way each sitter
could see that ten other sitters had received the same request. Who-
ever wanted the job had to respond quickly, because Kojo simply
gave the job to the first person who was available. At first, I thought
Kojo's sitter-finding method was rude, so much so that when I ran
into one of our sitters at the bank I apologized to her. Her response
surprised me. She actually *liked* that Kojo texted everyone, because
if she knew she couldn't do it, she didn't have to feel bad for declining or take the time to notify me via e-mail. I quickly came to appreciate the efficiency of his approach, too. Not only did it allow me to
take advantage of networking opportunities I would previously have
declined, but it also reduced the amount of time that one task—
"Find a sitter"—remained on my to-do list. Best of all, I could now
Drop the Ball on finding a sitter because my husband was clearly
better at it. Kojo and I were becoming true domestic equals. And
our home was becoming a place that benefited from the diversity of
different perspectives.

—————

Even with the need for more women in leadership, many workplaces
are light-years ahead of homes when it comes to leveraging diversity. These companies already understand how a diversity of employee experiences, backgrounds, and skills can lead an organization
to the best possible outcomes. A 2011 *Forbes Insights* study detailed
the importance of a diverse and inclusive workforce for innovation
and creativity,[1] while an article in the *McKinsey Quarterly* draws a
clear connection between the diversity of a company's C-suite and
its financial performance, finding that "for companies ranking in the
top quartile in terms of executive-board diversity, ROEs [average re-
turns on equity] were 53 percent higher, on average, than they
were for those companies in the bottom quartile."[2] Another study

conducted by researchers at the University of Michigan gave quantitative proof that a heterogeneous staff results in a more diverse pool of problem solvers who can offer unique strategic contributions.[3] Eighty-one percent of respondents to the survey revealed that they had instituted gender and diversity programs in their recruiting processes and human resource initiatives.[4] Clearly, more and more companies agree that diversity is important.

Barbara Annis, founder and CEO of Gender Intelligence Group, has made it her life's work to harness the benefits of gender diversity in the workplace. For more than thirty years, Annis has helped companies to identify and unravel gender "blind spots," which she defines as "the incorrect assumptions held by men and women that cause 'accidents' of miscommunication and misunderstanding and help maintain the status quo in gender relations in companies."[5]

Annis holds that there are four primary blind spots that characterize the way men and women engage at work:

1. The belief that equality means sameness, which "leads us to make uneducated assumptions that may be completely off the mark about the meaning and motivations behind the behavior of others."

2. The male-designed organization, the business model that has been in place since the Industrial Revolution, is tailored to accommodate male qualities such as "speed, efficiency and clear hierarchy" on an organizational level.

3. Fixing women to think and act like men, which "perpetuates the belief that women's contributions and styles are inferior to those of men."

4. Assuming that the off-putting behaviors of men (such as entertaining clients at male-centric establishments) are intentional when the majority of men are "just doing what often feels right for the company and not really thinking about the effect their actions tend to have on women in the workplace."[6]

Annis believes that leaders in the workplace can disrupt the status quo and achieve optimum synergy and productivity by acknowledging these blind spots. I now know that the same is true on the home front.

Let's start with her first blind spot that "equality means sameness"—as in *When it's his turn to dress the child, it should be done exactly the same way that I do it.* This blind spot also leads to assumptions about the intentions of our spouses' behavior. *He clearly doesn't care about how our child looks.* This "equality means sameness" blind spot was at work the night I yelled at Kojo because I couldn't understand why he was chilling on the blue couch watching a basketball game when our child was screaming. I realize now that Kojo was unperturbed because he knew our son was not in the slightest jeopardy and that he was being cared for by Lucinda, a beloved and trusted member of our village. Kojo's way of dealing with the situation was just different from mine.

This "equality means sameness" approach at home increases the sheer amount of work that women take on since we're always trying to fix our spouses' "work product" to make it the same as ours. One U.K. study showed that women spend three hours every week redoing chores that they think their men have done "badly."[7] We would free up the time by accepting the job as complete, even if it wasn't accomplished the same way we would have done it.

Now let's move to Annis's second blind spot about the male-designed organization, which has been in place since the Industrial Revolution. For about the same amount of time, home management has been a female-designated zone, biased toward women who often excel at multitasking. In fact, many men find it difficult to plug into the complex structure of tasks, events, relationships, and practices that govern a well-run home. This is why, when women leave for more than twenty-four hours, they often feel the need to leave detailed instructions about what to do in their absence.

One reason the home remains a female-designed organization is because women are often privileged with firsthand information about management issues. This is because most external stakeholders, including child-care and health-care providers, schools, and extra-curricular program staff, default to communicating with the "woman of the house," even when men are listed as the primary contact. Sociologists call women's control of this type of household management information "maternal gatekeeping."[8] For much of my marriage, I was gatekeeper in chief.

I had a rude and delightful awakening one day when one of our new babysitters disrupted my gatekeeping by texting Kojo directly. Every time she sent a text message, she included both Kojo and me. I would leave her a grocery list, and she would text us from the store, *What kind of apples?*, or I'd ask her to buy a birthday present, and she'd text, *What's the gift budget?*

I hadn't asked her to keep us both in the loop, and at first, it drove me crazy. I thought it was futile for her to text Kojo, too, since I was obviously the only one who knew the answers to her questions. But then something amazing began to happen—something I hadn't anticipated. I'd finish a meeting or public presentation to find a string of exchanges on my phone between the babysitter and Kojo. Sometimes he didn't answer her questions correctly (I needed green apples, not red), but after a few weeks, I grew to appreciate that the world didn't end with red apples. Just as important, I realized how stressful it had been to feel like I needed to be on call for the sitter while at work. My focus during meetings would often be split between the discussion around the table and whatever text was popping up on my screen. But now I saw that Kojo could be receptive to her questions as well. My anxiety dissipated, and my ability to be fully present at work improved. Female-designed organizations and home management systems that bias women leave us with more work and prevent men from being All-In Partners.

Blind spot number three: "Fixing women to think and act like men." We've long known that when women model male behavior in the office, it doesn't leverage what both genders bring to the table.[9] And yet I know many women who are trying to fix men to think and act like women at home. Sure, we can learn from each other and adopt some useful behaviors, but we inhibit men's creative problem solving by insisting they take the same approach we would.

Of all my failed strategies to encourage Kojo to do more, the one

I'm most ashamed of was my sticker incentive program. That was why I was so impressed with Felicia's, the educator who ran such a tight ship at home. My home management theory was rooted in the core idea that things shouldn't pile up. In my mind, the longer you waited to take care of something, the more work you'd have to do. But Kojo didn't see it this way. He figured that whether you took care of it now or later, it was still, cumulatively, the same amount of work. So he didn't feel any rush to address it. Despite his logical approach, I tried to coax him into adopting *my* timeline. I'd write a list for him of a few things that I wanted him to do, such as take out the recycling or return the wrong box of breakfast cereal to the grocery store. Then I'd stick the list on the refrigerator and add a bright yellow happy face sticker to all the tasks that were completed on the day *I* would have finished them. One day, the ridiculousness of my exercise really hit home when Kojo observed, "I keep randomly getting stickers and I don't even know why." I explained that he was getting a sticker next to a task he had completed "on time."

"But you've never written a deadline next to a task, so how am I even supposed to know what 'on time' is?" Kojo found the whole experiment patronizing, and I knew it was defeating its purpose when one afternoon I found myself writing on my to-do list, "Get new stickers." Needless to say, the sticker program was abandoned after three weeks.

Finally, the last blind spot: assuming that the off-putting behaviors of men are intentional. At home, too, it's important to understand that women aren't snapping at their husbands for fun or sport. Like the men whose off-putting behavior is not ill intentioned but is merely "what often feels right for the company," a woman who repeats the same phrase over and over each morning, each time a bit more forcefully, is simply trying to ensure that everyone gets to the right place at the right time with the right backpack. Usually, it's the stress of the morning rush in our voices and not some intentional desire to nag our family.

In general, Kojo exhibits less stress than I feel because, unlike me, he is able to compartmentalize most issues, keeping them simple and separate. I discovered this only because our physical distance forced us to communicate less spontaneously. With Kojo in Dubai, our primary form of communication was over Skype, and we had to be deliberate about scheduling regular check-ins. Since our time together was often limited, we developed agendas to ensure we covered everything. Kojo's agenda items were always straightforward. We always got through his list quickly. But more often than not, my seemingly "small" agenda items led to bigger issues that were too complicated for us to address on one call. For example, I'd write "diapers" to suggest to Kojo that we could start ordering them to be delivered directly to Kofi's day care, which would then lead me to express that I was concerned Kofi was still wearing diapers at all. What began as a quick note about buying diapers devolved into a much larger discussion about our son's development.

"Do you think that we should start the potty training process?" I would begin. "There are other kids in Kofi's preschool class who are out of diapers. What potty training method do you think we should use? I heard of one method where you allow the child to go bare bottom at home. That seems kind of extreme—and messy!" This would then launch me into a discussion with Kojo about our different parenting styles. Finally, Kojo would interrupt to say something like, "Babe, I thought we were just talking about diapers." He thinks in bullet points; I think in paragraphs.

In his video *Tale of Two Brains,* pastor and comedian Mark Gungor crafts a humorous metaphor for the differences in how men and women think.[10] He describes men as having brains that are full of boxes. For example, one box for the car, one box for work, one box for kids, and their favorite box—the nothing box. The male brain's unofficial rule is that none of the boxes ever touch.

Women, on the other hand, have brains full of connected wires. This connectivity can be a blessing. Because women can hold divergent viewpoints at once, their "connected" mode of thinking allows them to intuit and cater to other people's emotions while keeping more concrete objectives in mind, such as inspiring teams to achieve a shared purpose in the face of uncertainty.[11] This connectivity can also be a curse, however, particularly when it becomes necessary to separate one concern from another—or chat about basic household tasks over a late-night Skype call.

For me, having a brain full of connected wires means I have a difficult time separating my value as a human being from my performance. As much as I've tried to let go of my HCD, there is still some small part of me that believes my value as a mother is tied to how well my kids' hair is maintained. To this day, if my daughter's hair isn't neatly combed or my son hasn't been to the barbershop, I'm anxious that I'm going to get a mom pink slip. Yet for the sake of my own sanity, I strive to put the two ideas into separate boxes. Kojo's ability to do this means he experiences less pressure; it would never occur to him that he was a terrible father because his son was overdue for a haircut.

A man's "box brain" may also explain why men can crave pleasure at times when women's minds are too occupied to even consider it. My female friends often exclaim, "How could he want to have sex when the house is a complete wreck?" Women can immediately see the relationship between sex and housework. The wire goes something like this:

The housework required for tonight, which involves, among other things, emptying our bedroom closet so that maintenance workers can install the new shelving tomorrow, is going to take me three hours. I'm already exhausted, and getting my mind in the mood and my body ready to make love will take even more of my time. I'd need to sit for a while (with a glass of wine), then head to the bathroom to shower because in my haste to make my first meeting this morning I skipped shaving my legs. Unless he's going to help me clear out the closet (yeah, right), all of this presex prep, plus the act itself, will require an additional two hours, at least. I'm exhausted just thinking about it. It's already 8:00 P.M., and the kids aren't even in bed yet, and I can't cancel the maintenance man—it took me weeks to get this appointment. He can't wait, but my husband can.

Meanwhile, the man is ready to get into bed because he genuinely sees no relationship between the housework and the sex. In his mind, there's no logic wire connecting the two. Sex and housework are two boxes that do not touch.

Understanding these differences, combined with becoming aware of our blind spots, can ease tension and turn potentially combative situations into moments of connection. Instead of just rolling our eyes at our husbands' advances and assuming their desire to have sex means they don't care how we are feeling, we could share why we can't get in the mood. We might even try Delegating with Joy by renegotiating the evening to make space for an activity that would bond us in a deeper way.

The rewire could go something like this:

"Hon, I've got a deal for you. I'm going to take a long hot shower. While I'm doing that, it would be awesome if you emptied the closet. The maintenance guy is installing new shelves tomorrow morning, and I'm a little stressed about everything that needs to happen before then. When I emerge from the bathroom, if our bedroom closet is empty, I promise, I'm all yours."

Most men would then put "clean closet" and "sex" in the same box and get to work.

Too often, women's super-wired brains keep them from accessing simple solutions because they involve asking our husbands to do more at home. This was the case with Jackie, a woman I met through Mocha Moms, a national support group for mothers of color. When we talked at the end of her maternity leave after having her first child, I could sense the stress in her voice. For the past four weeks, Jackie had been visiting day cares, and with six days left before she had to be back at her desk, she still hadn't made a final decision on her child-care plan. None of the places she visited had seemed like the right fit for her beautiful baby girl, Olivia.

Meanwhile, her husband's employer (he was a maintenance worker for the local utility company) had recently implemented a new family leave policy that offered twelve weeks of paternity leave. Henry would not lose his job if he stayed home to care for his infant, but the leave was unpaid. Fortunately, Henry had nearly four weeks of unused vacation time that could be applied to his paternity leave so that he could, theoretically, be paid for the first month of being at home. Despite all this, Jackie told me that Henry would stay home with their daughter only as a last resort. Her first choice was to find adequate day care. Her second choice was asking her own boss if she could take an additional two weeks' leave. Having her husband stay home and care for their child was the backup plan.

This train of thought didn't make sense to me. I asked Jackie why she would risk jeopardizing her relationship with her boss, and her career, when Henry had a four-week paid-leave option. She explained that because their family relied more heavily on Henry's salary, his taking leave posed a greater financial risk than if she extended her leave. Jackie also believed that because it was rare for men to take paternity leave, doing so would hurt Henry's good standing with the company's higher-ups.

But my closer inquiry revealed another reason for her reluctance to have Henry take over Olivia's care: Jackie didn't think Henry would do a good job. "Henry has changed diapers, and he knows how to feed Olivia," she told me, "but he still doesn't know anything about the timing of either. She'll end up with a diaper rash. And he never feeds her on time or puts her to bed on time. He doesn't know her schedule."

I had so much empathy for Jackie as I thought about my "Top Ten Tips for Traveling with Kofi." But I now saw more clearly the unintended ramifications of such low expectations. Our assumptions that men can't handle caregiving deny them the benefits of participating at home—benefits for them, for our children, and to us. Jackie's first choice to extend her maternity leave rather than have Henry initiate his own leave would deprive him of the chance to bond with his infant daughter. It would also potentially compromise her own career. It's a scenario in which everybody loses, because studies show that men who have this opportunity early on are more engaged fathers down the road.[12]

Low expectations also lead many women to elevate their husbands' careers over their own, putting their families' financial future entirely in their husbands' hands. Pamela Stone, author of *Opting Out?: Why Women Really Quit Careers and Head Home,* probes the logic behind women's choice to forgo their careers to manage the home full-time, even when their husbands have been supportive of their professional lives. Stone describes women as "co-conspirators in privileging their husbands' careers." According to Stone, women often place higher value on their husbands' careers over their own, "for reasons that reflected culture, values, cold hard dollars, and most of all, time. The fact that men's careers came first was the underlying and unspoken 'reason' women quit, but men's careers almost always come first; they come first in couples in which women continue working."[13]

Even when men's engagement at home is the most practical solution, we often deny them the opportunity to care for their children because we've relegated them to breadwinning. Worse, we do this without asking them how they feel about it. Jackie had never actually discussed with Henry whether he wanted to take paternity leave to be with Olivia. When she finally did bring it up, he leaped at the opportunity! Jackie was happily surprised, but still harbored concerns. In her eyes, his desire did not equate to competency, and she doubted his motives. More than once when he'd come home to find Olivia and his wife sleeping, he'd commented how he wished that he could stay home and nap with the baby. Jackie wondered, *Does he think that taking a paternity leave will be a break?*

I assured Jackie that even if Henry harbored such an idea, he would manage. Perhaps not the way she would, but Olivia would be fine. I shared with her a pivotal moment from my own marriage, when I saw with a flash that my way was not always the only way, and sometimes not even the best way. I had awoken one morning to find Kofi asleep in his baby bouncer, which he had already outgrown. Even more confusing, the bouncer was lined with garbage bags, and Kofi had another bag tied to his neck like a giant plastic bib. Except for his diaper, my child was naked. When Kojo, who was working at his laptop nearby, saw the horrified look on my face, he explained that Kofi had been vomiting all night and that the garbage bag/baby bouncer strategy prevented him from having to wash bed linens and clothes continuously. It wasn't a solution I would have dreamed up in a million years, but I had to admit, it was brilliant.

There is a popular phrase "Done is better than perfect." It's supposed to help those of us with HCD feel better about things not being done exactly right. We are encouraged to resign ourselves to the simple fact of accomplishment, based on the idea that we can get more done by compromising on quality. What I learned after dropping a few balls and watching my husband pick them up and run with them is that quality is relative; one person's "done" can be another person's "perfect." Sure enough, the next time Kojo came home from Dubai, the first thing he remarked on after walking into our apartment was my lovely kitchen eyesore.

"Cool faucet, huh?"

CHAPTER 15

------◆------

Affirm with Gratitude

As I continued to strategize about how to create the strongest possible All-In Partnership between Kojo and me, I often thought back to my mother's early affirmations. When I was growing up, she would look me in the eye and say, "Tiffany, you are so smart. You are so beautiful. You are so loved." She said it so often that by the time I was a teenager I found it annoying. I didn't know it then, but her message became part of my consciousness; whenever I'd experience moments of difficulty or doubt, I'd hear my mother's words in my mind and feel renewed confidence. Once, in the midst of a heated argument, my mother told me she didn't love me. I refused to believe her.

"That's not true," I responded. "You're just upset." Her love for me was undeniable. After years of reinforcement, I trusted it implicitly. My mother's words of affirmation were the greatest gift she gave to me.

An affirmation is the assertion that something positive exists or is true, and it has the power to inspire great good. Conversely, a lack of affirmation has the power to do great harm: research shows that an absence of early affirmation in a person's life can result in emotional deprivation disorder, which is characterized by the inability to handle criticism, develop healthy relationships, or feel worthy.[1] Affirmation's potency is rooted in its ability to alter human behavior in the future, long after the affirming words are spoken. Whether we believe in ourselves or not, we are heavily influenced by people who believe in us. As every movie script about an inner-city educator who turns around a failing school illustrates, great leaders understand the relationship between their people and their people's performance. Effective leaders use affirmation to motivate others, often to phenomenal heights.

Sometimes affirmation can come across as harsh. It isn't always delivered gently and doesn't always feel good in the moment, especially when someone is pushing us to exceed the expectations we have of ourselves. But only people who truly believe in us can demand a lot and motivate us to deliver. The late University of Tennessee women's basketball coach Pat Summitt, known for racking up the most all-time wins in the NCAA (even more than the men's division), was a legendary example of the power of affirmative leadership. Summitt's success was rooted in her focused, goal-oriented guidance as well as a commitment to letting her players falter and learn from their mistakes. However, her style wasn't always easy for her players to take. As former University of Tennessee point guard Michelle Marciniak said of her coach, "Pat is a champion—thinks like a champion and coached me with endless passion and gutless determination. She didn't care if I liked her or agreed with her. Pat wanted results." Even though Coach Summitt's affirmations weren't delivered in a warm and fuzzy way, her players nonetheless *believed* they could win championships because she told them that they could.

In life, we could all use a coach to reaffirm our potential. Personally, I've been blessed to have Marie Wilson, a prominent figure in the women's movement, as my Sage Mentor and Sponsor. Marie's unwavering support motivated me to give my best for her and the organization—even in moments of struggle. More than once, I doubted myself or made a mistake and then worried Marie would fire me. The most notorious incident was when I blew an opportunity for the White House Project to receive significant funding from the shipping giant UPS. We had spent months cultivating the relationship with UPS and had received a verbal approval of the company's sponsorship. We just needed to submit a formal proposal, which my team completed in record time. We sent the proposal by overnight delivery to meet the deadline, but the next day, our contact went silent. After several attempts to follow up to confirm that UPS had received the proposal, our contact finally took my call, only to explain that, yes, our proposal had arrived—via FedEx. Needless to say, we didn't receive the corporate grant.

The hardest part for me was calling Marie to tell her I'd screwed up. I hated to disappoint her, and I was still feeling awful when I accompanied her to an event she was keynoting later that week. As always, during the speech, Marie acknowledged her staff members who were in the room. I'll never forget what she called me that night: a superstar. I had made a big mistake, yet it didn't change Marie's fundamental belief in me. Her continued faith in my abilities, especially in the wake of a failure, empowered me to forge ahead with confidence and to not define myself by that one misstep.

One of the biggest benefits of affirmation—through good times and bad—is that it simply communicates to an individual, "I see you, and I recognize your value." To be on the receiving end of this sort of affirmation is motivating and empowering. Especially as a woman of color climbing the career ladder, I understand how it feels to be invisible in the workplace. According to a 2015 study by Center for Talent Innovation, black women's advancement in particular is limited by the fact that our contributions often go unrecognized.[2] Being recognized is, in and of itself, a huge motivator.

Today I not only aspire to follow Marie Wilson's example of affirmative leadership when I manage others, but I also try to stay cognizant of its power when I work with my All-In Partner at home.

—

In the 2013 documentary *American Promise,* Joe Brewster is an All-In Partner and devoted father, adamantly invested in the academic success of his teenage son, Idris. Unfortunately, Joe's attempt at affirmative leadership is jeopardized by the negative reinforcement he dishes out, albeit with righteous intentions. "You're lazy!" he tells Idris, trying to motivate the adolescent, whose school performance only continues to decline.

Instead of affirmative leadership, Idris experiences negative reinforcement, which occurs when we feel our contributions are being ignored or when our behaviors or traits are labeled as negative qualities. When someone tells a little girl who has a clear voice and high leadership capacity that she is "bossy"—as if by organizing teams on the playground or assigning roles for make-believe play she is doing something wrong—we risk negatively reinforcing her. In 2014, the Lean In movement, which focuses on encouraging women to pursue their ambitions, and Girl Scouts of the USA launched the Ban Bossy campaign with the goal of supporting girls to be strong and confident. My own mother had had a different approach to this scenario. When I came home crying because someone had told me to stop being so "bossy," she squealed with delight. "Oh, but I *love* that you're bossy, sweetheart. Keep it up!" she would say. Whether we reappropriate the "bossy" insult or ban it altogether, it's critical that we combat the negative messages that girls too commonly receive.

Despite having been robustly affirmed at home, I learned at an early age that the boy next door and I could exhibit the exact same leadership qualities, but the people around us might interpret our behavior differently. Outside my home, it was often *my* behavior that was negatively reinforced, like the time in fifth grade when my Sunday school teacher reprimanded me for volunteering to lead a prayer in a class that included boys. As a preacher's daughter, I excelled at praying, yet I was being told that when boys were present, I should allow them to take the reins. As Jessica Bennett poignantly illustrates in her book, *Feminist Fight Club,* most girls grow up to experience this exact same phenomenon in the workplace.[3]

When our behavior is more negatively than positively affirmed, we feel disempowered and devalued. I've heard women say they feel this way when, for example, they offer a viewpoint during a meeting, but no one acknowledges that theirs is a great idea until the guy next to them repeats the same thing. Here's what happens next: women become less eager to speak their minds, and their companies are denied their potentially valuable contributions. Being ignored or negatively reinforced can affect the degree to which women feel comfortable vouching for themselves at work, whether that be inquiring about a promotion or seeking out a professional mentor.[4] It can also affect whether women hold back their ideas and opinions for fear of being perceived as too brash or talkative.

Even Superwomen who are politicians, a job that requires a lot of talking, know that for women, speaking up can be kryptonite. A study conducted by Victoria Brescoll of Yale University in 2012 examined the relationship between gender, power, and volubility based on observations of the United States Senate. Brescoll discovered that men with power talk more on the floor, while women with power talk less—but not because they have less to say. Women are concerned that being highly talkative will result in negative consequences. Brescoll's findings suggest that whether it's on the Senate floor or in the executive boardroom, "high-powered women are in fact justified in their concern that they will experience backlash from being highly voluble: a female CEO who talked disproportionately longer than others was rated as significantly less competent and less suitable for leadership than a male CEO who was reported as speaking for the same amount."[5] Negative reinforcement does affect our performance and, over time, can undermine our belief in ourselves.

Even though I'm incredibly fortunate to have had champions like my mother and Marie Wilson, like most women, I still need to remind myself of my value. We all need to be our own champions. I have coached many women to create their own self-affirmations, phrases that reinforce positive truths about themselves, such as "I am creative" and "Everything I need to be successful is within my reach." Some women write their affirmations on cards and post them in their homes. Others print and cut them as small as fortune cookie messages and tuck them into purses, pockets, and drawers to surprise themselves later. One of my friends, Chrissy Greer, regularly changes her security passwords to make them affirmation acronyms. After one of my breakfasts with Chrissy, in which I expressed anxiety over writing this book, she encouraged me to change all my security passwords to include "IAAPW," which stands for "I Am A Phenomenal Writer." (For security reasons, I've changed them all again.)

Such self-affirmation gives women the permission we sometimes need to prioritize our own success. It's one thing to Drop the Ball because our life-go-rounds have made us so dizzy; it's another to Drop the Ball because we know that we're worthy of a full night's sleep, a fit and healthy body, and time to think and create. When we're negatively reinforced, we lose sight of our potential, and we don't aspire to advance our leadership. Going for that next promotion feels like too much work. Ambition feels daunting. But when we are positively affirmed by ourselves and others, we feel *deserving* of the support that's required for us to excel. When we recognize our value, we don't hesitate to solicit help from others; we are able to recognize the upside of collaboration, not just for ourselves but also for the other person, for our organization, for our families, and for the world. We are confident that we're worth the investment.

Just as affirmed women are more likely to rise to the highest levels of leadership at work, so, too, can affirmed men rise to the highest levels of leadership at home. When I mentioned to a friend I was writing this book, she insisted that I interview a man she knew who had risen at home like a rock star. Karim had always aspired to be an involved father to his children. Raised by his mother and grandmother, he had yearned to know his own father, who died before Karim's anger over his absence had subsided enough for Karim to go looking for him. Karim's worst fear was that his two small sons would grow up feeling he wasn't there for them in the way he wished his own father had been there for him.

At first, Karim and his wife, Lisa, had a traditional arrangement.

She was the primary caretaker of the home as he pursued a career in medicine. When their youngest turned two, they decided Lisa would reenter the workforce. I met them less than a year after Lisa began her new job, when she and Karim were just emerging from her tense back-to-work transition.

Lisa's job often required her attendance at evening events. In the beginning, Karim wasn't accustomed to altering his schedule to accommodate his wife's. Their food bill skyrocketed, as they ordered takeout on weekday evenings when neither partner had time to prepare dinner. Plus all of the tasks that Lisa used to accomplish during the day, such as laundry and grocery shopping, were being pushed back, making weekends hectic for the family. Karim admired his wife and wanted her to succeed. He understood that meant he needed to do more at home so Lisa could devote the necessary time and energy to her own career, but in the beginning, he was overwhelmed. Over the course of several months, however, he was well on his way to being a true All-In Partner to Lisa. They were able to negotiate household chores almost evenly, and Karim was thrilled that he was spending more time with his sons. What was the clincher in Karim's motivation to do more on the home front?

Lisa's gratitude.

As Karim spent more time with the boys, he discovered a secret to altering their behavior—praising the good more often than reprimanding the bad. Sometimes Karim suspected that Lisa was using the same strategy on him, and he had to admit that it felt good. Karim spoke fondly of the written and verbal messages Lisa routinely served up. Because he was on to her tactic, he often found her comments funny because of how far she stretched to find something positive to say. One night, Lisa arrived home to find that their youngest son had dumped his dinner on the floor.

"Wow, thanks, honey," Lisa said to Karim without disdain. "So wonderful that you're cultivating Noah's food art potential!"

Karim told me that the more Lisa affirmed his efforts and expressed gratitude for his contributions, rather than disappointment when he didn't do things exactly the way she would have, the more he felt valued and confident in his newly expanded role at home.

Karim's success makes sense in light of the latest research on the effects of positive emotion. Barbara Fredrickson is a social psychologist and principal investigator of the Positive Emotions and Psychophysiology Lab at University of North Carolina at Chapel Hill. According to Fredrickson, affirmation sparks positive emotion, which in turn widens our consciousness and increases our creativity, our resilience, and our belief in what is possible.[6] Karim's broader mindset was the prerequisite for his discovery of new skills and knowledge.

Unfortunately, Lisa's deliberate and consistent use of gratitude to motivate Karim and fortify their All-In Partnership is not the norm in most households. Too many couples never quite realize how an absence of gratitude might be undermining their relationship. Seeking outside counsel can help, yet according to *The Science of Clinical Psychology,* the average couple spends six unhappy years together before scheduling their first appointment. At that point the therapist arrives, "less like an emergency-room physician who is called upon to set a fracture that happened a few hours ago and more like a general practitioner who is asked to treat a patient who broke his or her leg several months ago and then continued to hobble around on it, [having] to attend not only to the broken bone but also to the swelling and bruising, the sore hip and foot and the infection that ensued."[7]

Couples can avert such dysfunction by adopting healthy behavior patterns early in their relationships. For Kojo and me, this meant getting clear about what mattered most to each of us, leveraging our highest and best use, creating a MEL, and setting aside time to discuss our challenges and our goals. All these habits ensured we would be on the same page. But perhaps the most significant action we took to strengthen our All-In Partnership was to regularly express gratitude to each other as a way of making sure we both felt affirmed. A lovely bonus was the fact that expressing gratitude also has a positive effect on health and mood: studies show that its physical and psychosocial benefits are profound. In one study, research participants who felt grateful were more likely to offer another person emotional support, get more exercise, and have a higher quality of sleep.[8] In short, when we actively bring an attitude of gratitude to the proceedings, everybody wins.

Gratitude is a particularly powerful form of affirmation because it enables value[9]—and everyone wants to feel valued. However, gratitude requires intentionality because, as a practice, it's not encouraged by our culture, which has a knee-jerk inclination toward dissatisfaction. We can always use a bigger house, a leaner body, a faster car. We can always be better, quicker, smarter, richer. In contrast, gratitude— the act of showing appreciation for a thing, a person, or an act *as it is*—reinforces that what we currently have, who we currently are, and what we are currently capable of is enough. In this way, gratitude greases the wheels of an All-In Partnership, motivating our spouses to pick up our dropped balls and to master whatever tasks are necessary to allow us to flourish.

—◆—

In Fante, Kojo's native tongue, the word for "thank you" is *madasi,* and it's the most important word to know. Expressing gratitude is a cornerstone of Ghanaian culture. Kojo and I have always said thank you to one another. He did so the first time I told him that I loved him. I'll never forget that moment. It was just a couple of months after our first Red Robin date. He still referred to me as his friend, while I thought of him as my boyfriend. It was my birthday, and he had just presented me with a gift—a small beaded necklace from Ghana. The simplicity of his gesture stood in stark contrast to my previous birthday, when my ex-boyfriend had treated me to a four-course dinner, sent me roses and a balloon bouquet, and made a video of himself serenading me with Bobby Brown's "Roni." A week later, I discovered that boyfriend was cheating on me. What I most appreciated about Kojo was that his words and his actions were aligned. Though I considered myself his girlfriend, the necklace was exactly the gift a man would give a woman whom he called his friend. I swooned at his integrity. My "I love you" spilled out as he was adjusting the clasp. His gratitude was unexpected. "Thank you for loving me," he said. That's when I decided: *He's going to be my husband*.

For the first part of our marriage, I was very intentional about affirming Kojo's value as provider and protector. I called him "my lion" and thanked him often for taking care of me—even though we both knew I was perfectly capable of taking care of myself. But after our two children were born, our work and home management life-go-round grew so hectic that the affirmations that first kindled our love in a college dorm room became a distant recollection. My HCD and stealth resentment had all but smothered the feelings of appreciation I'd once held so consistently. My gratitude practice needed a reboot.

After Ekua's birth, I was awed by Kojo's willingness to support me in ways I had never imagined and had often overlooked. I was most impressed with his ingenuity and his ability to operate in our time zone, despite being nine hours ahead of us in Dubai. One cold morning, I awoke to discover there was snow outside and no running water, and I called him in a panic. He calmly instructed me to fill a large pot with some of the snow and to heat it on the stove. By the time the water was boiling, Kojo had made enough calls to report that the water would be back on by noon. "You are *so* not from a developing country," he joked when I finally calmed down.

Another time, when Kofi was so sick I couldn't leave the house, Kojo enlisted the help of a neighbor who rang our doorbell with Pedialyte within an hour. When we ate dinner at seven in the evenings, Kojo joined at the table via Skype, connecting with us, even though it was four in the morning his time. I could send him a text message at any hour of the day or night, and his response would come within the hour.

In addition to his creativity and responsiveness, I also appreciated Kojo's sacrifice. As difficult as it might have been for the kids and me to be without him, he was missing us, too. On many nights, Kojo would wait up until I arrived home, then after we caught up, he'd ask me to take my laptop into the bedroom so that he could watch our children sleep. Sometimes, I'd go back into the room after having cleaned up the kitchen and washed a load of clothes to find Kojo on my computer screen fast asleep. Knowing his alarm clock would buzz in less than an hour, I'd close my laptop and crawl into bed feeling fortunate that I had seven hours of shut-eye ahead of me.

Though I worried about Kojo forgoing his sleep, I was grateful to him because his support at home allowed me to thrive in new ways. You'd think with my husband on the other side of the world that I'd have less time and feel more pressure, but in fact the opposite was true. I had more time and felt less pressure with Kojo in Dubai. It's true that our greater fiscal security was calming my nerves—but there were three other reasons that I felt more relaxed at that time.

First, our geographic distance required that we check in regularly with one another about the status of our tasks or any other details mapped out on MEL. In addition to connecting each night via Skype, we instituted weekly meetings to update one another on household business. I knew more clearly than I ever had that I wasn't alone in managing our home. Kojo and I were a team.

The second reason I felt more relaxed was that we spent less physical time together. Of course I missed Kojo's presence, but the dirty little secret was that his absence meant that after I put Kofi and Ekua to bed and did a few chores, I had a couple of hours each evening to respond to e-mails, catch up with an old friend on the phone, or even put on a yoga DVD. With Kojo away, I discovered what some couples already know: time spent alone can be as valuable to the relationship as time spent together.

The third reason I felt less stress was that Kojo's now-unwavering commitment to our home management freed up my mental energy. I didn't have the constant itch to check to see if Kojo was completing his end of the bargain—because he was.

Everyone thought I was incredible (and a little crazy) to be holding down the fort in New York while Kojo was across an ocean. Even Kojo was becoming more aware of how much effort went into keeping our household running smoothly. Before, he'd assumed that I was like Samantha from *Bewitched*, twitching my nose to make everything happen while he was at the office. Now, he could see there was no magic involved—just a lot of careful planning and hard work. Despite a steady stream of compliments from other people—from "You're such a superwoman" to "I don't know how you do it all"—I knew that I *didn't* do it all. Yet I rarely shared the full truth: Kojo was right there with me as a partner, as involved as he would have been in person. I realized, however, that Kojo needed to know that *I* knew the truth of how much his support meant to me and to our family.

I made a resolution to be more proactive in expressing my gratitude. I wanted to fulfill this goal intentionally and meaningfully, so over one of our Skype calls I asked him, "How have I expressed gratitude to you in the past that's meant the most to you?" My second question was going to be, "Is there any *new* way that I can express gratitude that would be meaningful to you?" But we didn't get that far.

I thought I knew what his answer to my first question would be: my letters. In the beginning of our marriage, before kids and the demands of our careers kicked into overdrive, I'd gotten into the habit of handwriting letters to Kojo. Especially on special occasions, I'd share how much he meant to me and express the difference he made in my life. I'd adopted the practice from my father, who was a prolific letter writer.

The month I left home for college, my father wrote me a letter expressing his pride and expectations. It included scriptures and life lessons. I received more of these letters throughout my college career. As with my mother's affirmations, I didn't fully appreciate them at the time, but in hindsight, they were a great source of reassurance and wisdom, so much so that in August 1997, just one month after Kojo and I wed, I called my father to find out if he had mailed my letter; it had been a while since I'd received one. "You don't need those anymore," my father said matter-of-factly. "Kojo will take care of you now." My father had passed the baton. From that day on, I adopted my father's letter-writing tradition as my own.

To my mind, my letters to Kojo were the most meaningful expression of my gratitude, so I was not expecting that in response to my question he would say, "The hot pics you text me when you're traveling." In fact, I was horrified. *Meaningful* is not the adjective I would have used to describe the scantily clad photos of myself that I'd send to my husband during business trips. They were just playful banter. "How are hot pics of me a *meaningful* expression of gratitude?" I asked incredulously. "What about my letters where I pour my soul out?" There was a long pause, then, "Oh, your letters are great, babe."

I knew he was just saying that so I wouldn't get upset, like the automatic skid prevention on a car that activates to avoid a deadly accident. I didn't probe further, but that exchange got me thinking: maybe in expressing gratitude to Kojo I should do so on his terms, not mine. Clearly he appreciated different things from what I did. I loved words, and the most meaningful expression of gratitude for me was a letter. But for Kojo, it was something else. And so, to execute my gratitude resolution, I texted my husband more pictures, which took far less time than writing love letters. Using the power of positive affirmation, I had delegated to Kojo with joy. He had the ball now. Gratitude would ensure that he'd keep possession of it.

CHAPTER 16

Don't Buy the Stereotype

One warm summer evening in 2011, I invited a few of my friends, all working moms, for a girls' night of cosmos and conversation at my apartment. As soon as we exchanged hugs and hellos, we dove deep into discussion, grateful for the chance to connect with one another away from husbands, kids, and work obligations.

More than one of my friends talked about how thrilled they were to have a night out, but they also said they felt uneasy about leaving their children at home with their husbands. One girlfriend joked that she planned to have enough drinks to not care that her husband was probably feeding her kids McDonald's for dinner. Another said she had every intention of relaxing that evening because she knew there'd be a big mess waiting for her in the kitchen the next morning. I couldn't help but notice that although everyone was appreciative that their husbands had taken over for the night, they were all also anticipating that the men's performance would be lackluster.

As for me, I was only able to host this get-together because Kojo had taken Kofi and Ekua to Ghana for the summer. "You're so lucky, Tiffany," one woman commented, "to have a husband who can take care of two kids for three months!" I was too embarrassed to tell her there was a time, just four years prior, when I didn't trust Kojo to take care of one child even for a plane ride.

That evening, after my friends had said their good-byes and I'd loaded the dishwasher with all of the empty glasses, I plopped myself down on Kojo's well-worn corner of our blue couch. There was a near empty bag of tortilla chips next to me, and as I nibbled at the remnants, a thought occurred to me: *I should have told them the truth.*

Having a husband who took our kids to Ghana for the summer had nothing to do with luck and everything to do with practicality—and a lot of progress on my part. The cost of summer camp for two kids in New York City was far more than the cost of two round-trip tickets to Ghana. And since Kojo needed to be in Ghana for work, one of us would have to care for the kids solo anyway. Kojo traveled so much during the school year that if you added it all up, I was the solo person six months out of the year. So it made perfect sense for us to switch primary caretaking roles for the summer. Sure, I'd miss them. But the separation was worth the rich cultural experience Kofi and Ekua would have in their father's homeland. By taking the kids to Ghana with him, Kojo was doing what any reasonable and thoughtful parent and partner would do: he was sharing the load.

But because society's expectations of men are so low, my girlfriends heralded Kojo as a hero and rendered their own husbands incompetent.

I recognized their thought process because I had once shared it. After being married to Kojo for fifteen years, though, I had come to know at least one thing for sure: my success at work and in life was directly correlated to the high expectations I held of my husband. The more capable I assumed he was at home, the more energy I was able to direct outside the home, and the less time I wasted worrying about how well the kids were being taken care of when I wasn't there. My high expectations of Kojo on the home front also proved to be self-fulfilling. The more I expected of him, the more incredible an All-In Partner Kojo became.

So why had I resisted going all Oprah on my girlfriends by singing my husband's praises? Instead, as if to further affirm my friends' low expectations of their husbands, I'd bashed my own: "Oh, please. Kojo has so much help staying with his family in Ghana. It's not like he's bathing and feeding the kids or even washing their clothes," I'd said.

Why was it that no matter how much Kojo engaged on the home front, I hesitated to give him the appropriate amount of public credit? Could I have been perpetuating a larger problem? I realized that if I had been more honest with my friends about my own situation, we might have had a productive conversation about how women can get past the bungling husband stereotype to create true All-In Partnerships of their own.

———

On June 23, 2014, Roger Trombley sat down to eat with four other people at a Chipotle in Washington, D.C. It was a perfectly ordinary lunch—except that one of his dining companions was the president of the United States.

A thirty-eight-year-old father of two from Ann Arbor, Michigan, Roger had been invited to lunch with President Barack Obama as part of the White House Summit on Working Families. Roger is a safety engineer at Ford Motor Company. He is also raising his children with his wife, Shimul Bhuva, another Ford engineer. Roger and Shimul have flexible schedules that allow them both to be intimately involved in managing their home while pursuing their careers. Two to three days a week, Roger and Shimul work remotely, which allows one parent to be with the kids at all times. In stories about the couple that appeared in the press at the time of the lunch, most of the credit for their All-In Partnership went to Ford, which allows its employees to work from home. To that end, companies that offer flexible arrangements do enable their male and female employees to curate more integrated lives. America needs more companies to follow this example.

But after I met Roger and we had a chance to talk, I was struck by one particular aspect of his relationship: it is the messages he receives from Shimul, not the messages he receives from his employer, that motivate his participation at home. Unlike my friends at girls' night, Roger's wife *believes* that he's capable of everything that domestic life requires.

"She isn't the gatekeeper," he told me. "She allows me to lead and make decisions and make my own mistakes." The result is that Roger is confident in the role he plays at home. "No one thing is all that complicated," he reflected. "Most men just don't have the experience to know what to do because women do so much."[1]

Our culture is really tough on men when it comes to our expectations about what they are capable of in the home. While women fall prey to stereotypes of the perfect wife and mother whose home is impeccable and whose kids are saints, men suffer from an equally damaging stereotype—that of the dumb dad.

Advertising is one major promoter of this stereotype. Consider this commercial from Lowe's: From a hotel room, a woman Skypes her husband and three children, who are home while she is on a business trip. Her husband, surrounded by their two young boys and toddler daughter in a high chair, calmly assures his wife that everything is under control. The children all nod. Their backdrop is a perfectly clean yellow wall. After an exchange of I-love-yous and good-byes, the Skype call ends and the camera pulls back, giving the viewer a panoramic shot of the kitchen in horrific disarray, with food splattered all over the walls. The only exception is the one small clean square of yellow wall behind the husband and kids. The colors fade, and the voice-over intones, "Finally, a paint that's stain resistant and scrubbable. Valspar Reserve paint."[2]

The presumption is that any working mother will be in on the joke. She laughs at this husband's foibles because she's the one who leaves detailed to-do lists for her own spouse in preparation for her business trips. She's the one who feels pangs of guilt and worry as the plane takes off, wondering whether her husband will actually feed the kids the broccoli she left in the fridge. She checks in countless times a day, never fully assured that he has it all under control. That's because, despite her smile over Skype, underlying this working mom's pervasive anxiety is the belief that her man is useless.

In *Throwaway Dads: The Myths and Barriers That Keep Men from Being the Fathers They Want to Be,* Ross Parke and Armin Brott discuss the concept of "framing"—presenting an obscured version of reality to appeal to a certain targeted viewership—to explain negative male stereotypes in the media, particularly in advertising. "In a world where women make the overwhelming majority of family spending decisions," Parke and Brott note, "it makes sense for advertisers to worry more about keeping female viewers happy than about alienating male ones."[3] Here's the problem: while we may enjoy watching dumb dads, the humor glosses over a reality that is simply not funny. Laughter doesn't help to fix our culture's lopsided division of labor on the home front, and ultimately, the joke is on women. Low expectations of men as husbands and fathers, and the idea that our children and homes will barely be able to survive men's poor management, make women's lives so much more difficult than they have to be. The belief that men are incompetent weighs on our psyche, sapping our energy and influencing our choices. We'd rather do the housework ourselves or, if we have the means, outsource tasks to people we deem more competent than our husbands. And when we can bring ourselves to delegate, we're often quick to micromanage. It's no wonder we expend so much energy feeling concerned about what's happening at home when we're not there.

Such overengagement contributes to women's ongoing struggle to find a balance between work and homelife. Professional women who travel for business and who don't have a fully engaged partner at home will always need to plan ahead—their children's perfectly matched outfits ironed and on hangers, one for each day they'll be gone; the frozen lasagna in the freezer; the kitchen-counter notes explaining drop-offs and pickups; the instructions about overseeing homework. Indeed, research shows that "many working mothers seek to save time by multitasking at home and at work. For these women, multitasking maximizes time use and serves as a time-management strategy that allows them to deal with the double duty they experience being wage earners and care givers."[4] But studies also show that multitasking can reduce productivity by up to 40 percent.[5] Our minds might be shuffling through that to-do list in meetings, making it difficult to focus fully on the task at hand. The end result: more work for women in both the professional and the domestic spheres.

—✦—

"How do you get your husband to coordinate all the playdates?"

I have been asked this question so often, and with such consistent incredulity, that I am tempted to remark, "I put a gun to his head." Instead, I respond with a smile and a laugh that hides my frustration.

Recently, at morning drop-off at my son's school, I was asked this same question by another mother. I was wearing a dress, jacket, and black patent-leather pumps. My questioner was decked out in Lululemon and neon sneakers. Both of us were rushing as she approached me to confirm an after-school plan that, clearly, I knew nothing about.

On cue, she followed up with, "My husband would *never* coordinate playdates."

I remember when I thought that way, too. "Have you ever asked him to?" I inquired.

She rolled her eyes. "I wouldn't even bother. That man can't manage a detail to save his own life."

"What does he do professionally?"

"He's a tax attorney."

I laughed again—but this time it was genuine.

"Girl, how did you end up with a tax attorney who can't manage a detail?"

She laughed, too, and we agreed to have lunch the following week. I promised I'd share with her how I got my investment banker husband to coordinate playdates.

—✦—

If women truly want men to step up at home, we have to start seeing them not as dumb, useless, or selfish, but as intelligent, capable, and generous agents of change in our lives. When we do this, we increase the likelihood they'll measure up as husbands, fathers, and human beings. We also ignite our own possibilities. On the other hand, our perpetuation of the dumb-dad myth stifles everyone's potential. By refusing to wrap our brains around men's ability to perform at home, women fail to empower men as true partners who can help us achieve our own professional aspirations. In the end, we only hurt ourselves.

Understanding the psychological dynamics that influence our beliefs about the delineation of responsibility on the home front can help us to instigate change. In his popular TED talk "The Psychology of Your Future Self," psychologist Dan Gilbert notes that it's easier for us to remember the past than it is to imagine the future. This influences our decision making, especially in relationship to time. If, for example, we look ten years back and ask ourselves how much we've changed, we would answer, "A lot." But if we look ten years forward and ask ourselves how much we think we'll change, we would answer, "Very little." Gilbert's point is that we have a tendency to view ourselves in the present moment as static, assuming that our current selves are more permanent than they actually are. We have a limited imagination for how we will evolve, and we are inclined to view our spouses through that same lens.[6] We think, *If my husband isn't a planner today, he won't be one tomorrow.*

I now know how limiting that thinking can be. Nevertheless, when I suggest to other women that the secret to being healthy, happy, and making an impact on the world is for them to expect less from themselves at home and more from their partners, I'm usually met with cynicism and disbelief. They might think it's a great idea in theory, but when we start naming actual household tasks that their partners could take on, they are universally skeptical that their spouses can do what they do. When I'm working with these women as a corporate consultant or even just offering advice as a friend, I'll ask them to play a game with me. "Close your eyes," I say, "and think about three things that your spouse has never done at home. Things that, if he were to complete them, would make your life a million times easier." I instruct them to imagine him doing those things regularly, on his own, without being reminded and pestered.

"What a wonderful fantasy," they respond when they open their eyes.

We chuckle. I can relate. Then I ask them to close their eyes again. "This time, I want you to imagine three things your kids can do now that they couldn't do years or even months ago—reading, walking, riding a bike, dressing themselves." They always smile, but they are ready to explain to me the difference.

"But, Tiffany, our kids are rapidly developing. Reaching those milestones are all a part of being a growing child. Adults are much more set in their ways."

I understand this response. Sometimes I address it by explaining that it's easy to forget that everyone is capable of learning how to do new things, but there's no reason our spouses can't take on new roles at home and learn how to do them in the ways that feel right to them. But reflecting on our spouses' and our children's growth is actually not the point of the exercise. What's most important to reflect on during these visualizations is *our response* to their development, not the development itself. I can vividly recall when I was trying to teach Kofi how to eat from a spoon. I kept pushing the puréed carrots into his mouth, and he just kept pushing them out with his tongue. At the time, it felt like I was doing this for an eternity. I legitimately wondered whether my son would ever eat from a spoon, let alone feed himself with one. And yet, despite my skepticism, of course he eventually learned to eat from a spoon. I expressed the same level of frustration and doubt about every subsequent milestone. Will he be wearing a diaper in kindergarten? Will he ever tie his own shoes? Despite my seeming lack of faith in Kofi's growth process, he still grew. Without our faith in our spouses' growth process, they likely won't. *That* is the big difference.

Women do not want to feel that they're always nagging or cajoling their spouses—and I get that. Nor do we want to treat them like kids when trying to encourage them to assume more responsibility at home. I've learned that it helps to remind our spouse that carrying more of the load at home is a way for him to capitalize on his investments. Maybe his investment is his word: he promised "till death do us part," and he has no intention of reneging on that. Maybe he's invested in ensuring that his children are happy and healthy, and he needs their mother to be happy and healthy, too. Maybe his investment is economic: to relieve his own breadwinning pressure as well as pay the bills, he needs his wife's income. Or maybe he's invested in his wife's potential as a human being. Perhaps he understands that her success is his success, and he will do whatever he can to facilitate it.

Seeing our spouse as "invested" instead of "useless" opens the way for us to expect more from him at home, allowing us to redirect our time and energy outside the home—just as I did when I joined the board of Harlem4Kids and Kojo took over meal prep for the week. Being on that board remains one of the most rewarding experiences of my life, yet I almost missed out because I didn't give Kojo credit for being invested in my fulfillment—or being willing and able to slice and dice a week's worth of food. In both cases, my initial thinking was wrong.

One of the things that matters most to me is advancing women and girls, and I have a hard time saying no to a woman who reaches out to me for advice or support. I get a lot of "I'd-love-to-connect-with-you" e-mails, and I say yes to nearly all of them. Three days a week, I do morning meetings. On an average week, I meet with five people. Since I have no interest in listening to me talk about myself over and over, I've gotten very good at asking enough questions that my coffee date does most of the talking. Over the course of a few years, I've listened to close to a thousand different women's stories. Not surprisingly, our struggles navigating work and family life are a familiar theme, as are the common messages we send to the men in our lives. There are three messages that I hear all the time that I believe particularly inhibit our partners' ability to make meaningful contributions at home. Until women stop sending these messages, consciously or not, we'll never be able to cultivate a true All-In Partnership. The three messages we need to retire:

1. "He can't manage the details."

Perhaps the most common reason women give for why they don't endow their men with full, or at least more, responsibility on the home front is that "too many things would fall through the cracks." It's true that there are a lot of moving parts involved in transporting kids, coordinating extracurricular activities, and shopping lists, and many women simply don't believe our husbands can manage the minutiae. This assumption that men are not adept at managing details does have some basis in biology. Men's and women's brains are, in fact, hardwired differently in adolescence, and brain-mapping studies indicate that women tend to be stronger at tasks that engage memory and intuition,[7] which are helpful when it comes to keeping a lot of balls in the air on any given day. But the ability to manage details is not the only skill required to run a home well, and men bring other abilities to the table.

In her book, *All Joy and No Fun: The Paradox of Modern Parenthood,* Jennifer Senior shadows a couple, Angie and Clint, who hardly see each other because of incompatible work schedules. The fact that each partner is forced by circumstances to single-handedly manage a shift at home creates a perfect opportunity for Senior to make pointed observations about the couple's different parenting styles. Whereas Angie, like most mothers, "is more alive to the emotional undercurrents of the household" and tends to get caught up in the stress of the "moment to moment handling of the kids," Clint is less frazzled and more composed, approaching child care with the bigger picture in mind. Hence, he is able to see certain tasks through with more ease than Angie because he is less hung up on the minutiae of the kids' lives; his attention is less "fractured."[8]

Clint's tendency to see the bigger picture and not sweat the small stuff does not make him a better parent than his wife. Nor does Angie's attention to detail make her superior to Clint. The point is that when both partners play to their strengths, they complement each other's efforts, and the family as a whole benefits. Our husbands need not be experts in managing details to be All-In Partners.

2. "He isn't here."

A husband's absence is another common explanation women give for why their spouses aren't more active in the home. This, too, is not an unfounded complaint. In *Opting Out?: Why Women Really Quit Careers and Head Home,* author Pamela Stone observes, "Just over half (60 percent) of women mentioned their husbands as one of the key influences on their decision to quit. . . . For most of these women, it turns out, husbands were, quite literally, absent. . . . [I]n never being around, husbands had an arguably greater effect on women's decisions to quit than the more immediately pressing and oft-cited 'family' demands of children."[9]

Women tend to accept men never being around because males' identities have historically been tethered to their roles as primary breadwinners. Their absence at home is excused on account of their being at the office to satisfy this sociocultural expectation. But in our digital age, the "he's not here" complaint need no longer exempt men from fully participating in homelife. Working women are also absent from the home, but that doesn't stop us from texting sitters, ordering groceries to be delivered, and registering the kids for summer camps online between client meetings. The expectation that our husbands cannot be engaged at home because they're at work doesn't take into account that technology can loop them in from wherever they are. My own husband proved this admirably when he replaced our kitchen sink from the other side of the world.

3. "He doesn't know what's best for our children."

This third assumption may be the saddest and most troubling of all, because it reinforces society's limited definition of masculinity— that of the hard-charging breadwinner who is only capable of leading outside the home. This narrow definition of what it means to be a man denies our partners the opportunity to express their more nurturing sides and to develop their home management chops.

Women contribute to this problem when we insist that we can't hand off tasks to our spouses because men do not understand the fundamentals of child-rearing or aren't sensitive to the needs of their kids. Some women go so far as to opt out of their careers altogether or spend huge sums of money on outsourced child care in lieu of handing child-rearing responsibilities off to their men.

One of the components researchers use to measure maternal gatekeeping is women's traditional attitude that they enjoy and perform housework and child care better than men.[10] Our belief that Mother knows best contributes to a vicious cycle that has a damaging effect on men's actual involvement. Specifically, the more a mother believes the father to be incompetent, the more gatekeeping she does.[11] The more gatekeeping she does, the less practice he gets fulfilling parental responsibilities. The less competent a father is, the less motivated he is to spend time with his children.[12]

I'll never forget the first time I witnessed Kojo's response to Kofi falling as a toddler at the playground. My first instinct was always to rush to my son's aid, picking him up quickly and wiping away his tears. But Kojo, upon seeing his son fall onto the turf, grabbed my arm to prevent me from running and simply called out, "You okay, buddy?" I held my breath for Kofi's wail, but it never came. Instead, our two-year-old picked himself up, dusted his hands, and ran off to play. Apparently, even without practice, Father *can* know best. "He can't manage details, isn't here, and doesn't know what's best for our children." These three messages, rooted in stereotype and woven through our culture, block a range of creative approaches to home management to which men might otherwise contribute. And these inhibiting messages fail to take into account that for many women, nurturing behavior does not come naturally and has to be learned. One writer, Meaghan O'Connell, pointed out in *New York* magazine that she was "the slacker parent" while her husband was "the natural" who fulfilled the more traditionally maternal roles.[13] In short, either parent may possess a more instinctively nurturing sensibility, yet by default, women are expected to take the lead at home. It's time for us to recognize that men are as fully capable of taking care of their families as women are, even if they may approach household and child-rearing tasks differently. Indeed, a 2014 study published in the *Proceedings of the National Academy of Sciences of the United States of America*[14] found that the very act of parenting promoted the development of a "parental caregiving neural network" in the subjects, regardless of gender or the relationship status of the parents.[15] Men might not have as much practice caregiving, but they are just as capable as women when given the opportunity.

So what stops women from embracing the notion that our husbands may really have a strong wish to be engaged? One reason may be that men seldom express the desire directly, in part because cultural stereotypes make it hard for them to be honest about their caretaking desires. A few years ago, for example, Kojo decided that he wanted to make a career transition that would allow him to spend more time in New York with the kids and me. At least that's what he said to me. In the weeks that followed, I'd get increasingly frustrated when I'd hear him on the phone with prospective employers explaining that he needed to be stateside more "because the wife is nagging me." One day, after another one of these phone calls, I blew a gasket.

"Why do you keep making me look bad?" I asked him. "I don't nag you about coming home! I've been totally supportive of your career." I suspected his male bravado was causing him to typecast me in a falsely stereotypical way, but I didn't like being put into the "nagging wife" box, especially when I had worked so hard to be a good All-In Partner. It turned out that his nagging wife comments weren't about me at all.

"What am I supposed to say, Tiffany?" Kojo said. "That I want to spend more time with my family? That I want to take my kids to school? I'm not allowed to say that."

Kojo's perception of how he would be perceived by potential employers for simply wanting to be an engaged father was not off base. As R. Kirk Mauldin writes in "The Role of Humor in the Construction of Gendered and Ethnic Stereotypes": "[Society] so thoroughly devalues whatever thoughts, feelings, and behaviors are culturally defined as feminine that crossing the gender boundary has a more negative cultural meaning for men than it has for women—which means, in turn, that male gender-boundary-crossers are much more culturally stigmatized than female gender-boundary-crossers."[16] In other words, men have a more difficult time engaging in gender role fluidity than women because of external pressures for men to present themselves in ways that are deemed masculine. This expectation, in turn, makes them feel insecure about expressing their domestic desires to their peers for fear of appearing anything less than manly.

Sadly, even as the advertising world evolves to show men taking on a larger role in the domestic sphere, cultural commentary still seems one step behind. In 2015, for example, several Super Bowl commercials featured strong and nurturing fathers who were intimately engaged in the lives of their children. In a spot for Dove's #RealStrength initiative, which asserts that a man's demonstration of sensitivity and love toward his child does not make him any less of a man, viewers were bombarded with a montage of fathers engaging with their children of various ages, who responded by uttering variations of the word *daddy* in sweet and grateful tones.[17] Another commercial, this one for Nissan, was entitled "With Dad." It portrayed a young boy's adoration for his hypermasculine, race-car-driving father over an extended period of his life.[18]

The next day, media outlets praised these brands for playing against gender stereotypes. But was that really what the ads were doing? They melted our hearts and did indeed counter the dumb-dad stereotype, showing an involved and engaged dad—why was that a unique and amazing concept? The presence of these stereotypes was what made the ads noteworthy, not the ads themselves. Viewers may have been brought to tears in between bites of buffalo wings, but true progress won't be made until the image of a competent father spending time with his children is as expected as that of a mother spending time with hers.

CHAPTER 17

Happiness Motivates Everyone

After our daughter, Ekua, was born, Kojo was home for two weeks before heading back to Dubai. Toyia was there to help out, and one evening, she made an unusual request. She asked me to come and sit down with her because she had observed that the only time I ever sat down was when I was eating or nursing my daughter.

"You're always on your feet," she said as if something was wrong with my nonstop busyness.

She explained she couldn't recall my ever just sitting and relaxing. *I don't have time to sit,* I thought. *There's too much to do!* I continued to wipe the table, or whatever it was I was busying myself with, as I mulled over Toyia's comment. It occurred to me that when Kojo was home, he spent an enormous amount of time sitting on our blue couch. I started to think about the differences in the way we handled deadlines and stress. I'd feel the need to push through, never taking a break for fear I'd fall further behind. He'd turn on the TV, take a nap on the couch, and then wake up early the next morning to get his work done. This approach drove me crazy.

How can he just sit there not doing anything when there's so much to do?

The more I reflected on the differences in how Kojo and I moved through our daily lives, the more I understood why I was the one who was usually the stressed-out mess. I wasn't pacing my energy. Maybe there *was* something to Kojo's strategy. Life is an endless to-do list. As I thought about what Toyia had said, I realized occasionally, intentionally relaxing might be a more sustainable approach to managing a hectic schedule.

Intrigued by Toyia's observation about my relentless approach to life, I decided to test Kojo's tactic. To make myself slow down, I forced myself to sit on the blue couch twice a day. I called this exercise Stop & Sit, and I set the timer on my iPhone to remind myself to actually do it. In the beginning, I couldn't endure simply sitting there doing nothing. Precious time was being squandered, at least in my eyes. So while I sat, I'd fold a load of laundry or bring my laptop to check e-mail. Over time, though, I was able to sit and just breathe for a few minutes.

One night after putting Kofi to bed, I made myself a cup of tea and grabbed the previous month's *O* magazine (I was always behind on my issues, which I tended to read only on airplanes). With Ekua in my lap, I made a nest in Kojo's corner of the blue couch and read and sipped my tea for half an hour before dozing off. When I woke up twenty minutes later, I was a new woman. I couldn't believe how refreshed I felt after such a short nap! I was hooked.

As frustrated as some of our spouses' habits and behaviors might make us, we can often learn and benefit from them. The moments of stillness I experienced during my Stop & Sit sessions prompted me to do something that the spinning Tasmanian Devil in me would never have allowed—assess whether my perpetual motion was absolutely required. *If I went to bed right now, what difference would it make if I didn't respond to that e-mail? Would an armor-clad battalion of mice really descend on my kitchen if I left that one dirty*

dish in the sink overnight? Whose life would be altered if I left that
load of clothes in the dryer? In the swirl of trying to get it all done,
I had never taken the time to ask myself such questions. But in the
quiet of my Stop & Sits, after breathing and assessing for as little as
six minutes, the urgency of my to-do list would teasingly subside. It
began to make sense to me how Kojo could drift off to sleep with
little, if any, worry about what still needed to get done.

The connection between a happy woman and a thriving All-In
Partnership cannot be overstated. Research has proven that happier
women make for happier men. As Deborah Carr, professor and chair
of sociology at Rutgers University, points out, "The more content the
wife is with the long-term union, the happier the husband is with
his life no matter how he feels about their nuptials."[1] Happy men
are also better All-In Partners. They participate at home out of love
for their wives and commitment to their families, and they are rewarded with partners who are infinitely more serene, joyful, and
clear on their priorities because these women now have the bandwidth to participate in activities that nourish their souls.

The more I thought about it, the more I began to understand the
connection between a woman's physical and emotional well-being
and a thriving All-In Partnership with her spouse. Such partnerships
can falter when a woman doesn't prioritize her own happiness. And
yet prioritizing our own happiness is extremely hard to do. Why is
this so? I reached out to Dr. Christine Carter, a sociologist and senior fellow at UC Berkeley's Greater Good Science Center, who is a
happiness expert and coach, to find out. "We tell women again and
again that you have to put on your own oxygen mask first," she explained, "but we don't provide the tools to understand that it requires
a lot of courage to do that. Women are trained to maintain harmony
even when it hurts us. To honor ourselves when it creates dishar-
mony with other people's needs goes against everything we've been
taught."[2]

I've heard women speak of countless barriers that prevent them
from reaching for a life of joy, but there are three happiness hurdles that women mention most frequently in our conversations: the

first is our incessant feeling of culpability; the second is our tendency to dishonor our boundaries; and the third is a lack of happiness habits—regular practices that bring us pleasure and replenish us creatively. When faced with any one of these three happiness hurdles, we're somewhere on the spectrum of dissatisfaction. When we confront all three hurdles at once, we're downright miserable. On the other hand, when we are free of guilt, respectful of boundaries, and engaged in happiness habits, we are filled with positive energy and can sustain an All-In Partnership at the highest level of cooperation and joy.

Let's examine each of the happiness hurdles more closely:

1. Break Free of Guilt

The first hurdle women have to overcome is a perpetual feeling of culpability. If I had a dollar for every time a woman apologized to me, I would be rich. Unfortunately, saying "I'm sorry" is a tough habit to break, because as women, we've been trained by society to feel culpable for just about everything. In 2014, Pantene's groundbreaking "Not Sorry" TV commercial drew widespread attention to women's propensity to preface statements, observations, and interactions with men—in the boardroom or in the bedroom—with arbitrary apologies. In the commercial, a man sits down next to a woman in a waiting room and accidentally bumps her arm with his elbow, and *she* apologizes. Another man enters a conference room full of coworkers and asks, "Mind if I squeeze in here?" The women adjacent, who are doing him a favor by moving over, mutter that they are sorry. Similar scenarios unfold through various other professional and domestic tableaus. To underscore the absurd and unnecessary nature of these apologies, the commercial concludes on an empowering note by presenting the same scenarios *without* the apologies.[3]

The commercial prompts women to ask ourselves why we feel our actions and words need to be excused. As women, we are conditioned to act as caretakers and prone to always prioritize others' happiness above our own. When we don't, we feel bad. And when apologies are not enough, we're quick to offer explanations to prove that our intentions were good and selfless: *I had a deadline. I needed to take cupcakes to my daughter's school for her birthday. My boss asked me to. I had an event I needed to attend.* Never once have I witnessed a woman rush in five minutes late to a meeting and say, "I'm so sorry. I was getting a massage." The guilt we feel when we actually do something for ourselves often prevents us from fully enjoying the experience.

Karina Schumann and Michael Ross of the University of Waterloo conducted a study to determine whether women's apologetic impulses are grounded in differences in how men and women perceive culpability. The researchers found that "[w]omen reported offering more apologies than men, but they also reported committing more offenses. Men apologized for the same number of offenses they believed they committed, but they believed they committed fewer overall offenses. This finding suggests that men apologize less frequently than women because they have a higher threshold for what constitutes offensive behavior. . . . [W]e tested this threshold hypothesis by asking participants to evaluate both imaginary and recalled offenses. As predicted, men rated the offenses as less severe than women did."[4] This explains why I was the one apologizing to our babysitter in the bank for Kojo's mass texting, a strategy that he thought was fantastic.

It's difficult to feel happy when you're constantly feeling as if you're doing something wrong. I have often declared, not at all facetiously, that we should embark upon a post-apology era for women. The feeling that we are constantly behaving in a way that warrants apology is a social mechanism that trains us to put others' needs before our own. Women should stop apologizing, not because we do everything right, but because we need to understand that it is okay to do some things wrong. We can be happy and imperfect at the same time. Jen Santoleri, program director for Allegis Global Solutions, said it best when she accepted a performance award at the company's annual gala I was privileged to attend. "I didn't win this award because I'm perfect," she said. "Perfection isn't possible, but excellence is."[5]

2. Respect Our Boundaries

The second happiness hurdle we need to overcome is dishonoring our boundaries. I know this particular hurdle well. Early in my career, I had a boss who frequently e-mailed me on weekends. I would easily spend half of my weekend responding to her messages, assuring her that everything would be taken care of by Monday. It sucked. I worked so hard during the week that I needed and deserved a break on Saturdays and Sundays. After many lost weekends, I finally screwed up the courage to broach the subject with her. I was extremely nervous and had practiced my speech over and over again. I started by expressing to her how committed I was to the organization and to doing my part to ensure that we would meet our goals. I then confessed that I was finding myself working more and more on the weekends and that it was affecting my productivity, especially on Monday mornings when I had stayed up late to work on Sunday night.

My greatest fear materialized when my boss responded with annoyance. "Why should I respect your weekends when you don't?" she huffed back. "I'll send you e-mails when it works for me. It's *your* job to respond when it works for you. I never said I expected anything before Monday. You've taken it upon yourself to work every weekend. Don't blame me for that."

At first I was mortified. Then I became angry. She clearly didn't appreciate my dedication. *Well fine, then,* I thought. *I'm not responding to your weekend messages ever again.* And you know what? I don't think my waiting until Monday to respond made any difference to her. But it did make a huge difference to me.

I recognize that there are managers who e-mail, text, and call their employees on weekends and fully expect them to respond. In fact, it's a national epidemic. Technology has effectively dismantled the clear division between work and home. In a 2013 survey of over four hundred North American workers, Right Management found that 36 percent said that their bosses send them e-mails after work hours and expect an immediate response. A further 15 percent of respondents felt this expectation on weekends and during vacation. These numbers are significant, especially when we consider how difficult this type of communication was in the pre-Internet era.[6] Of course, there are some workers who understand that they signed up for this and are happy to oblige, but many others comply—as I once did—because they don't realize they have a choice. But if we don't respect our own time, how can we expect other people to honor our boundaries? We have to treat ourselves as we expect to be treated. And to be forgiving of ourselves as we learn how to do so. As Dr. Carter says, "Very little takes as much courage as a woman taking care of her own needs."

3. Develop Happiness Habits

The third hurdle that women must surmount is a lack of happiness habits—regular practices that bring us joy. Happiness is a state that evolves from actualizing what matters most to us. It's different for everyone. For some of us, a happiness habit may be attending church or reading spiritual books. Others may find joy in advancing their careers, spending time with their children, hiking in nature, or engaging in artistic pursuits. Whatever our happiness practices are, what's most important is that we turn them into habits. Researchers have found that intentional activity is the most promising way to alter one's level of happiness.[7]

We, too, often underestimate how vital our happiness is to the well-being of those around us, especially our spouses and children. Our concentrated focus on taking care of everyone else has to be balanced against our capacity to feel like vibrant, fully functioning human beings. When we take time to regularly practice our own happiness habits, we are better able to delight in caring for our family members, to nurture ourselves, and develop a sense of life's adventure, possibility, and joy.

One of my Sage Mentors, Alice, learned this the hard way. When she and her husband, Paul, met as first-year Vanderbilt law students, both were committed to supporting each other's professional ambitions. But after their children arrived, Alice began to feel boxed into the mommy track. During each maternity leave, clients she had secured were assigned to other lawyers. When she returned to work, she felt as if she had to prove her commitment all over again. Alice blamed the firm, which she felt didn't support any of its working mothers. She also blamed Paul for her dissatisfaction. She was carrying most of the load at home, and she knew that his taking on less household responsibility had contributed to his professional success. She loved him, and she loved how much he had achieved. It just didn't feel fair.

One day, Paul arrived home earlier than usual and found Alice in the driveway. She was in the driver's seat crying, something she admitted she had been doing a lot lately, though she couldn't explain exactly why. All that she could articulate was a feeling of suffocation, of drowning. Paul was concerned that she might be clinically depressed, and he knew that something had to change. That's when he started voluntarily doing more around the house. Not until that moment had he realized the toll his laid-back role at home had taken on the woman he adored.

Their transition to an All-In Partnership was bumpy at first. Paul didn't understand the intricacies of managing their household. In the first few months, multiple cashmere sweaters were shrunk in the dryer and social events were missed. Paul often found his lack of information about basic household tasks to be a stumbling block to getting things done. Asking Alice for someone's phone number became such a common occurrence that he finally just imported all her contacts into his address book.

In addition to his taking on more responsibilities at home, Paul also encouraged Alice to redirect her energies into activities that replenished her spirit. The most important change, though, was to the family's morning routine. This was the only time of day that Alice felt she could carve out time for herself. She started practicing yoga while Paul got the kids ready and off to school and day care. Within a year, not only was Alice more centered and joyful, but she had also arrived at an exciting new point in her career. She and two other lawyers decided to leave their firm to start their own private practice. It was an enormous undertaking, and Paul felt the pressure to further adjust his life to allow for his wife to flourish, too. That was over a decade ago.

These days, Alice rises at 5:00 each morning for her yoga practice. For the first few minutes, her mind swirls with all of her to-dos, but by the time she says "Namaste" at the end of her practice, she feels peaceful, strong, and ready to conquer the day.

Given my personal experience with Alice as a calm and wise counselor to me and so many others, it's difficult for me to imagine the old Alice, the one who sat crying in the driveway. Paul told me that back then, Alice had been perpetually stressed, worried about everything, and quick to anger. "It's like the kids and I would have to run for cover," he admitted. Paul was sensitive to at least one source of Alice's earlier frustration. He had been made partner at his firm while she was still struggling to get the recognition she felt she deserved at hers. Considering it now, Paul says his only regret was that they didn't change their household dynamic sooner. Seeing Alice's law practice take off and observing how fulfilled she is makes it all worth it, he said, adding simply, "Alice is happy."

—◆—

For me, Stop & Sit would eventually become one of my core happiness habits, always with a cup of tea and the latest issue of *O* magazine. That simple pause in my evening rippled out to ensure that I included other activities in my week for no reason other than they made me happy. Every night now, I put on music and dance. I used to do this when I was a little girl. In my head, I'm in a music video. Sometimes the kids wake up and tell me I'm making too much noise. I laugh and put them back to bed. I also love running in the park; that's when all my best ideas come to me. Ditto long, luxurious soaks with yummy LUSH Bath Bombs or marathon catch-up phone calls with girlfriends. Remember when we used to talk to our friends for *hours* on the phone? Like *that*. Joy.

CHAPTER 18

Why We Need Men

When I was growing up, my dad had a theory about how the world was run by an elite group of people. It was similar to being worried about the Man, but more insidious because this group was plural. Many years ago "these people" had denied my father a Sears credit card, and with it the opportunity to buy necessary household appliances. Ensuring that there was a class of people who didn't have easy access to technological advances like microwaves and dishwashers was just one way "they" held on to their power, my father said. To this day, my dad still refuses to set foot in a Sears department store as a raised fist to "them."

I used to think my dad was crazy. I would be embarrassed when he would warn me about "them" in front of my friends. As I've grown up, though, I've come to understand what my father meant. There is, in fact, a group of people at the highest echelons of corporations, social enterprises, and our branches of government that is making big decisions that affect each and every one of us. With few exceptions, these people are white, male, straight, able-bodied, and wealthy. This lack of diversity is problematic—research shows that a hetero- geneous group of people solving a problem can lead to more innova- tive solutions.[1] In *The Difference: How the Power of Diversity Creates Better Groups, Firms, Schools, and Societies*, Scott Page, a professor at the University of Michigan, details how "diverse cities are more productive, diverse boards of directors make better deci- sions, the most innovative companies are diverse, breakthroughs in science increasingly come from teams of bright, diverse people."[2] In short, the presence of more women at the top levels of leader- ship and management can help to solve some of society's toughest problems.

Ironically, one of the stubbornest of those problems is the fact that the percentage of women at the highest executive levels hasn't increased significantly in the past fifteen years.[3] Excluding the few true superwomen in this country, it seems that what's really prevent- ing women from ascending the corporate ladder is their dual roles: professional employee and home manager. The average woman can't be convinced to continue climbing in a fiercely competitive career pipeline when she still has a full-time job at home. Women are not crazy. Even though we've been told we can do both, we know that it's literally impossible. In response to a *Harvard Business Review* study surveying the time allocation of working women following the birth of a child, the Catalyst Research Center concluded that "the reality is, if a woman wants to obtain a top management position, she cannot be the primary caretaker of [her] child."[4]

Assuming a female worker doesn't have the desire or economic privilege of opting out, or the means to hire an in-home staff, once she gets to a certain level, her bandwidth will become so thin that she'll simply decide to remain in a middle management position. Of course, I've used the words *simply* and *decide* loosely here. It's far more complicated and usually doesn't *feel* like a choice to the woman grappling with society's conditional promise—that we can have it all, as long as we *do* it all. And that's exactly where we find ourselves now, with half the population trying to do everything at work and at home to fulfill the dream of having it all. The net effect is personal and societal: too many women are discouraged from or cannot continue advancing their careers, and our society suffers from a lack of diversity in the upper echelons of decision makers who are shaping our world.

What we all need most is for women to juggle fewer balls at home. This is where men come in. An All-In Partner helps us to accomplish our professional goals in three complementary ways. First, with less domestic pressure, women have more time and energy to pursue the activities that will support their advancement at work. Second, men's engagement at home opens the gate to innovation and efficiency on the domestic front. After being tasked with unloading the dishwasher, for example, it was Kojo who insisted we group cutlery together in baskets so he could just grab all the forks or the spoons together and put them in the drawers. Third, men are generally okay with a healthy degree of imperfection, from which women can learn in their quest to expect less of themselves. In *Family Man*, sociologist Scott Coltrane rationalizes men's relaxed attitude this way: "Because men usually don't have responsibility for initiating housework and because their identity is usually not tied to doing it, they often don't pay much attention to it in the first place."[5]

Richard Zweigenhaft is a professor of psychology at Guilford College in North Carolina and the coauthor, with G. William Domhoff, of *The New CEOs*, a study of women and minorities who are chief executives. Zweigenhaft and Domhoff detail how "statistics suggest that aspirants to America's top corporate jobs had better have a spouse, a partner, or someone else willing to be devoted to the aspirant's career."[6] In their study of women who previously held or currently hold a chief executive role at a Fortune 500 company, they note that "many of the women C.E.O.s said they could not have succeeded without the support of their husbands, helping with the children, the household chores, and showing a willingness to move."[7]

The upshot is that men who do laundry free women up to advance their leadership. Women who are freed from managing it all at home have more mental space to be strategic in their careers.

They are healthier and have more stamina. They have more flexibility to travel and put in the hours required to achieve their next career milestones. And they have more time to cultivate relationships with a network of individuals who can support them on their professional journeys. Perhaps most important, women who Drop the Ball have the ability to climb the ranks at the office without sacrificing the well-being of their families because they are freed from the imposed expectation that it's their job to manage everything at home. They've also witnessed their partners' success at home and aren't worried that things will fall apart.

Ursula Burns, who was the first woman of color CEO at Xerox and is a mother of two, espouses a more relaxed attitude toward "having it all." At *Fortune* magazine's 2013 Most Powerful Women Summit, she urged her audience to "chill out." "Pick the places where you want to be great, focus your energies there, and then go do it," she implored. "Understand you're not going to be great at everything, and then relax."[8] Ursula Burns has been able to relax because of her All-In Partner, Lloyd Bean, whom she met at Xerox. He was an equal contributor on the home front for many years, allowing Ursula the time she needed to climb the ranks.

The World Economic Forum estimates that at our current rate we won't reach gender parity in workplace leadership until 2095.[9] All-In Partnership is one way to fast-forward this appalling statistic. It should come as no surprise that when the professional services firm EY (formerly Ernst & Young) commissioned research to identify the best ways to accelerate women's leadership, the top-ranked strategy by high performers was "implementing flexible arrangements for *men*."[10] Men's participation normalizes flexible work arrangements and counteracts their mommy-track stigma. It all comes back to the same refrain: when women are freed from having two full-time jobs, they are better able to execute the strategies and adopt the mind-sets necessary to transcend the glass ceiling.

The potential for transformation that occurs when men are fully engaged at home extends beyond our individual households. More men being intentional about participating at home, whether as nonpaid working dads or employed All-In Partners, will fast-forward initiatives that support all working families. When men have problems, public response is quicker, policies are enacted to address them faster, and products go to market to solve them sooner than when women do. Case in point: Ashton Kutcher.

Shortly after the birth of the model-turned-actor's first child, he lamented the scarcity of changing tables in men's public restrooms, rousing fans to #BeTheChange[11] on his Facebook page. When men speak up, awareness is set into motion. Within days, Kutcher's status received 245,266 likes, 14,065 shares, and a slew of responses in the form of user comments. He created a Change.org petition that quickly garnered 104,391 supporters demanding that Target and Costco implement changing tables in male restrooms. "It's 2015, families are diverse, and it is an injustice to assume it's only a woman's job to handle changing diapers," Kutcher wrote to rally his supporters. "This assumption is gender stereotyping and companies should be supporting all parents that shop at their stores equally—no matter their gender."[12] The campaign was considered an all-around victory, with both Costco and Target, two of the country's largest retailers, dedicating themselves to the implementation of family-friendly restrooms in their stores. Would the same response have been generated if a female celebrity publicly lamented the issue, highlighting that the changing tables indicated a different kind of gender disparity, one in which only women were expected to take care of matters regarding child care? Or would she have been considered whiny and ungrateful, unable to accept the responsibilities assigned to motherhood?

Another case in point: Daniel Murphy. There was a bit of a firestorm in 2014 when the New York Mets player took paternity leave after he and his wife had their first child and he missed the first two games of the season. A few radio hosts criticized him for doing so. One commentator, unable to wrap his head around Murphy's decision, expressed his opinion that since Murphy was a Major League baseball player, he could afford to hire a nurse. Another personality complained that Murphy's wife should have scheduled a C-section before the start of the season. The criticism of these few, however, precipitated a round of defense by pretty much everyone else. The baseball player soon delivered a public explanation accounting for his leave, which should have been entirely unnecessary. "I decided to take paternity leave to be able to support my wife and give her peace," he said.[13] If being a Major League baseball player hadn't already secured Daniel Murphy's hero status, this statement etched it into stone. All of a sudden, the airwaves were filled with talk of how to support professional athlete fathers. Fewer than two months later, Murphy became the poster dad at the White House, where they hosted the first Summit for Working Fathers. (No White House administration, by the way, has ever hosted a summit for working mothers.)

Finally, the most ironic case: Paul Ryan. When the former vice presidential Republican candidate was being courted for the Speaker of the House job, which he repeatedly said he didn't want (but eventually took), he made time with his family a bargaining chip. The same man who declined to sign legislation that would allow Americans to earn paid sick time to care for themselves and their families[14] told reporters in a press conference, "I cannot and will not give up my family time."[15] Once again, a man's public declaration of his desire to embrace caregiving made headlines as the national conversation turned toward work-life balance in the swirl of Ryan's statement. Even a man who insists on the importance of his own family time while making it more difficult for the rest of Americans to spend time with theirs gets serious airtime.

Some of the wonderful outcomes of these firestorms are the attention that they bring to men's engagement at home, the lack of workplace policies that support it, and the scarcity of men taking advantage of them when they actually are offered. Unlike Facebook's CEO, Mark Zuckerberg, who took a two-month leave after the birth of his daughter, very few men pursue lengthy paternity leaves. Even when there are other leave policies they can use, they still largely don't consider the opportunity. The concept of fathers taking advantage of such policies carries a stigma as potent as women's fear of appearing bossy or domineering by speaking up at meetings. "A lot of men who might otherwise be interested in breaking through the glass wall that separates them from their families are hindered by the fear that getting on the 'daddy track' will hurt their careers," note Parke and Brott in *Throwaway Dads*. I know a young lawyer who opted out of his firm's family leave policy, and he put it this way: "All the male associates knew it [taking paternity leave] would be career suicide."

A 1986 Catalyst study on the topic revealed that "41 percent of respondents said no amount of paternity leave was reasonable," even at companies that offered flexible policies to support working families, which was not common at the time. "Ten years later, nothing had changed."[16] Today, the reluctance remains. While companies have become more generous in offering fathers paternity leave options, it's still a hurdle for men to overcome the stigma associated with them. A 2014 study conducted by the Boston College Center for Work & Family reveals that although 89 percent of fathers felt it was important for employers to offer paid paternity leave, 96 percent of these same fathers returned to work a mere two weeks after the birth of a child.[17] This window of time hardly amounts to the duration of the leave a woman who just gave birth must take by necessity.

One of the men with whom I spoke in researching this book, Keith, is a computer systems analyst. When we first met, Keith and his wife were expecting their first child, and Keith was elated. He wanted to take time off after the baby's arrival to help his wife and to bond with their infant, but he described an uncomfortable experience he had at an information session his company hosted on work leave and flex policies. When Keith arrived at the session, he found a roomful of women and discovered that he was the only man in attendance. Later, a male colleague told him, "Those rules really aren't for the guys." Keith ignored this colleague's remark and pushed through his initial discomfort to enjoy four weeks' leave after the birth of his son. His experience as an All-In Partner has made him a strong advocate of men taking advantage of flex leave policies—and he was never penalized at work for taking advantage of the benefits his company offers to all its employees.

Men who participate at home have more empathy for women because they experience their own life-go-rounds. Their empathy helps fuel our ambitions and leads them to redefine their own roles as men. Men who have daughters are more supportive of corporate practices and public policies that work to advance women.[18] All-In Partnership ensures this reality for men who also have wives. Men who are juggling their own careers with coordinating with the plumber and helping the kids with their homework hold a greater appreciation for the struggles of their female colleagues at the office and the other women in their lives.

Most importantly, though, men who are engaged at home are better able to Drop the Ball on the unrealistic expectations society has set for them, too. For all my HCD, I thought it was irrational of Kojo to get "unnecessary" maintenance on our Jetta when he was leaving for Dubai. I wasn't obsessed with the condition of our car the way I was obsessed with what I served for dinner. That's because I was socialized to be responsible for the nourishment of my family. Kojo was socialized to feel responsible for the protection of his family. Men feel omnipresent pressure, too, of being sole protector, provider, and breadwinner at all costs, especially the painful cost of being absent in their families' lives. They must also find the courage to Drop the Ball.

As Daniel Murphy put it, "Long after I'm no longer good enough to be a baseball player, I'll still be a dad . . . I can someday talk to my son about the day he was born because I was there (instead of telling him about how Stephen Strasburg hung me a curveball!)." And the creation of All-In Partnerships doesn't just make women happy; it makes men happy, too. "Being a father has transformed me," Murphy shared. "It is humbling and exciting, it is stripping me of my selfishness, has led me to seek wisdom from the men in my life, made me closer to my wife, and connected me to God's love for his children."[19]

Scott Behson, a notable blogger on work-life balance, articulates how "the equality of women at work is inextricably tied to the equality of men as parents."[20] Until the contributions that women make at work are seen as just as valuable as the contributions women make at home, the contributions that men make at home will never be considered as valuable as the contributions men make at work. Just as women need affirmation on both fronts, so do men. But men receive far less affirmation when it comes to their value at home, so much so that domestic engagement can lead to an identity struggle.

Real men know that all boats rise with the tide. Real men have discovered that the best way to provide for their families is to unleash the full creative and economic capacity of the women in their lives by being All-In Partners. The commitment of Dan Mulhern, husband of former governor of Michigan Jennifer Granholm, to an All-In Partnership empowered his wife's career. While Mulhern has admitted that taking a backseat to his wife's career initially "left [him] vulnerable and caused [him] to rethink what it means to 'be a man,'" he affirms that the choice did not precipitate a "tragic end to [his] manhood, but a wondrous beginning."[21] He learned "to exult in [his wife's] strengths," declaring with pride in an editorial addressed to his son: "Her success freed me to see a man can be good—or great—without being a hero in war, sports, business, or politics. A strong man, Jack, is not threatened by others' greatness. He's comfortable with his own."[22]

Because the tug-of-war between climbing the career ladder and raising children is largely perceived as a women's problem, innovative solutions to address it have evolved at a turtle's pace. Now that we have a new generation in the workforce and millennial men are demanding the workplace flexibility women have always needed, companies are responding with progressive policies to retain them.[23] Fortunately, solving this pain point for men will benefit everyone and go a long way toward changing traditional attitudes.

Men who participate at home are good for children, too. Their kids grow up with a vision of what an All-In Partnership can look like, which disrupts their socialization regarding traditional gender roles. Girls who see Daddy cooking and taking them to birthday parties aren't planted with the seed that they will eventually become the primary caregiver just because they're female. In fact, research has found that for men who are engaged at home, their daughters expressed a greater preference for non-traditional-gendered jobs.[24] Millions of girls only need their fathers to pick up a dustpan for them to aspire to be engineers. Similarly, boys who see Daddy making grocery runs and folding laundry aren't raised to believe that in the future, their wives will exclusively be taking care of these kinds of tasks.

I experienced the power of innovative fatherhood when I was in the fourth grade. I had chicken pox, and since my mother needed to stay home to care for me, she sent my father to school that week to pick up my homework. Even as a nine-year-old, the idea of getting behind on my work was enough to generate more red spots. Not to mention, I was missing all the latest playground gossip. My mother consoled me with affirmations about how smart I was and reminded me that everything would be fine. My father had a different idea. "Don't worry," he'd reassure me each evening when he delivered that day's assignment and collected what I had completed. "You'll be the coolest kid in class when you get back."

On the morning of my return, my father drove me to school and escorted me to my classroom. This was rare, since it was my mother who primarily dropped me off and communicated with the school. As soon as I walked through the door with my father, mayhem broke out. I will never forget the image of my friend Molly with her freckled cheeks screaming at the top of her lungs, "It's Michael Jackson! It's Michael Jackson!" And then he did it. Before I even understood what was happening, my father leaped ahead of me and gracefully slid across the linoleum, executing a perfect moonwalk in front of my entire fourth-grade class. The room erupted in thunderous applause and cheers as one of the boys yelled out, "Yo, Tiffany! Your dad is awesome!" Before that moment, I had never imagined my dad as a cool parent, yet that day he made me the coolest girl in class. Privately, my mother was the consummate consoler, but I couldn't imagine her going to such public lengths to make me feel better.

It would be decades before I understood the deeper lesson of what my father did for me that week. He provided a lasting example of the magic two parents can create for their children when each one plays to his or her strengths.

Children watch us carefully and are very susceptible to what they see. I once had one of my son's friends, a white boy from a privileged family, ask me if I was a nanny. His mother was horrified when I told her, but I explained that it was a perfectly reasonable question from a young child whose only other close experiences with black women were with his nannies. Regardless of the beliefs of the adults in their lives, children connect their own dots about race, ethnicity, socioeconomics, ability, and gender based on their own observations. My son has asked me why I don't do the same things other moms do and why his dad does things that other fathers don't. By asking these questions, he introduces a space where we can have a conversation about what it means when people do things differently from what we've come to expect.

Children of All-In Partners also learn early how to negotiate two different parenting styles. When two full-time working parents are both engaged at home, they don't have the bandwidth to be on the same page every moment. Certainly they need to have their opinions aligned about big things like values, school choices, and media consumption. But it's not practical to be in perfect unison on small day-to-day preferences. All-In Partners must adopt a "When in Rome" strategy to prevent stepping on each other's toes and to make each other interchangeable caregivers.

When our kids are with Kojo, for example, he frequently plays football with them in our apartment; they must eat all their dinner; and there is no dancing on furniture. When the kids are with me, there is no ball throwing allowed; they can choose how much dinner they want to eat; and dancing on furniture is a nighttime ritual (especially to Michael Jackson). Our kids are accustomed to adjusting. They understand that Mommy and Daddy love them the same but have different ways of doing things, as will other people in their lives. Being interchangeable caregivers means that kids get to experience whatever unique aspects one offers to them as their parent. It also means that neither parent has to leave a page full of notes and instructions when he or she isn't there.

All-In Partners also have a stronger case to make with their children about their own contributions at home. First, when the kids see their parents pitching in equally, they can more easily see that they, too, have roles to play as family members. Kofi and Ekua now have their own columns on MEL. Second, the benefit of the "When in Rome" strategy is that it makes any rules or discipline both parents agree to instill that much clearer. There are household responsibilities that my kids habitually fulfill without being reminded. They include folding their pajamas each morning and putting their dirty dishes on the counter after meals. They complete these tasks automatically because Kojo, I, and everyone else in their village consistently hold them accountable. Since Mommy and Daddy sometimes have different rules, the ones we have in common are taken that much more seriously.

I'm not suggesting an All-In Partnership is the only strategy for raising healthy children. I don't know what stories Kofi and Ekua will choose to tell about their childhoods when they grow up. Maybe they will say they've been able to build strong marriages because of the model that their parents set. Maybe they will say we ruined their lives because neither one of us was always there. I hope they both say that they have the power to curate the kind of relationships that work for them and enable their success—based on what matters most to them. I respect their right to tell their own future stories. What I do know is that an All-In Partnership is a healthy strategy to ensure the well-being of two full-time working parents. And happy parents are good for their children and for the world.

PART FIVE

Looking Ahead

CHAPTER 19

✦

The Four Go-Tos

By the spring of 2009, the novelty of Kojo's stint in Dubai had completely worn off. Babies are a lot more work after they're born. And the numbing, sleep-deprived existence of newborn parenting is more exhausting when you can't just roll over and give your partner the you're-on-duty nudge. Kojo was doing an amazing job comanaging our household from afar, but getting through those first couple of months alone made me miss him terribly.

Two other events solidified my doubt that we could continue our cross-Atlantic family situation. First, I was nearing the end of my maternity leave with Ekua, and I wasn't sure how I was going to manage working full-time with a two-year-old and a three-month-old without another grown-up in the house. This concern was brought about by the second event: Toyia had been accepted into graduate school and would be moving to Seattle by the end of the summer. Words were insufficient to express my gratitude for all she had done for us. I was simultaneously thrilled to see her move on to the next phase of her life and terrified about how I'd manage without her.

Fortunately, Kojo had an impending work transition as well. He'd still be assigned to oversee projects in sub-Saharan Africa, but he was moving back to New York. He'd have to travel out of the country for long stretches of time, but he'd have long stretches at home, too. It was infinitely better than his near-permanent residence being in Dubai. The stars weren't just aligning, they were kissing each other!

I knew that it was important that Kojo be around not just for bonding time with our infant daughter but also as a support during my transition back to work. While I was on maternity leave, I had read *Getting to 50/50,* a book I realized could have been helpful to me much earlier. In the book, authors Sharon Meers and Joanna Strober identify a primary caregiver's reentry into the workforce as a period that's critical to determining the future of a family, because the couple is forced to reckon with whether they will continue with one person assuming primary care for the child or whether they will become All-In Partners.[1] According to Meers and Strober, the degree to which the primary caregiver, usually the mother, allows her spouse to take over day-to-day caregiving responsibilities is the key to determining the direction their future will take. After having Kofi, I had gone back to work and continued to be responsible for the bulk of the caregiving at home. With Ekua, I would do things differently.

At about the same time that Kojo moved home full-time and I went back to work, I decided that I needed to do something for myself: exercise. I'd never been athletic; in my school years, I was always too busy planning dances and running for student government to play organized sports. Then in 2002 when we were still in Seattle, my friend Daveda convinced me to participate in a mini triathlon. I laughed heartily when she first suggested it. I didn't know how to swim (not even doggy paddle). I might jog if I was crossing the street and a car was approaching a little too quickly. And I hadn't been on a bike since riding my hot-pink, flowered banana seat to 7-Eleven to buy Now & Laters. Daveda didn't want to do it by herself, though. She told me I was her one friend whose *only* barrier to finishing a triathlon was in my head. Then she played the women-and-girls card: we'd be raising money for breast cancer research. I apprehensively agreed.

The Danskin triathlon turned out to be the greatest gift Daveda ever gave to me. During the training process, I developed an entirely new relationship with my body. I especially found the rhythm of running therapeutic and clarifying. I would breathe in. I would push it out. I would have so many aha moments during my early-morning runs. I loved Seward Park because it was a forested peninsula in Lake Washington. Once you began your run around the peninsula, you had to commit. I respected nature for encouraging discipline, and the stillness of the lake fortified me. After the triathlon, I continued to run and stay fit at the gym—until I had kids. That was when my exercise habit soared out the window, leaving me in a constant state of fatigue. I knew I had to get back in the gym to replenish my energy, and not just because I had children who needed me to be healthy; I needed more stamina to fuel my success at work.

Another thing happened around the time Kojo moved back from Dubai: challenges at the office were heating up. During the twelve weeks that I'd been on maternity leave, a restructuring at the White House Project had positioned a colleague and me to colead the organization under Marie Wilson, who would remain president. I was thrilled. My coleader, Sam, was one of the smartest people I'd ever worked with. I respected her and was confident that we'd be a strong team. So I was blindsided when she respectfully revealed that she was concerned about coleading with me because of my obligations outside of the office. She was worried that she'd have to carry more of the load at work, especially now that I had an infant at home. Sam was single with no kids. I was floored.

Similar to Alice's fight to maintain her professional legitimacy as a corporate attorney while on the mommy track, many women have faced stigma at the office for choosing to manage their dual roles as worker and mother. Even other women sometimes have trouble accepting their coworkers whose obligations lie in both camps. In a 2015 *Fortune* magazine article, Katharine Zaleski, cofounder and president of the female tech placement company PowerToFly, shuddered to think about the cruel way she treated her peers with children before she had her own. "I sat in a job interview where a male boss grilled a mother of three and asked her, 'How in the world are you going to be able to commit to this job and all your kids at the same time?'" Katharine recalled. "I'm ashamed to say I didn't give any visual encouragement when the woman, who was a top cable news producer at the time, looked at him and said, 'Believe it or not, I like being away from my kids during the workday—just like you.'"[2]

It was not until Katharine had her own child five years later that she realized the profound prejudice harbored toward mothers in the workplace. She understands now that her own behavior mimicked many of the microaggressions that women encounter from men who unfairly assess and exclude colleagues based on their status as mothers. To help redress the situation, she started her company PowerToFly, which is devoted to placing working mothers in tech jobs that they can do from home.

Even though I had never personally confronted this stigma, I was conscious of it, and I had always gone the extra mile to counter the stereotype, which is why Sam's comments stung. I had worked with her for three years and could count on one hand the number of times she had arrived at the office before I did. I could also count on one hand the number of times I'd had to stay home because of a childcare issue. Despite my family obligations, my work ethic was stellar, as evidenced by the nickname scrawled on my office whiteboard when I returned from my maternity leave—"Welcome Back, Tiffinator."

As Sam shared her concern with me, I remained calm on the outside, but inside I was seething. I thought, *You have no idea what "carrying more of the load" even means. I can tie one baby on my back, put the other on my hip, and still excel at this and any job.* After walking away from our meeting, I decided I would make it my mission to vindicate all working mothers on the planet. I would prove Sam wrong and anyone else who doubted us.

I was sitting in my office alone, staring at my computer monitor with my elbows on my desk and my forefingers on my temples. I was angry about what Sam had shared, but even in my anger, I had to admit she was right about one thing: I did have a lot on my plate. I had a new baby at home, and the promotion meant more responsibility at work. That one thought began to wreak havoc on my mind, and my heart started racing. I felt overwhelmed yet again. I had come so far in my evolution of Dropping the Ball. I had figured out how to apply my highest and best use at home to accomplish what mattered most to me. I had freed myself from the constant pressure of feeling that I needed to do everything at home. And Kojo really was a phenomenal All-In Partner in sharing the load. But I was still feeling the pressure of high performance at work, even more so now that Sam had explicitly expressed her doubt about my capacity. I was proud that I had discovered a system for success at home. What would be my system for success at the office? Clearly it wasn't going to be working nonstop like a machine. The Tiffinator needed a new approach.

Sitting there alone in my office, my first instinct was to do what I always did when I needed help figuring things out: go ask a Sage Mentor for advice. The closest one to me in that moment was Marie. She was literally in her office down the hall. Plus she was well qualified to offer insight. Of all the impressive things Marie had done in her career, serving in her city council in Iowa, launching the largest women's workforce reentry program in the country, building the Ms. Foundation for Women, and founding the White House Project, I respected her most for the fact that she did all this *and* raised five children. Normally, I'd schedule a separate coffee date outside the office to solicit personal advice from my boss, but my swirling emotions propelled me to make an impulsive move. I couldn't wait to speak to her.

As I was walking down the hall toward Marie's office, I tried to formulate my question to her, but someone else's thoughts were crowding my mind. I was ashamed of the thoughts. I tried to ignore them.

Tiffany, don't let your pride get in the way. You know Sam is right. You want this promotion, but Sam is smarter, and she runs the

*program whereas you've only raised money. Tell Marie you don't
want to colead. Just let Sam do it. Kofi and Ekua will only be young
once. Why are you making this so difficult? You're not your mother.*

The last thought made me want to cry. That's when I knew I
wasn't in a good place to talk to Marie, and I should have turned
around, but my stubbornness made me stick to my commitment.
When I got to the end of the hall, I could hear her talking on the
phone, so I stopped to wait. I tried even harder to figure out what I
would say to her, but the voice in my head kept getting louder. *Marie,
I need help. No, I need advice. I think you've made a mistake
promoting me. I can't do this. I'm so sorry to disappoint you.*

At the end of the hallway was a huge window. The White House
Project offices were on the eighth floor of a building on the far west
side of Manhattan. Looking out of that big window, I could see the
Hudson River. There were billions of tiny waves crashing, constantly
contradicting each other, and still the entire river moved in one direction. I closed my eyes, and I could feel myself moving alongside it.
I breathed in. I pushed it out. I could feel myself floating next to the
Charles River in Boston, and before that, along Lake Washington
when I was training for the triathlon. *Marie doesn't have your answer. You do. Run.* I could hear the click of Marie's receiver, and she
saw me standing near her door.

"What can I do for you, hon?" she chirped with Southern famil-
iarity and authority.

"Oh, nothing," I said, "I was just taking in the view."

That moment, of simply looking out at the Hudson, brought such
clarity about what I needed to do next: start running again. I didn't
have to have a perfect work strategy all figured out immediately.
After all, it had taken me nearly two years to figure out how to let go
at home. I just needed to carve out the time to run. Running would
help me to be strong, alert, strategic, and creative enough to figure
out the rest. It would also give me a healthy outlet to manage all my
conflicting thoughts. The biggest challenge would be carving out the
time. With a full-time job and two small children, one of whom was

still breast-feeding, and child care that only extended through office hours, where would I find a free hour in my day to run?

Like Alice, the only time slot I could allot to exercise was just before dawn, which meant I wouldn't be running outside since it was too dark and therefore unsafe. That also meant I'd have to wake at 4:45 A.M. to pump milk, then head out at 5:20 A.M. so I could be there when the gym opened at 5:30. This could only happen, of course, if someone *else* was at home to take care of my kids in the apartment.

Once again, I needed Kojo's help, and so I Delegated with Joy the task of getting the kids ready in the morning so that I could exercise. We agreeably retooled our MEL, but executing it turned out to be a rocky road. In order for the plan to work, Kojo would need to be up and showered by 6:15. The first morning, when I returned from my run at 6:40, I found Kojo and both of our kids asleep in the same bed. Both of us ended up late to work. The second morning, Kojo asked me if I could "just go tomorrow" because he had an early meeting for which he needed to prepare. I still went to the gym that day but cut it short by only running twenty minutes. On the third day, Kojo rolled over and nestled his arm around my waist after my alarm went off. It was still dark outside. I was very tempted to stay in bed.

It would have been so easy to skip many of these morning workouts, but I defended them ferociously, even to myself (on most mornings, a little voice would whisper, *But we went yesterday. Do we really have to go again?*). It was always grueling to make myself leave the house, but I felt so strong and proud of myself on the run back home. And with each passing day, Kojo and the kids ran a little less late. Eventually, the family fell into a new rhythm.

I knew that my routine was having a positive effect on Kojo when one morning I walked into our apartment and he greeted me with a kiss on the forehead.

"Did you have a good workout?" he asked.

"I did," I responded enthusiastically.

"Good," he replied, and I knew he was proud of me, too.

Though my morning runs meant an earlier rise for him, my

physical fitness meant a happier wife and mother throughout the day for our family. For me, it also meant professional success. On those morning runs, my breath was so in sync and my head was so clear that within a few weeks I was able to formulate a new success equation for work. I would maximize the new freedom that my All-In Partnership afforded me to be more strategic, and I would cultivate a village of support that would ensure I wasn't a victim of the Lone Ranger syndrome at work, just like I had been at home. It wasn't too long before I was thanking Sam for sharing her concern with me that day. As difficult as it was, that meeting with her was the catalyst for my creation of the Four Go-Tos, my new strategy for handling the pressures at the office.

As I have stated, there continues to be a dearth of women in top leadership positions, and the root of the problem is that the leadership pipeline for college-educated women breaks down at middle management. It is at this point in a professional career that energy expended at work needs to shift from a focus on performance to a focus on what it actually takes to get to the top—stamina, people who've got your back, a platform, and creativity. Many women reach this point at the precise moment they're starting their families, and if they don't already have significant support at home, the life-go-round begins to spin. It's no wonder, then, that women represent 53 percent of corporate entry-level jobs but only 14 percent of the executive committee level,[3] or that they make up 47 percent of law students, 45 percent of associates in law firms, but only 19 percent of partners.[4] The overwhelming majority of male executives—94.6 percent—are married with children, but only 46 percent of top corporate women are married, and only 52 percent of them are mothers.[5]

As my own experience taught me, working mothers who are serious about getting to the proverbial C-suite have to be crystal clear about what matters most; we have to understand what constitutes our highest and best use; we have to Delegate with Joy at home; and we have to prioritize our own happiness and success. Even all of that is still not enough. The point of lightening our home to-do lists is not so that we can spend more time at the office. Rather, the best reinvestment of our increased bandwidth is in four activities that will most effectively help us advance our careers and raise our quality of life. When women are physically fit, well networked, visible, and well rested, their leadership is inevitably advanced. We have to institute regular and repeatable practices that allow us to flourish. The practices, which I call the Four Go-Tos, are most effective when integrated into our daily routines. They are the following:

1. Going to exercise (building your stamina)
2. Going to lunch (building your network)
3. Going to events (building your visibility)
4. Going to sleep (building your renewal)

These practices are not rocket science, but they are essential to women's ability to prosper at work and in life, and they are nearly impossible for women to incorporate into their daily calendars unless time is freed up. Freeing up time requires that we apply the same intentionality to our calendars that we apply to our to-do lists, then proactively fill our remaining time with go-to activities that will support our success and well-being. That means asking ourselves questions like these: *How does this appointment match up to what matters most to me? Is making brownies from scratch for the school bake sale my highest and best use? Am I the only person who can clear the bathroom cabinet of expired medicine?* It is only by being intentional about what we should remove from our lists and calendars that we can gain control of what they should contain.

The first Go-To is *Going to Exercise*. Physical activity improves our stamina. Women who are managing full-time careers, family, and community have a lot to juggle, and their lives require an enormous amount of energy. The benefits of exercise are widely touted, but when it comes to women, the stress-reduction factor is the real kicker. I am a more relaxed wife, mother, and worker when I'm fit. Exercise increases concentrations of norepinephrine, the chemical that moderates the brain's response to stress.[6] Whether we're actually going to a gym, working out to videos in our living rooms, or dancing at a nightclub, movement is critical to our physical fitness and can add a couple of hours to our day in terms of increased energy. Even working out for just thirty minutes a day a few times a week can boost the brain's release of endorphins.[7] Furthermore, a recent study suggests that a rigorous workout can increase levels of BDNF, a brain-derived protein, which is understood to aid decision making and learning.[8] And the most significant study on the impact of exercise on professional life demonstrates that employees who work out maintain more energy and perform with higher rates of productivity.[9]

Women who have the resources and the child-care options in place that enable them to go to a gym only need to muster the discipline. One woman I know, Seiko, sleeps in her gym clothes to remove that one extra step in her morning routine. Another friend of mine, Devon, sets her iPhone alarm to her favorite workout song. I love using wearable trackers (my favorite is the UP fitness band) to set fitness goals with friends. I'm competitive enough to spend thirty minutes before I go to bed dancing to Shakira just to rack up my step count and watch my avatar on the app move to the top.

Women who don't have the money for a gym or for child care can still find creative ways to get fit. A bit of floor space is all that's needed to become a yogi like Alice or to work out to a fitness video on the computer or TV. When I don't have a babysitter and I need to move my body, I take my kids to the park across the street. They play or time me while I do sprints in a big grassy area or run up and down the steps of the amphitheater. Everything counts when it comes to exercise. People used to ask me how I got my arms so toned. They were always requesting specific weight routines or nutritional advice. The truth is, my arm muscles were largely the result of schlepping a stroller loaded with a toddler and a day's worth of bags up and down the New York City subway steps. One of my friends plays Wii tennis while her baby naps. When all else fails, some of us just put on music and dance our hearts out—whatever it takes to *move*.

The second Go-To is *Going to Lunch*. Of course, I don't mean lunch specifically—you can also go to breakfast, dinner, coffee, or drinks. The point is to connect with others to cultivate a professional network. This will prove vital as we move up the ranks. Just as our village offers support shouldering the burdens of our home lives, our networks—or what I prefer to call *ecosystems*—help us thrive in our work lives. Ecosystems are interdependent and require nurturing to expand. It takes an ecosystem to propel a career. In one study on the approaches that executive women take to move their careers forward and strike a healthy balance between work and family, Souha R. Ezzedeen and Kristen G. Ritchey found that "a complex and diversified network of social support . . . is necessary for women to advance in their chosen fields and to have a fulfilling family life."[10] Ezzedeen and Ritchey further found that "social support was not only a coping mechanism but also a creator of a context and a determinant of the life course strategies devised by women."[11] In other words, the existence of these ecosystems helped women shoot higher, perform better, and experience more satisfaction in all areas of their lives.

But ecosystems serve as more than social support; they can define who will speak for us when we're not in the room. A McKinsey report on the strategies high-achieving women adopt in order to thrive at work found that an effective ecosystem includes people who are willing to serve as sponsors, meaning they believe in our potential enough to advocate for us behind the scenes. Rosalind Hudnell, the chief diversity officer for Intel, explained that at the level where decisions about women's careers are no longer at the discretion of an individual manager, feedback from sponsors can make all the difference. "Having a sponsor who can provide that endorsement is critical," she noted.[12] Without it, women can work hard and know their stuff, yet they might never rise to the highest ranks of leadership.

Sponsors are only one brand of talent in our career ecosystem. I've already explained how I found it helpful to create a village comprised of Family Members, Neighbors, Nonpaid Working Moms, Babysitters, and Specialists to help with the demands of our home lives.

Similarly, our ecosystems need several types of talent to best help us thrive professionally.

The most precious members of our ecosystems are our *Sage Mentors*. They include our aunties, senior executives, and civic leaders—all of whom have been around the block more times than we have. They help us to achieve clarity through guidance and encouragement. They know the good, the bad, and the ugly about our challenges because we've been meeting with them regularly, at least once every six months for several years. We seek out Sage Mentors for their wisdom, as they have enough experience to see patterns— industry patterns, business patterns, our mind-set patterns—and they ask us the right (and often tough) questions to help us with decision making. Their wisdom transcends the specifics of any particular industry, so they don't have to be experts in our field. It was my Sage Mentors who told me, "Go for it, but wait to have kids," when Kojo proposed to me in college. That suggestion seemed personal at the time, but it turned out to be the best career advice for a woman in her twenties who was hell-bent on changing the world.

Then there's the counsel we receive from members of our own cohort group: *Peer Mentors*. Peer Mentors have a lot of empathy about our career challenges because they're dealing with the same thing. We're all going around the block together. We meet with them once every few months to get help mapping out and executing our plans. Sometimes a group of us will do this together. We seek out Peer Mentors who will hold us accountable, helping us keep our feet to the fire on our dreams. We do the same thing for them. Negotiation expert Selena Rezvani writes about how women who discuss their goals and strategies with others end up being more confident negotiators and that "talking to others not only gives us a sense of what's possible, but it also helps us form an accurate and honest picture of who we are and what we are worth. This kind of interaction endows us with . . . 'accountability partners,' those who will keep us on track and make sure we are asking for what we want."[13] In fact, the book you are currently holding is largely the result of two years of prodding from one of my Peer Mentors, Reshma Saujani, founder of Girls Who Code. "So when are you writing a book?" she'd ask each time I saw her. And now I have.

Peer Mentors engage in transactions that make us an interlocking chain of power and a safety net for one another's careers. It often feels like we're tethering each other as climbers would on a mountain. When my Peer Mentor Janessa Cox, Head of Diversity & Inclusion at AllianceBernstein, needed a moderator for a panel her company was hosting, she invited me because she knew I was seeking more visibility. Unfortunately, I had to decline due to a travel conflict, but I pitched another of my Peer Mentors, attorney Candice Cook, who got the gig. When Keisha Smith-Jeremie needed clients to complete her executive coach accreditation, I connected her with brand and image consultant Kali Patrice, who was thrilled to hire Keisha to help her curate the next phase of her career. When several of us learned that Penny Abeywardena was in the running for international affairs commissioner for New York City, we all picked up the phone to endorse her. Our girl was definitely getting that job. The point? Wherever we are in our careers, we must foster an ecosystem of other women who are at our level so that we can all help pull one another up the mountain, together.

Then there are the *Sponsors*—people who are willing to use their social and political capital to lobby for our success. I don't connect with my Sponsors as often I do with my Peer Mentors, but Sponsors have facilitated every big career transition I've made. One of my first Sponsors was Janie Williams, a social justice leader and philanthropist in Seattle who helped me get into a fund-raising management program early in my career. Sponsors generally have the ear of the right person during clutch moments, making them invaluable members of the team. They don't need to know the good, the bad, and the ugly about us, nor do they always need to know our career plans. They just need to consider us to be superstars and feel confident nominating us for influential networking organizations or advocating for our promotion.

We must be sensitive to the fact that Sponsors have to be extremely judicious about how they spend their capital, because when they convince others to give us an opportunity, they're putting their own reputations on the line. If we don't heed the advice that a Sage Mentor gives to us in private, only two people will know. But if a Sponsor endorses us and we don't deliver, we make them look bad publicly. A Sponsor regretting that he or she invested in me? I do everything to avoid that scenario. The flip side is that when we do deliver, we've built credibility for our Sponsor. And if we keep delivering, we'll be in a position to help our Sponsors in the future.

I was recently talking to my friend Kelly Parisi, a brilliant communications professional, about our mutual Sponsor, Marie. Kelly was early in her career when Marie, then president of the Ms. Foundation, invested in her. Kelly eventually went on to become chief communications executive at Girl Scouts of the USA and also ran communications for LeanIn.org. I expressed to Kelly my own gratitude for Marie's sponsorship. "I would do *anything* for Marie," I told her. "Me too!" Kelly responded with enthusiasm. We then thought about all of the people who were just like us—women and men in high-level positions who feel indebted to Marie for her early investment in them. Whatever Marie needs, she has only to pick up the phone and call any one of us. That's when it dawned on us: Marie's sponsorship of so many people is one of the reasons she's so incredibly powerful.

Promoters are the fourth group of people in our ecosystem. They are the team benchwarmers rooting for us off the field, but they'll fly onto the field in a heartbeat to offer support should we ever ask them to. They don't know us as intimately as some of the other members of our team, as we keep them posted mostly via social media or group e-mails, but they know enough about us to say yes when we need quick advice, an introduction, a reference, or a resource. The unspoken rule is that we'll return the favor in a heartbeat, too. We seek out Promoters for smaller transactions that will facilitate our personal and career success but that don't require a major commitment on the part of the Promoter. For example, we'll ask Promoters to forward a job description when we're looking for talent or to retweet an article we've written.

Finally, there are the members of our ecosystem who inspire us the most: our *Mentees*. Our Mentees are people who are earlier in their careers than we are. They often solicit us for the same kind of advice and encouragement we receive from our Sage Mentors, and when the opportunity arises, we don't hesitate to act as their Sponsors. But what we do for our Mentees pales in comparison to the insight, cheerleading, and support we receive from them—at least that's how it feels to me. Our Mentees' primary value is in keeping us relevant and grounded. We invest in Mentees who remind us what's possible and who make us beam with pride when we recommend them to others.

My Mentees have supported my leadership journey in countless ways. I once got so preoccupied trying to meet a deadline that I completely forgot to send invitations to an event I was hosting for a major foundation—one that was only three days away. Since it was an event targeting millennials, I sent out messages to several of my Mentees who responded within minutes saying they'd be there. One of them, Damali Elliott, who is the founder of Petals-N-Belles, an organization to empower girls, wrote back that she couldn't attend herself but would spread the word. She recruited several of her friends, who packed the room. Damali saved me! Another one of my Mentees, Samira DeAndrade, has worked her tail off as a fashion executive for major brands such as Donna Karan, Diesel, and Alice+Olivia. Samira has made sure that I'm well dressed for public appearances, and I happily promote her brands. My Mentees help me with everything from research projects to babysitting when I'm in a pinch. I wouldn't be where I am today without them.

Anyone—work colleagues, bosses, sorority sisters, in-laws, neighbors, babysitters, family, and friends—can be members of our ecosystems. The biggest challenge is usually prioritizing the time to cultivate these important relationships. There are many ways to go about it. One of my friends, Katherine Mossman, sends handwritten notes to people. There are also multiple contact management tools like FullContacts and Contacts+ that allow women to stay in touch. And ever since graduating from college, I've sent an update e-mail twice a year to people with whom I want to stay connected. I sent the first update to the three professors who had the largest impact on me, and also included a handful of friends. Now, nearly twenty years later, my updates go out to more than three hundred people, all of whom I've studied or worked with in some capacity. Above all, I want the people in my ecosystem to know that their advice and support continues to make a difference in my life.

In addition to regular updates, it's important to dedicate real time in our schedules to cultivating our ecosystem. Several women I interviewed for this book set aside regular time slots each week for networking meetings—I do mine on Tuesday, Thursday, and Friday mornings. Our ecosystems should be so diverse and plentiful that when we need something—anything—if we don't know someone who can help, we know someone who knows someone who can. As my friend Erica Dhawan, a leadership consultant, would say, "Connectional intelligence is how we get big things done."

The third Go-To is *Going to Events* that raise our visibility and public profile. These can be in-person events where we're addressing an audience or serving on a panel, or virtual events like Twitter chats, but what's important is that we're practicing using and hearing our own voices. I was lucky enough to be on the ground floor of launching Seattle Girls' School, an all-girls' middle school that focuses on math, science, and technology. One of the most powerful aspects of the institution's approach is its focus on the Greek oral tradition. By the time a girl is in the fifth grade, she can stand in front of a group of her peers and adults and verbally demonstrate her knowledge with confidence. These whip-smart girls are getting early and invaluable training in how to raise their profiles and augment their visibility.

Smart people who can meet goals are a dime a dozen, and most of them are languishing in middle management. In order to kick our careers into high gear, women need to be willing to step onto public platforms that reflect our passions and help differentiate us from our peers. The best way to stand out in the workplace is to use our voices. I seek out opportunities to make presentations, serve on panels, and give talks because these are the most effective ways to build my credibility and position myself as a thought leader. Warren Buffett once told a class of business students that he would pay anyone in the room $100,000 for 10 percent of their future earnings, but if they were good communicators, he would raise his bid by 50 percent. Their ability to motivate others through their deft communication skills would make his investment more valuable.[14] Even if the idea of speaking publicly makes us want to vomit, there are many ways to exercise our voices without making our palms sweat, such as social media, writing for publications, and leadership roles in professional organizations, to name just a few. In a 2013 survey, the consulting firm BRANDfog determined that 75 percent of Americans believed that CEO participation in social media resulted in better leadership techniques and outcomes.[15] Translating our vision of what matters in the highly accessible and informal way that social media platforms allow can help us connect with people who have the right expertise to support us on our leadership journeys.

Going to events that raise our visibility also makes networking more efficient. If I'm on a morning panel at a conference or in a Twitter chat, I can easily meet twenty new people who heard what I had to say and want to follow up. I'd have to give up four of my weekday evenings, precious time for a busy working mom, to attend enough cocktail events to meaningfully connect with the same number of people singularly. Raising our profiles increases the number of people who want to connect with *us*, which means far less work.

The final Go-To is *Going to Sleep*. Getting our z's is probably the toughest task for women juggling the responsibilities of work and home, but as Arianna Huffington espouses in *The Sleep Revolution*, it is an essential activity because of the positive impact it has on how we approach everything else that we do. By getting enough sleep each day, we replenish our energy, bolster memory and learning ability, and unleash our creativity.[16] Interestingly, there can be a direct correlation between workplace stress and the sleep patterns of employees: a recent study found that employees with less supportive managers slept less and were more than twice as likely to be at risk for cardiovascular disease than those with more creative and responsive managers.[17] I've been fortunate to have the latter in Caroline Ghosn, the rock star CEO of Levo.

My sleep evolution was somewhat forced by Caroline. During my first performance conversation with her, she expressed her appreciation that I had hit business milestones but said she was concerned about the amount of sleep I was getting. Most team members at the technology start-up wore UP bands, and Caroline had some sense of my sleep patterns from the device and my e-mail time stamps. Let's just say my activity showed that I wasn't getting a lot of shut-eye, though in all fairness to me, it wasn't any less than what the average working mother tends to get—about five hours.[18]

At first, Caroline's comment felt intrusive. At that time, the majority of employees at Levo were in their twenties, all of them single, and I was the only one with kids. *She just doesn't understand,* I thought to myself. As if she were reading my mind (which, after three years of working with her, I seriously believe she might have been), Caroline acknowledged that I was the only parent in the company and offered to do anything to accommodate my getting more sleep, even if that meant my taking naps during the workday. To her, it was more strategic to have an executive running on a full tank for a shorter period of time than one who is running close to empty all day.

I would have shrugged Caroline off were it not for Kojo's comment that night when I told him about our meeting. "I think everyone's world would be better if you got more sleep," he said. *Ouch.* Thus began my "eight for eight" experiment of getting eight hours of sleep a night for eight weeks in a row, which I hadn't done since having kids.

In order to make it happen, I had to disrupt the typical working-mom schedule that plagues our life-go-rounds. It basically works like this: We spend the morning prepping others and ourselves for the day. Then we head to the office, often getting there early because school drop-offs require us to leave our homes before our childless colleagues. Once we reach a certain professional level, we're in meetings all day. We take notes in every meeting, piling up a long list of to-dos that we'll get to later in the day. Sadly "later in the day" never comes. We rush out of the last meeting to pick up our kids from after-school programming or to relieve our caregivers. After dinner, bath, and bedtime for our kids, we clean up and then finally sit down at our computers to wade through a bunch of e-mails that have been sent between the time we left the office and when we tucked our kids into bed. We respond to all of them. By the time we complete that task it's 10:00 P.M. and we're just beginning to tackle our lists from the day. We hit the pillow by midnight, if we're lucky, but if there are any family issues or school paperwork to attend to, it's more like 1:00 A.M. Because I was committed to my workouts as another vital Go-To, I'd be up at 5:00 A.M. to do it all over again.

The only way I could interrupt this vicious cycle was to get my work done during the day, which meant taking control of my calendar. I sought advice from women who had already done it. One of my Sage Mentors had long abandoned scheduling hour-long meetings. All her meetings were forty minutes, followed by a ten-minute window to check off any to-dos from that meeting and to take a break. Another senior leader with an open-door policy used a timer whenever someone popped in to speak with her "for just five minutes." That tactic alone easily shaved an hour off my day. One of the best time management tools I adopted from an executive was a simple question: "Why do you need me in this meeting?" Simply asking that question often caused people to apologize and rescind their invitation.

The result of my "eight for eight" experiment was astounding. After turning in by 9:00 P.M. each night for two months straight, I discovered I had been exhausted for seven years. I had been making things happen but not really functioning at optimal capacity. A foggy haze that I had not even been aware of lifted, and I was infinitely more alert. I'm embarrassed to admit that before this experiment, I had prided myself on my lack of sleep. Worse, I thought it was a positive trait in others, too, a sign of a solid work ethic, grit, and commitment. But my "eight for eight" experiment reminded me that it was the tortoise, not the hare, that triumphed in the end. Slow and steady wins the race.

———

Often when I'm tucking Kofi in at night, he reminds me, "Mom, you can make us go to bed, but you can't make us go to sleep!" This logic applies to our spouses as well. *Getting* him to do more is not the same as him *wanting* to do more. And the best strategy for getting our spouses to hold on to the ball we've dropped is to show them how doing so allows us to thrive. When women execute the four Go-Tos, men see the fruit of their labor.

A year after I had reestablished my morning routine of going to exercise and was also actively going to lunch and events (it would be another few years before I regularly got to sleep), I asked Kojo how he thought our MEL was going. He admitted that when I first enlisted him in doing more at home, he had been frustrated because it had felt like a bait and switch. He had married the queen of domesticity, after all. Gradually, though, his frustration abated. "Look," he said, "it's not that I enjoy doing all this stuff. But I remembered that we got married because of the impact we believed we could make in the world. Your passion was advancing women and girls. My passion was advancing sub-Saharan Africa. You have always supported me when I had an opportunity to do that. I felt committed to doing whatever it took to ensure that you were in the position to change the world. That's what motivates me still."

In just two years, Kojo's All-In Partnership and the implementation of my Four Go-Tos resulted in the biggest promotion of my career. I was named president of the White House Project.

CHAPTER 20

✦

Final Frontier

I became president of the White House Project at the end of 2010, and over the next five years, a lot changed for me. First, my career skyrocketed. After running the White House Project for two years, I joined the launch team for Lean In, a movement focused on encouraging women to pursue their ambitions, and became chief leadership officer of Levo, the fastest-growing network founded for millennial women. Levo mentors and arms young professionals with the tools necessary to build excellence and to create lives they're passionate about. It's attracted the attention of leaders such as Warren Buffett, Soledad O'Brien, and Kevin Spacey, all of whom have inspiring video interviews featured on the site.

My public speaking platform also exploded. I was invited to present at top women's conferences like *Fortune*'s Most Powerful Women and TEDWomen. I was humbled to receive a rousing standing ovation at BET's Leading Women Defined, and I cried when the event's producer sent a note saying the last person to receive such a response was Michelle Obama. I joined boards, advisory committees, and powerful women's networks. On top of all this, I was receiving a lot of recognition for my work, which, for the first time in my life, I wasn't constantly seeking. I had retired from trying to be perfect. *How ironic*, I thought, when *Fast Company* named me to their League of Extraordinary Women, *that this accolade comes as soon as I give up on being extraordinary and simply focus on doing what matters most to me.*

Kojo was kicking butt, too. He had joined the founding team of Atlas Mara, a new financial venture that was the brainchild of former Barclays CEO Bob Diamond and entrepreneur Ashish Thakkar. Their goal was to revolutionize banking in Africa, and they were well on their way, having raised $325 million through an initial public offering on the London Stock Exchange. Just a little over a year later, Atlas Mara had grown their assets to $2.6 billion. Kojo was doing what mattered most to him: advancing sub-Saharan Africa.

In the meantime, Kofi and Ekua grew from babies to vibrant young people in the blink of an eye. Our son, whom I once found swathed in garbage bags in a baby bouncer, was now bouncing a basketball all over our apartment. And the same daughter whose hair I had worried about managing was now swinging her gorgeous beaded braids (courtesy of a salon) to Taylor Swift. Some days, Kojo and I felt like we needed white-and-black-striped shirts and whistles to referee the kids' arguments, but most of the time, we felt like we were on the right track toward raising conscious global citizens.

I had reached a point in my career where I was busier and more in demand than ever before, yet I felt more on top of it than I ever had. And this composure came from the same woman who, just a few years prior, couldn't fathom attending a two-hour neighborhood board meeting once a month because it would interfere with her Sunday food-prep routine. The biggest change: I Dropped the Ball. The result: Kojo picked it up.

You know when something new happens to you—you get a new car, a new pair of shoes, you get visibly pregnant—and all of a sudden you start noticing tons of Jettas, Chloe scalloped slip-ons, and waddling bellies? That's what happens when we Drop the Ball, too. All of a sudden, we start running into women who confidently declare, "I stopped cleaning the top of my refrigerator *years* ago." For a while, when I met this new breed, I felt as if I had missed an important memo. As it turns out, more and more women are motivated to redefine success by relinquishing the myth of the superwoman and enlisting their spouses as All-In Partners. But for many, the highest bar to battle is our unrealistic expectation around motherhood. I especially felt this as my kids got older and they began to articulate for themselves what they needed from me.

One Saturday afternoon, six-year-old Kofi and I were nestled in the corner of the blue couch, talking. He had just returned from his summer in Ghana with his dad and his sister, and I asked him what his favorite part of the trip had been. He pondered with his eyes toward the ceiling and said wistfully, "When I was in Ghana, I didn't have to hold a grown-up's hand." He asked me why he always had to hold my hand in New York, and when I explained it was for safety reasons, he suggested that I should trust him more. "I'm a big kid now. It's not like I'm gonna run away." Because of my Drop the Ball evolution, I was surprised about where my mind immediately traveled when he said this: to an image of a woman walking down the street with her son running an entire block ahead and my immediate judgment that she was an irresponsible mom. Then I remembered the time I started to read a French parenting book that advocated allowing children to walk independently. I never finished it. I told Kofi definitively, "Honey, you'll be walking down your wedding aisle holding my hand." I was only half joking. As I'm writing this book, I trust my nine-year-old son to put on his own seat belt, make himself a cup of tea with scalding-hot water, and cut his English muffin with a sharp knife, but he is *still* required to hold my hand when we're walking down the street. The drive for motherhood perfection runs deep.

Although we logically know it's just not attainable, women today feel more pressure than ever to be flawless parents. According to *Time,* close to 80 percent of millennial mothers believe that it's important to be the perfect mom.[1] Even women who are recovering HCDers find it relatively easy to embrace imperfection on the household management front, but they often struggle to let go when it comes to the tasks related to parenting. Motherhood is the final Drop the Ball frontier.

Our fear is not simply generated from within. The social stigma of anything less than perfect parenting still tends to fall on women's shoulders. Women bear the brunt of criticism about their parenting, and millennials are particularly susceptible. A Pew Research Center study conducted among over two thousand Americans revealed a strong belief that today's young parents are not measuring up to the standards set by parents a generation ago. Although the respondents admitted that moms have a more difficult job than dads, over half (56 percent) believed that mothers today are doing a worse job than mothers twenty or thirty years ago. In contrast, only 47 percent stated that fathers are doing a worse job.[2]

Many have pointed the finger at paid working moms, which only exacerbates the pressure. Women who feel guilty working outside the home often compensate with überinvolvement, assuming total responsibility for their child's "successes" and "failures," a new form of HCD known as helicopter parenting. But a number of studies have shown that helicopter parenting can be more harmful than helpful. A 2012 study found that helicopter kids were less engaged in school, were overly dependent, and lacked problem-solving skills and the ability to advocate for themselves, while parents were more stressed.[3] Apparently, hovering works better for pilots than it does for parents, but we missed that memo, too.

As if social pressure to parent well isn't enough, now we have social media–generated peer pressure to contend with. Ninety percent of millennials use social media—and for good reason; it's a treasure trove of valuable information and offers many of us an easy, efficient way to stay abreast of loved ones' lives. However, when parents post information and photographs about their children and families (perhaps in a subconscious attempt to crowdsource praise), the domino effect is that every "friend" who sees one mom's post announcing that her two-year-old has mastered sign language can feel a little less perfect herself. So, she jets off to buy Little Pim language CDs to get her little Feliz a jumpstart on learning Chinese. Moms who see more feel the need to do more.

However, social media presents a one-sided image of people's lives, as many tend to post only the best parts of their days rather than airing the dirty laundry of our kids' temper tantrums, arguments with the spouse, in-law drama, or problems at work—you know, all that other stuff that makes us human and, therefore, relatable. The truth is that feeling worried, confused, guilty, overwhelmed, and even inadequate from time to time is the new normal—as is a woman working full-time outside the home. America's June Cleaver days are largely over.

In 2014, the number of stay-at-home parents among married-couple families was a little over five million—not even 20 percent of the U.S. population.[4] The skyrocketing costs of raising children, about $14,000 per child annually, make a nonpaid working parent unfeasible in most households. Yet even though the majority of us are in the workforce, a report for Working Mother Media found that 60 percent of millennial moms still believe one parent should be at home raising children.[5] This gap between our economic reality (most women need to go to work) and our unrealistic cultural expectation (that women belong at home) can't be closed with guilt. But it can be narrowed with the truth: the critique that working mothers are the downfall of good parenting is largely unfounded and may reveal more about national discomfort with the evolving role of mothers than it does about the well-being of children today.

When compared with previous generations, it's actually unlikely that moms today are failing in their duties. As Judith Warner writes in her book *Perfect Madness*, an eight-year study in 1955 "found no significant differences in school performance, psychosomatic symptoms, or closeness to their mothers" between children of paid and nonpaid working mothers.[6] A study in the mid-1970s that controlled for such factors as family life, day-care quality, class, and ethnicity found that "there were no significant differences in intelligence, language, social skills, or attachment" between kids cared for by mothers versus day-care workers.[7] The same conclusion was drawn in 1988 and again in 1996. Another meta-analysis entitled "Maternal Work Early in the Lives of Children and Its Distal Associations with Achievement and Behavior Problems" looked at sixty-nine case studies to determine the long-term effects of maternal employment during a child's infancy and early childhood. With a few exceptions, a mother's employment had no bearing on her child's overall well-being and success in later life.[8] There is no reason for us to continue to self-flagellate when it comes to parenting.

So how can moms block out all that white noise? Instead of striving to meet unrealistic expectations and hustle for "likes," we can refocus energy on what matters most to us—as any insecurities we might experience are being spurred by an incomplete picture to begin with. And instead of turning into comparison junkies, we can harness the connective power of social media. Sites like Facebook offer us the opportunity to share our struggles and triumphs in a more transparent way, which can generate more authentic conversations around the frustrations and fears that are associated with parenting.

Of course, this is easier said than done. The pressure to be the perfect parent is so pervasive that even women who don't have children feel it. They receive the same societal messages and are viewing the same posts. But instead of directing their anxiety to overparenting their own children, they are forced to manage external expectations that they are inadequate, and they often feel pressure at work to stay late and do more, since they don't have kids to pick up from soccer practice or a family for whom they need to cook dinner. In fact, my colleague Sam was responding to this exact pressure when she shared with me her concern about sharing more of the load at work. Many of us tend to unconsciously conflate the roles of "woman" and "mom." And with the territory of the latter comes the directive to be everything to everyone, offer constant nurturing, and love every moment of it. Women who don't want children may not have to deal directly with these expectations, but at the same time, they are perceived as "not normal," as if they have chosen not to prioritize caregiving and nurturing. Often, these women do prioritize caregiving and nurturing in ways that do not necessarily involve children. In addition, women who would like to have children but are struggling, either because they wish to do it in a partnership or because they are having difficulty conceiving and are facing infertility, are being spoon-fed the same message.

Every single one of these women needs to be free to Drop the Ball.

Our collective dependency on one definitive model of parenting is stifling women's ability to be happy with themselves and their choices. Perhaps, in the words of the Indigo Girls, "There's more than one answer to these questions / Pointing me in crooked line."

———

I should be honest about a couple of privileges that have made Dropping the Ball easier for me. For starters, I'm an African American woman who was racially socialized. From an early age, my parents told me I was black, and they helped me put my black identity into context. They would say things like, "Because you're black, you'll have to work harder than white people. Life isn't fair." This might seem a harsh message to give a young child, but I've found that having clarity about how the world actually operates has come in handy. I'm not saying that these kinds of messages didn't create a burden for me. When I'm the only black person in the room, I do sincerely believe that if I screw up, it's a ding on the entire black race. I'm just saying that, unlike some of my white sisters, I was heartbroken but not shocked when Hillary lost to a man who joked about assaulting women and had never served in public office. I was never under the illusion that the most qualified person gets the job. Most of the time, my racial identity allows me to quickly put my experience into a larger perspective and to feel a sense of gratitude. Yes, my child has just thrown herself on the sidewalk like a civil rights protester because I said she can't have ice cream, but she is not being sold away from me. If my ancestors could get through that trauma, I can get through this tantrum. So contextualizing my personal life-go-round within

women's collective experience was a similar leap and was very helpful to me in realizing what I wish other women understood sooner:
we're not going crazy, and we're not alone.

The second privilege that has made it easier for me to Drop the
Ball is my spiritual belief. I believe that we are all souls, and we exist
because God loves us. I believe that when Kofi and Ekua, as souls,
were looking down deciding which woman would be their mother in
this lifetime, they picked me. I don't know why. Discovering the answer to that question is an awakening for each of us to have about our
own mothers, and my children will have that about me in their own
time. But I trust that if they needed a less ambitious mother, they
would have picked a different woman. So when I'm rushing out of
the house and I glance at the babysitter removing Ekua's cornrows,
a childhood bonding experience I used to have with my mother that
I recall vividly, I experience a tinge of guilt because I'm not doing it
for her myself, but I quickly recover. By the time I reach the bottom
of my stoop, I'm confident that what I *am* doing will hopefully change
the work environment to allow my daughter to wear her cornrows
proudly. I'm confident that she knows better than I what she was
getting herself into when she decided I should be her mom. I can't
blame myself for that one. I can only do my best to guide her on her
unique path. Finally, my spiritual outlook has helped me to understand the ultimate source of our pressure to be perfect. It's helped
me to understand why our identities as mothers are often so wrought
and complicated: our relationships with our own mothers are often
just that, tangled.

———

Since 2006, when I found myself drenched in breast milk on the
floor of an office bathroom stall, I've spoken to my mom only three
times. I hate the word *estranged* because it's the antithesis of how I
feel about my mom. She is always with me. But technically, that's
what we are. Not long ago, I was having a conversation with my sister,
Trinity, who was expressing anger that our mom wasn't present in
our lives. She didn't understand why I wasn't angry, too. "Kofi and

Ekua don't know her," she said. "Doesn't she want to know her own grandchildren?" Sisters have a special way of saying things that make you want to burst into tears. I held mine back. Regardless of history, all children will tell their own stories about their mothers. Here is mine:

From the time she found out she was pregnant with me until I was sixteen, my mom gave me everything I needed to be strong. She taught me that I was the most powerful change agent in my own journey. And she did it, despite not having anyone do it for her. Because of her, my children have a mother who is healthy and empowered. That's the greatest gift she could give. She doesn't owe us anything else.

As soon as I told myself this story again, I had my awakening. I spent my entire life forgiving my mother's imperfections but refusing to forgive my own. If I was too busy to check on an old college buddy, I was a terrible friend. If my yeast rolls didn't rise just so, I was a terrible cook. If someone on my team quit, I was a terrible boss. If my husband fed my kids pizza, I was a terrible mother. I wasted so much time trying to prove that I was perfect—a futile endeavor given that we're all human and imperfect by design. In fact, our imperfection is what makes us endearing. And then I finally got it.

I picked her so she could teach me how to love myself as imperfect.

Loving ourselves as imperfect is the prerequisite to Dropping the Ball.

—

One morning, Kofi and I were in the bathroom when Ekua walked through the door with her arms outstretched in a huge circle. "Look at this big barrel of apples I picked!" she exclaimed, her breath heavy from carrying such a huge, albeit imaginary, load. I continued applying my mascara. Kofi stopped brushing his hair to engage with his little sister. He pretended to reach his arm deep into her barrel and pulled out an apple, holding it high above his head. "Ha!" he teased. "I'm going to eat one of your apples!" Ekua immediately became incensed. She jumped up and down, fruitlessly trying to grab her apple from her brother's clenched fist. He laughed, and she cried, eventually crumbling to the floor in anguish.

As this scene unfolded, I had my own epiphany. Just a few minutes earlier, Ekua had joyfully invited us into her imaginary world over which she had complete control, yet within minutes, she had allowed her brother to hijack it. Then *she* became the stressed-out mess on the bathroom floor. *Women have to stop doing this. We have to stop letting other people hijack our journeys.* Ekua looked up at me for help. Tears streamed down her face. I put down my mascara brush, got down on the floor, and whispered in her ear, "Your apples are magic, hon. Whenever your brother touches one, it turns to dust. He can't eat them." With that, Ekua smiled, pulled herself up off the floor, and began collecting her imaginary apples, placing each one carefully back in her barrel. As she waddled out of the bathroom, arms outstretched, she turned to give her brother the final word: "So *there!*" Later, I told her how proud I was of the decision she made not to let her brother's game get the best of her. I told her, "You are so smart. You are so loved. You are so beautiful."

CHAPTER 21

Freedom

It's Thursday, February 12, 2015, and I'm going to miss another Valentine's Day. I'm thrilled, however, to be flying to Aspen the next morning to participate in Anne-Marie Slaughter's Socrates Seminar, "Competition and Care: How Can We Strike a Balance Between Work and Family for Women and Men?" It's 6:00 P.M. when I finish up my last meeting, and a new e-mail appears in my inbox from Ekua's school. Subject line: Valentine's Day. *Oh, shoot. We forgot the kids' Valentine's Day cards for their classmates. They'll be exchanging them tomorrow.* My phone rings less than a minute later. It's Kojo, and he's whispering, which means he has had to step out of a meeting to call me. "Babe, check your e-mail. We forgot the kids' Valentine's Day cards!" We decide that I'll go grab the cards since I'm finished with my meetings and he still has one more to go. Then I'll go home and get the kids started on writing their messages. When Kojo gets home, he'll help them finish their cards while I pack for my trip.

The old Tiffany would have designed an original Valentine's Day card for each child and rushed to Michael's craft store to get all the supplies. (Note: she would have done this two weeks prior, too.) That nonsense is now a thing of the past, thankfully! The newer Tiffany would have headed to a Target to purchase prepackaged Valentine's greetings with the latest cool superhero featured on the front. But there is no Target on my train ride home, and I'm not about to jeopardize our parking space once I get there to drive to one. So that leaves the current Tiffany with only one option: head to the Staples next door. I grab a ream of red paper that the kids can write messages on and a bag of heart-shaped lollipops that I see at the register. The kids can just tape the lollipops onto their "cards." Problem solved.

Unfortunately, Kofi and Ekua are not happy with my solution when I proudly unveil the paper and lollipops. First, Kofi: "Seriously, Mom? I'm not even allowed to bring candy to school!" Then, Ekua: "I can't either! Private schools don't believe in sugar! *You should know this, Mom!*" The last line stings a little, but I shake it off. I have to admit that I'm surprised by these new rules. "Since when have you not been able to bring candy?" I ask. "Since kindergarten," says Kofi, "and now I'm in the *third grade!*" I start chuckling, which frustrates them so much that they send me to my room to pack while they start writing their friends' names on the cards. As I'm walking down the hall, I can hear Ekua saying to her brother, "We'll just have to wait for Dad to help us figure out the rest."

And figure it out he does. When I awake early the next morning to catch my flight, there are thirty-two cards with drawings from the kids. On each one is a message: "Being your friend makes good 'sense.'" But instead of the word *sense* there are two pennies taped to the paper. They are the most adorable (and least expensive) Valentine's Day cards I ever laid my eyes on.

Until our public and corporate policies catch up with the reality of today's world, All-In Partnership is the most practical solution to end women's dizzying, exhausting life-go-rounds. Society can no longer afford to have half its talent pool stifled by the unrealistic demands of doing it all. Executing a vision for career achievement requires space, thought, careful planning, creativity, and a good night's sleep. And it's really hard to have space for any of those things when we think we need to stay up all night making valentines.

Women need to know that it is perfectly okay for us to do 50 percent of what's currently on our to-do lists. We need to give ourselves permission to expect less of ourselves and more from the partners with whom we've signed up to change the world. We need women's ingenuity, perspective, and voices to be heard at the highest levels of leadership in this country. Whether we care about education, health care, the economy, food deserts, immigration, the environment, or any other issue that affects our lives and our futures, at the end of the day, it is the people at the highest levels of governments and corporations who are sitting at heavy marble tables trying to address these problems. Their decisions affect every single one of us. But there is a dearth of women in the chairs around those tables.

Like many of my colleagues in the women's leadership sphere, I'm a huge advocate of public policies that would institutionalize equal pay and affordable child care, which would address the most urgent needs facing working families. I've advised companies on inclusive practices, and I've been a part of some of the most groundbreaking leadership development programs designed to support women in making their way to the top. I am not suggesting that we discontinue these efforts, but I do believe that if we want something we've never had before, we're going to have to do something we've never done before in order to achieve it. In *Unbending Gender*, Joan Williams writes, "Allowing women the 'choice' to perform as ideal workers without the privileges that support male ideal workers is not equality."[1] The greatest privilege that men in the workplace have had isn't a corporate or public policy. It's a partner at home.

Kojo and I are not an anomaly. Most successful women in leadership today have spouses who are All-In Partners in managing their

homes.[2] Almost half of the women who lead Fortune 500 companies have spouses who play a significant role on the domestic front.[3]
Much attention is given to the socioeconomic privilege that allows
women to outsource domestic labor. I, too, am blessed with a part-
time sitter who does school pickups and can spend the night with
the kids if Kojo and I are both traveling. I understand this is a luxury that is not possible for the vast majority of families. What we
often overlook is the journeys that women take through lower- and
middle-management roles to get to those privileged executive positions. These are the years when women don't have powerhouse
compensation and when their partners' contributions at home are
critical to their success at the office and at home.

In the time it took for me to write and publish this book, many
of the families I was fortunate to interview successfully navigated
these middle-management years by cultivating deliberate All-In
Partnerships. Two years after Karim decided to spend more time at
home with his boys to allow Lisa the flexibility her new job required,
they were toasting her promotion to director of marketing. Susan,
the bus driver whose route change created havoc with her morning
drop-offs, enlisted the help of her sister who took her kids to
school each day until she could negotiate a more ideal time with
her boss. Jun, the ambitious pharmaceutical rep who once felt like a
failure at home, eventually got to her oldest son's baseball games
with the support of her husband. After going through her own inquiry process she decided one of the things that mattered most to
her was relentlessly supporting the endeavors *her sons* had chosen.
If *she* wanted them to learn chess, she could miss a tournament
guilt-free. But if it was their own passion driving their participation
in baseball, she'd move heaven and earth to be there. She and her
husband renegotiated their weekend schedules, giving her more
time on Saturday afternoons to devote to crossing things off her work
to-do list so that she could leave the office early to support her sons
whenever necessary.

—

A nonpaid working dad (a.k.a. stay-at-home dad) might be some working moms' idea of a superhero. And this does seem to be a choice more and more families are making; the percentage of men who are the primary caregivers of their children has risen from 10 percent to 16 percent since 1989.[4] But nonpaid working dads are not the ultimate solution. For one, this option just isn't feasible for the vast majority of families who cannot afford to have a nonpaid working parent, regardless of gender. Second, when men with full-time careers are also fully active at home, employers are more incentivized to create solutions that truly effect change for *all* working families. Third, if we now know that our workplaces benefit from diversity, doesn't it make sense that our homes would too? We do not need role reversal; rather, we need a new model of teamwork in which both parents are meaningfully engaged at work and at home, collaboratively making decisions that reflect what matters most to them. We need All-In Partnership, and women must lead the way.

It may seem counterintuitive to suggest that the secret to freeing women from being overworked is to hold them responsible for their spouses' stepping up. Haven't women been blamed enough? But for most American households, the power dynamic in the private sphere is the inverse of the dynamic in the public. Some researchers have even suggested that because women haven't been able to accumulate as much power at work, they've sought to maintain it in the family structure.[5] Regardless of their motives, at home women rule, even when they work outside of it. In dual-income households, women make the majority of decisions related to child care and home management, regardless of whether they earn more or less than their spouses. Only in 26 percent of American couples do men take the lead on domestic decisions, from household purchases to financial management,[6] thus the influence of the wife weighs heavily on whether housework is shared equally. In one study, nearly every man who shared housework had a wife who urged and/or welcomed his participation at home.[7]

Before someone else can take the reins, women have to release them first.

When *Lean In* author Sheryl Sandberg encouraged women to "make your partner a real partner," we all thought, *Amen to that.*[8] Then we went home and put in another load of laundry. That's because actually enlisting our spouses and other people in our lives to help manage the home requires more than delegating tasks. It isn't child's play—it necessitates a substantive shift in our beliefs and expectations. It requires being disobedient and pushing back.

In 2011, I had the honor of presenting filmmaker and philanthropist Abby Disney with an award at a luncheon to benefit Amref Health Africa. I have tremendous admiration for Abby because she pours her talent and resources into documentaries that tell the stories of the most marginalized women. In my short speech, I rattled off a list of all of the things that superwomen like her accomplish that make them worthy of such honors, including making oatmeal for kids in the morning. "Oatmeal?" Abby exclaimed when she got to the microphone. "My kids eat Cap'n Crunch!" The audience erupted in laughter. I thought, *Wow. Abby is pushing back.*

The next year, I attended the Womensphere conference, where I heard a memorable speech from another one of my sheroes, Shelly Lazarus. In 1971, Shelly joined the advertising agency Ogilvy & Mather as the only woman on the business side and rose up the ranks to become chairman and CEO. She's appeared on *Fortune* magazine's annual ranking of America's 50 Most Powerful Women in Business since the list's inception in 1998. To me, Shelly Lazarus epitomizes polish. So I was intrigued during the Q&A when an audience member asked how Shelly had managed to balance family and work as such a high-level executive and she responded, "If you'd seen the way my house looked at certain points in my career, you wouldn't ask me that question." Again there was thunderous laughter. *Shelly is pushing back,* I thought.

These powerful women understood that in order to be successful, they'd need to define what success looked like on their own terms. They had already figured out what I know now, too: success is imperfect.

I push back daily in micro ways. When I receive a kid's birthday party invitation that Kojo hasn't been included on because it was only sent to the moms, I kindly reply, "Thanks for including us! Please send to Kojo, as he's the Kid Calendar Maven." When Kojo leaves me at a cocktail party to relieve the sitter and a guest comments on how unusual that is, I smile and say, "We take turns." When a colleague asks who watches my kids when I travel I say, "Their father, and not just when I travel." When another mom tells me she can't imagine how I do all the things that I do, I respond, "That's because half the things you're imagining I do, I don't." Every day, I'm offered other people's idealized impressions of my life. Every day, I politely decline through tiny, intentional acts of defiance.

What would happen if we all started speaking honestly and openly about our priorities and the choices we make about how to spend our time? How inspiring would it be to the young women in our offices if they saw female executives who don't pretend to do it all, but who are open and honest about the balls they've dropped to get to where they are today? Women need to support one another by being honest about the compromises we make and by speaking openly about the help we require from our partners and other support systems.

I have listened to hundreds of women carefully. We talk about the demands on our time as if they are being imposed on us and we have no choice. *I have to sell the raffle tickets for the school auction. I need to check e-mail before I go to bed. I'd better call my uncle before he leaves another message.* Every day, we let others dictate our experience. In small, subtle ways we give our time and our power over to others, when our time is the one thing we should protect and control. The irony is that in order to control our time, we have to release control of half the things we're filling it with. We have to let go. Working-mommy martyrdom is *so* yesterday.

———

On April 5, 2012, the White House Project's EPIC Awards were under way. The theme, "The New Face of Leadership," burst magnificently in rich shades of purple and red through the smooth glass façade of Frank Gehry's IAC building in lower Manhattan. As the organization's new president, I was proud we were honoring individuals who were changing our culture's perception about what young women could accomplish. Emma Contiguglia had won the Girl Scouts' coveted Bronze Award for her community service, and Nikiya Harris was one of the youngest people elected county supervisor in Milwaukee, Wisconsin. Once again we had star power, as Geena Davis would be the host.

In my previous position, as the chief fund-raiser, my primary focus of the EPIC Awards was the money, and I was always proudest of the number of dollars that we raised to advance our mission of promoting women's leadership. As the new president, it was different. Yes, I was proud of the money and the honorees, but the accomplishment that made me giddiest had to do with a tiny pair of shoes.

Beginning in 2000, every four years the White House Project partnered with the toy manufacturer Mattel to produce President Barbie. It was a controversial marriage given feminists' disdain over the little blonde's unrealistic body measurements and superficial image. But if there's one thing I'd learned from the White House Project's founder, Marie Wilson, it's this: if you want to ignite real change in the world, you have to meet people where *they* are, not where *you* are. And millions of girls around the world were on the floors of their bedrooms playing with Barbies. As far as Marie was concerned, if we could use the doll to encourage girls to imagine themselves calling a joint session of Congress, instead of cooking dinner for Ken in a dream house, it was worth upsetting a few people. Plus, the partnership would allow us to have a voice in the creation of the doll. One of the features we were proudest to have influenced was her diversity; by election year 2012, President Barbie came in four shades—white, black, Hispanic, and Asian. But there was another feature that Marie had personally been needling Mattel over: the doll's feet. The message on every box said it all: "Doll cannot stand alone." This feature was the most absurd, and Marie did not mince words with Mattel executives. "How can the leader of the free world not stand on her own two feet?" she'd ask them in meetings.

As president, I adopted Marie's mantle, and I, too, pressed for this feature to be changed. Finally, the years of lobbying had paid off. I jumped up and down in my office like a third grader when Stephanie Cota, then a senior vice president at Mattel, called me to share the news. Engineers had designed President Barbie a special pair of shoes. For the first time in the doll's fifty-three-year history, millions of girls would now play with a Barbie who stood on her own. We would unveil her at the EPIC Awards.

As I stood on the red carpet, smiling for the media's camera flashes at the pre-awards reception, I relished the impact of those shoes and mulled over my opening remarks. Things had gotten so busy leading up to the event that I had Delegated with Joy and re-cruited a speechwriter friend to draft the remarks I would give that night to welcome the audience. She had written a rousing manifesto about the need to redefine leadership, and while I had memorized large chunks, I'd be relying on printed pages at the lectern to en-sure I didn't mess up. Ironically, I was nervous about this foolproof strategy because of something my father once told me after he saw me read a script during a conference speech: "You're a public speaker. Not a public reader. That was a waste of your gift." As I posed for the photographers, I thought about how disappointed my father would be that I wasn't unleashing my potential. But I felt it was more impor-tant to be prepared.

After the bright lights and press interviews, I was ushered into the main room and tasked with personally greeting my assigned list of donors and VIPs as they took their seats. By the time everyone was seated and the voice-over called my name, butterflies in my stomach began to flap their wings. As I walked up the steps to the stage, I glanced over at Kojo, who was seated at the front table. He smiled at me with that same smile that captured me when I first saw him in the lobby of our college dorm. His gesture prompted me to take a deep breath.

I stood at the lectern looking at hundreds of gazing eyes. In my mind, I knew the exact words that should have been coming out of my mouth, but they stalled in my stomach. I could feel my flesh warming and my chest contracting. All I had to do was look down at my notes to retrieve my first line, but I couldn't take my eyes off the people in front of me. I couldn't speak. Time must have been moving much slower than it felt because everyone was just waiting patiently. Finally, I heard my voice: *You're not on this stage to tell them what you want to say. You'll only make a difference if you tell them what they need to hear.*

I breathed in. I pushed it out.

I decided to abandon the notes. My heart pounded in my chest. Once I deviated from the script that had been written for me, I'd have to speak extemporaneously for the rest of my speech. There would be no going back. *If you want something you've never had before, you'll have to do something you've never done before in order to get it.*

This was the moment I decided to stop searching for what I was supposed to say, and I just spoke from my heart; this was the moment I unleashed my potential.

My life's work is advancing women and girls. It's why I'm on the planet. So my life is simple. I know what's on my tombstone, and I'm just project managing my life backward. Right now I feel incredibly fortunate that I get to execute my purpose as president of the White House Project. But don't let these flashing cameras fool you. I am not the superstar.

One of the popular questions I've been getting from journalists since I've become president is "Where did Marie Wilson find you?" I always just smile and respond, "Marie Wilson has her eyes open."

Over the next two hours, you're going to be introduced to some extraordinary young women whose determination and talents will blow you away. You're going to think, *Wow. She's going places.* The most important thing I want you to know tonight is that she needs *you* to get where she's going. The new face of leadership is only made possible by your investment in her. Keep your eyes open. Don't even blink. The more you believe in her, the higher she'll fly . . .

In 2006, on that suffocating train ride to Harlem after my first day back at work, I was pressed up against other commuters in my damp suit, carrying my breast pump in one bag and my heels and fund-raising management books in the other. I would never have imagined that five years later I would be standing on a stage in a glamorous dress as president of the White House Project. I was too preoccupied trying to figure out how I would continue to make everything function at home. For too long after that train ride I exhausted myself attempting to fulfill the expectation that I should excel in my career and simultaneously be the perfect wife and mother. I would never have imagined that the best solution would be letting go of that expectation. I wrote this book in hopes that it won't take another woman so long.

There is a parable that describes a woman who is swimming across a lake, and near the center, she begins to get tired and sink. People watching from the shore cry out to her, "Drop the rock!" but she initially doesn't understand them. She regains her momentum and swims a few strokes but again tires and struggles to stay afloat. Finally, she notices what the onlookers have seen. There is a rock tied around her, pulling her down. To the people on the shore, the answer to her dilemma seems so obvious: drop the rock! But as she sinks, they can hear her saying, "I can't. It's mine."[9]

Throughout the course of my work, and even more so during the process of writing this book, I have encountered many women who are struggling to swim while they carry their rocks. They are drowning in e-mails, carpools, playdates, PowerPoints, pitches, and grocery runs. They are drowning in unrealistic expectations that they are supposed to do it all to have it all. They are drowning in the guilt of failing at what is impossible: we simply cannot *do* it all. The workforce revolution that began in the 1950s has stagnated because of the lack of a parallel revolution at home. In 1970, Gloria Steinem declared, "The challenge to all of us is to live a revolution, not die for one." We're approaching fifty years later, and we're still barely living.

We need to ask ourselves what matters most to us. What is our highest and best use toward achieving it? What do we need to let go of to make it happen? Who in our lives will help us because they want us to be our best selves? The first step to Dropping the Ball is getting over the fear of letting that ball roll all over the floor. We have to let it roll to feel the freedom, laugh loud, and live fully.

ACKNOWLEDGMENTS

Amy Poehler said it best: writing a book is hard. Writing the acknowledgments is even harder. Since I am merely the cumulative investment of a lot of people, it would take an entire new book to name all those who have expended their social, economic, political, and heart capital to get me to this point. Please know that I am forever indebted. Here are my shout-outs to those of you who were especially pivotal during this, the birth of my third child.

Thank you . . .

- Bob Miller and the passionate team at Flatiron Books for believing in me and this project
- Debrena Jackson Gandy for telling me during our first phone call in January 1996 that the reason why boys couldn't plan events was because we never let them
- Reshma Saujani for pestering me about writing a book
- Chloe Drew and Arva Rice for dittoing Reshma
- Shelley Burke for teaching me how to keep writing
- Michelle Burford for modeling writer's grit and being my big sister in the literary club
- Erica Dhawan for schooling me on the saddest and most

brilliant networking strategy: "Just walk up and introduce yourself to the oldest white man in the room"

- To Chrissy Greer, Carmen Rita Wong, Keisha Smith-Jeremie, and Aadora Udoji for the emoji texts, multicolored fountain pens, and clutch pep talks
- To the prolific Veronica Chambers for your fresh eyes and giant Post-its
- Ken Matos for hipping me to Google Scholar—wow!
- Anne-Marie Slaughter for igniting insights in Aspen that shaped my arguments
- Levo cofounders Caroline Ghosn and Amanda Pouchot for starting a company where you can work and write a book and fulfill your dreams all at the same time
- Gina Bianchini, Fran Hauser, and Sheryl Sandberg, who invested in Levo and told me it would be a good bet—the wager has changed my life
- Rachel Rosenblatt for the jam session in your apartment while we made playlists (and John for whipping up the incredible cocktails)
- Courtney O'Malley for coming up with "all-in," which might have been the book title except for David Petraeus
- Liz Neumark for loaning me your beautiful quiet house out of the city. Every writer needs one.
- Auntie Gloria, Geena Davis, Gloria Feldt, Ilene Lang, Susan Taylor, and Davia Temin, your wisdom through the process has been immeasurable
- To my book club, Jennifer Allyn, Lois Braverman, Shifra Bronznick, Kym Ward Gaffney, Katie Orenstein, Naamah Paley, and Marie, because every writer has to read while they're writing
- Gabi Tudin and the Heleo team for your social prowess in racking up my views
- To my Harlem4Kids board moms for more than once excusing me from meetings with full support and no judgment: Satrina Boyce, Lisa Jones Brown, Remeise Chandler,

Cynthia Eytina, Amanda Fuller, Wanjiro Gethaiga, and Sabrina Tann-Harris

- To my Wonder Women: Daisy Auger-Dominguez, Cindy Pace, Yrthya Dinzey-Flores, Helene Yan, and Diana Solash for coaching me through the biggest struggle of all (you are *sworn* to secrecy)
- To my Sands: Rosalyn Anderson-Howell, Shana Beckwith, Jewel Dawn Hampton, Toyia Taylor, and Tiffany Tull, whose Delta love and devotion got me through many rough chapters
- Julia Gilfillan, Kathleen Harris, and Amanda Schumacher: your marketing, digital editorial, and PR guidance was golden
- To all the people who took the time to read ugly, unpolished versions of the manuscript and provide me feedback and/or editing: Joanne Gordon, Caroline Gray, Kathleen Harris, Elizabeth Hines, Vinca LaFleur, Rosemarie Robotham, Jovian Zayne, Lois, Marie, Michelle, and Veronica—*serious* yellow happy face sticker
- To my data hunters, Mackenzie Beer, Sava Berhane, and Emily Scholnick, for making me seem even smarter
- To my editor, Whitney Frick, for taking the time to know me and brilliantly rearranging my words (a masterful endeavor given I'm a recovering HCDer)
- To my agent, the indomitable Richard Pine, for being the oldest white man in the room and having your eyes open
- Uncle Kenny for still loving me even though I was terrible at returning your phone calls; I miss them
- Auntie Margaret and Uncle Dan for raising my children while I wrote this book
- Marie for being my political mother
- To my little sisters, Trinity, Tamika, and Desiree, for always knowing I was imperfect and still thinking I was really cool
- Mummy and Daddy for raising a brilliant husband and father

- Debbra for choosing to love me
- Mom for teaching me how to love myself
- Dad for teaching me how to work hard and how to treat people
- To my inspiration, Abiam and Amala, for all of the hard questions you ask that I don't know the answers to
- To my lion, Kojo, for replacing our blue IKEA couch with a beautiful gray Ethan Allen one after reading the first draft; I will put on a hot seventies dress for you anytime.

NOTES

INTRODUCTION

1. Kim Parker, "Despite Progress, Women Still Bear Heavier Load than Men in Balancing Work and Family," *Pew Research Center* (Fact Tank), March 10, 2015, http://www.pewresearch.org/fact-tank/2015/03/10/women-still-bear-heavier-load-than-men-balancing-work-family/. A 2016 study presented at the American Sociological Association reveals why: housework expectations are still drawn along gender lines. According to lead author, Natasha Quadline, nearly 75 percent of those surveyed thought that women in heterosexual couples should be responsible for "cooking, doing laundry, cleaning house, and buying groceries." Eighty-two percent felt women should take care of children's physical needs. See "Sex and Gender more important than income in determining views in division of chores," EurekAlert, August 21, 2016, http:///www.eurekalert.org/pub-releases/2016-08/asa-sag081616.php.

2. The average age of a college-educated first-time mother is thirty. "In Brief," *Knot Yet* (blog), accessed September 2015, http://twentysomethingmarriage.org/in-brief/.

3. Anne-Marie Slaughter, *Unfinished Business: Women Men Work Family* (New York: Random House, 2015).

4. Klaus Schwab et al., eds., *The Europe 2020 Competitiveness Report: Building a More Competitive Europe*, Insight Report (Geneva: World Economic Forum, 2012), http://www3.weforum.org/docs/CSI/2012/Europe2020_Competitiveness_Report_2012.pdf.

5. D'vera Cohn, Gretchen Livingston, and Wendy Wang, "After Decades of Decline, a Rise in Stay-at-Home Mothers," *Pew Research Center* (Social & Demographic Trends), April 8, 2014, http://www.pewsocialtrends.org/2014/04/08/after-decades-of-decline-a-rise-in-stay-at-home-mothers/.

6. Wendy Wang, Kim Parker, and Paul Taylor, "Breadwinner Moms," *Pew Research Center* (Social & Demographic Trends), May 28, 2013, http://www.pewsocialtrends.org/2013/05/29/breadwinner-moms/.

7. *Women in the Workplace: 2015*, Report (Lean In and McKinsey & Company, September 2015), http://womenintheworkplace.com/ui/pdfs/Women_in_the_Workplace_2015.pdf.

8. Felice Schwartz, "Management, Women and the New Facts of Life," *Harvard Business Review* 67, no. 3 (January-February 1989): 65–76, https://hbr.org/1989/01/management-women-and-the-new-facts-of-life/ar.

9. Claire Miller, "More Than Their Mothers, Young Women Plan Career Pauses," *The New York Times,* July 22, 2015, http://www.nytimes.com/2015/07/23/upshot/more-than-their-mothers-young-women-plan-career-pauses.html?_r=1&abt=0002&abg=1.

10. Robin Ely et al., *Life and Leadership after Harvard Business School,* Report (Boston: Harvard Business School, May 2015), http://www.hbs.edu/women50/docs/L_and_L_Survey_2Findings_12final.pdf.

11. Stewart Friedman, *Baby Bust: New Choices for Men and Women in Work and Family* (Philadelphia: Wharton Digital Press, 2014), 2.

12. Sylvia Ann Hewlett, "Executive Women and the Myth of Having It All," *Harvard Business Review* 80, no. 4 (April 2002): 66–73, https://hbr.org/2002/04/executive-women-and-the-myth-of-having-it-all.

13. Centers for Disease Control and Prevention, "QuickStats: Percentage of Adults Who Often Felt Very Tired or Exhausted in the Past 3 Months, by Sex and Age Group—National Health Interview Survey, United States, 2010–2011," April 12, 2013, accessed January 2016, http://www.cdc.gov/mmwr/preview/mmwrhtml/mm6214a5.htm?s_cid=mm6214a5_w.

14. U.S. Census Bureau, "QuickFacts: United States," accessed January 13, 2016, http://quickfacts.census.gov/qfd/states/00000.html.

15. Mitra Toossi, "Labor Force Projections to 2020: A More Slowly Growing Workforce," *Monthly Labor Review* 135, no. 1 (January 2012): 43–64, http://www.bls.gov/opub/mlr/2012/01/art3full.pdf.

16. Tiffani Lennon, *Benchmarking Women's Leadership in the United States,* Report (University of Denver—Colorado Women's College, 2013), http://www.womenscollege.du.edu/media/documents/newbwl.pdf.

17. Lean In and McKinsey & Company, *Women in the Workplace: 2015,* 3.

CHAPTER 1: A WOMAN'S PLACE

1. U.S. Department of Labor, Bureau of Labor Statistics, "American Time Use Survey Summary," June 24, 2015, accessed September 19, 2015, http://www.bls.gov/news.release/atus.nr0.htm.

2. Judith Shulevitz, "Mom: The Designated Worrier," *The New York Times,* May 8, 2015, http://www.nytimes.com/2015/05/10/opinion/sunday/judith-shulevitz-mom-the-designated-worrier.html.

3. Arlie Hochschild and Anne Machung, *The Second Shift: Working Families and the Revolution at Home* (New York: Penguin, 2012).

4. Robin Abrahams and Boris Groysberg, "Manage Your Work, Manage Your Life," *Harvard Business Review* 92, no. 3 (March 2014): 58–66, http://hbr.org/2014/03/manage-your-work-manage-your-life.

5. Alyssa Croft et al., "The Second Shift Reflected in the Second Generation: Do Parents' Gender Roles at Home Predict Children's Aspirations?," *Psychological Science* 25 (March 15, 2014):1418–1428, http://news.ubc.ca/wp-content/uploads/2014/05/FULL-submitted-version-PSCI-13-1163-R2.pdf.

6. John E. Williams and Deborah L. Best, *Measuring Sex Stereotypes: A Multination Study* (California: Sage Publishing, 1990).

7. Naomi Wolf, *The Beauty Myth* (New York: Doubleday, 1991), 22–23.

8. Teresa L. Thompson and Eugenia Zerbinos, "Television Cartoons: Do Children Notice It's a Boy's World," *Sex Roles: A Journal of Research* 37, no. 5 (September 1997): 415–432, http://link.springer.com/article/10.1023%2FA%3A1025657508010.

9. *Change It Up! What Girls Say about Redefining Leadership*, Report (New York: Girl Scout Research Institute, 2008), 20, http://www.girlscouts.org/research/pdf/change_it_up_executive_summary_english.pdf.

10. Seventy-six percent of *Us Weekly*'s and *People*'s 2015 magazine covers through November announced a celebrity's new baby, new boyfriend, new marriage, or end of the latter. I counted.

CHAPTER 3: WORKING MOM

1. Wendy Klein, Carolina Izquierdo, and Thomas N. Bradbury, "The Difference between a Happy Marriage and a Miserable One: Chores," *The Atlantic,* March 1, 2013, http://www.theatlantic.com/sexes/archive/2013/03/the-difference-between-a-happy-marriage-and-miserable-one-chores/273615/2/.

2. Nancy J. Briton and Judith A. Hall, "Beliefs about Female and Male Nonverbal Communication," *Sex Roles: A Journal of Research* 32, no. 1 (January 1995): 79–90, http://link.springer.com/article/10.1007%2FBF01544758.

3. "Modern Marriage," *Pew Research Center* (Social & Demographic Trends), July 18, 2007, http://www.pewsocialtrends.org/2007/07/18/modern-marriage/.

4. Elinor Ochs and Tamar Kremer-Sadik, eds., *Fast-Forward Family: Home, Work, and Relationships in Middle-Class America* (Berkeley: University of California Press, 2013).

5. U.S. Department of Labor, Bureau of Labor Statistics, "Employment Characteristics of Families—2013," April 25, 2014, accessed June 16, 2014, http://www.bls.gov/news.release/archives/famee_04252014.pdf.

6. Catherine E. Ross, "The Division of Labor at Home," *Social Forces* 65, no. 3 (March 1987): 816–33, http://www.jstor.org/stable/2578530.

7. U.S. Department of Labor, Bureau of Labor Statistics, "American Time Use Survey Summary."

8. Elizabeth Chuck, "Juggling Act: Why Are Women Still Trying to Do It All?," *NBC News,* January 14, 2014, http://usnews.nbcnews.com/_news/2014/01/14/22291797-juggling-act-why-are-women-still-trying-to-do-it-all.

9. Ellen Galinsky, *CCF Gender Revolution Symposium: Gender Evolution among Employed Men,* Brief Report (University of Miami—Council on Contemporary Families, March 6, 2012), https://contemporaryfamilies.org/gender-evolution-among-employed-men.

10. Tara Pringle Jefferson, "Resentment: #1 Enemy of Young Moms and Their Relationships," *The Young Mommy Life: Our Journey Together* (blog), March 28, 2011, http://www.theyoungmommylife.com/2011/03/28/how-know-youre-full-of-resentment.

11. Christy Lilley, "The Ballad of a Working Mom: Guilt, Anxiety, Exhaustion and Guilt," *NPR Special Series: The Baby Project* (blog), August 31, 2011, http://www.npr.org/blogs/babyproject/2011/08/30/140068781/the-ballad-of-a-working-mom-guilt-anxiety-exhaustion-and-guilt.

12. Conor Friedersdorf, "Why PepsiCo CEO Indra K. Nooyi Can't Have It All," *The Atlantic*, July 1, 2014, http://www.theatlantic.com/business/archive/2014/07/why-pepsico-ceo-indra-k-nooyi-cant-have-it-all/373750/.

13. Anne-Marie Slaughter, *Unfinished Business: Women Men Work Family*.

CHAPTER 4: HOME CONTROL DISEASE

1. "High-Powered Women and Supportive Spouses: Who's in Charge, and of What?," *Knowledge @ Wharton* (University of Pennsylvania), November 7, 2012, http://knowledge.wharton.upenn.edu/article/high-powered-women-and-supportive-spouses-whos-in-charge-and-of-what-2.

2. Kelly Sakai, "Work Is Not to Blame for Women's Lack of Free Time; Time-Pressure Is Often Self-Imposed, According to Real Simple/Families and Work Institute Survey," *Families and Work Institute,* January 11, 2014, http://www.familiesandwork.org/the-results-of-a-new-groundbreaking-national-survey-women-and-time-setting-a-new-agenda-commissioned-by-real-simple-and-designed-by-families-and-work-institute-released/.

3. Elisa Birtwistle et al., *Women 2020: How Women's Actions and Expectations Are Changing the Future*, Report (The Futures Company, 2013), http://www.wpp.com/wpp/marketing/consumerinsights/women-2020.

4. Joan Williams, *Unbending Gender: Why Family and Work Conflict and What to Do About It* (New York: Oxford University Press, 2000). Print.

5. Carol Martin and Lisa Dinella, "Children's Gender Cognitions, the Social Environment, and Sex Differences in Cognitive Domains," in *Biology, Society, and Behavior: The Development of Sex Differences in Cognition,* edited by Ann McGillicuddy-De Lisi and Richard De Lisi (Westport, CT: Greenwood Publishing Group, 2002), 207–42.

6. Andrée Pomerleau et al., "Pink or Blue: Environmental Gender Stereotypes in the First Two Years of Life," *Sex Roles: A Journal of Research* 22, no. 5 (March 1990): 359–367, http://link.springer.com/article/10.1007%2FBF00288339.

7. Elizabeth Sweet, "Toys Are More Divided by Gender Now Than They Were 50 Years Ago," *The Atlantic*, December 9, 2014, http://www.theatlantic.com/business/archive/2014/12/toys-are-more-divided-by-gender-now-than-they-were-50-years-ago/383556/.

8. Interview with Elizabeth Sweet, October 16, 2015.

9. Laura Meckler, "More Moms Staying Home, Reversing Decadeslong Decline," *The Wall Street Journal,* April 8, 2014, http://blogs.wsj.com/economics/2014/04/08/more-moms-are-staying-at-home-reversing-decadeslong-decline.

10. Melissa J. Williams and Serena Chen, "When 'Mom's the Boss': Control over Domestic Decision Making Reduces Women's Interest in Workplace Power," *Group Processes & Intergroup Relations* 17, no. 4 (July 2014): 436–452, http://gpi.sagepub.com/content/17/4/436.abstract.

11. "Creatures of Habit: Disorders of Compulsivity Share Common Pattern and Brain Structure," *The University of Cambridge*, May 29, 2014, http://www.cam.ac.uk/research/news/creatures-of-habit-disorders-of-compulsivity-share-common-pattern-and-brain-structure.

12. Deborah L. Rotman, "Separate Spheres? Beyond the Dichotomies of Domesticity," *Current Anthropology* 47, no. 4 (August 2006): 666–674, http://www.jstor.org/stable/10.1086/506286.

13. Cynthia Hanson, "I Hate Asking for Help," *Good Housekeeping*, February 1, 2008, http://www.webmd.com/women/features/i-hate-asking-help.

CHAPTER 5: LIFE-GO-ROUND

1. Allison Pearson, *I Don't Know How She Does It* (New York: Anchor Books, 2003).

2. U.S. Department of Labor, Bureau of Labor Statistics, "Employment Characteristics of Families—2013," April 25, 2014, accessed June 16, 2014, http://www.bls.gov/news.release/pdf/famee.pdf.

3. Jodi Mindell, *Sleeping through the Night: How Infants, Toddlers, and Their Parents Can Get a Good Night's Sleep* (New York: Harper Collins, 2005).

4. "Fewer Mothers Prefer Full-Time Work," *Pew Research Center* (Social & Demographic Trends), July 12, 2007, http://www.pewsocialtrends.org/2007/07/12/fewer-mothers-prefer-full-time-work.

5. Kelly Sakai, "Work Is Not to Blame for Women's Lack of Free Time."

6. Sarah Damaske, *CCF Research Brief: Really? Work lowers people's stress levels, Council on Contemporary Families*, Brief Report (University of Miami—Council on Contemporary Families, May 22, 2014), https://contemporaryfamilies.org/work-lowers-stress-levels.

7. Brigid Schulte, "Are You More Stressed at Home Than at Work?," *The Washington Post*, May 22, 2014, http://www.washingtonpost.com/blogs/she-the-people/wp/2014/05/22/are-you-more-stressed-at-home-than-at-work.

8. Betsey Stevenson and Justin Wolfers, "The Paradox of Declining Female Happiness," National Bureau of Economic Research Working Paper Series No. 14969, May 2009, accessed December 27, 2014, http://www.nber.org/papers/w14969.pdf.

9. Nathalie St-Amour et al., *The Difficulty of Balancing Work and Family Life: Impact on the Physical and Mental Health of Quebec Families*, Report (Québec: Institut National de Sante Publique Du Quebec, March 2007), http://www.ncchpp.ca/docs/633DiffBalancingWorkFamilyLife.pdf.

10. Natalie Slopen et al., "Job Strain, Job Insecurity, and Incident Cardiovascular Disease in the Women's Health Study: Results from a 10-Year Prospective Study," *PLoS ONE* 7, no. 7 (July 2012): e40512, http://journals.plos.org/plosone/article?id=10.1371/journal.pone.0040512.

11. Arlie Hochschild and Anne Machung, *The Second Shift*.

12. Barack Obama, *The Audacity of Hope: Thoughts on Reclaiming the American Dream* (New York: Random House, 2006), Amazon Kindle edition, 340.

CHAPTER 6: THE TURNING POINT

1. Gary S. Becker, *A Treatise on the Family*, enl. ed (Cambridge: Harvard University Press, 1991).

2. Clare Lyonette and Rosemary Crompton, "Sharing the load? Partners' relative earnings and the division of domestic labour," *Work, Employment & Society* 29, no. 1 (2014): 23–40, http://wes.sagepub.com/content/29/1/23.full.

3. Josh Katz, "How Nonemployed Americans Spend Their Weekdays: Men vs. Women," *The New York Times*, January 5, 2015, http://www.nytimes.com/interactive/2015/01/06/upshot/how-nonemployed-americans-spend-their-weekdays-men-vs-women.html?_r=0.

CHAPTER 7: WHAT MATTERS MOST

1. Ayala Malach-Pines, "Burnout: An Existential Perspective," in *Professional Burnout,* edited by W. Schaufeli, C. Maslach, and T. Marek (Washington, D.C.: Taylor & Francis, 1993): 33–52.

2. Joanna Barsh and Susie Cranston, *How Remarkable Women Lead: The Breakthrough Model for Work and Life* (New York: Crown Business, 2009).

3. Joan C. Williams and Rachel W. Dempsey, "The Rise of Executive Feminism," *Harvard Business Review* (blog), March 28, 2014, http://blogs.hbr.org/2014/03/the-rise-of-executive-feminism.

4. Stephen Covey, *The 7 Habits of Highly Effective People: Powerful Lessons in Personal Change* (DC Books, 2005).

5. Robert E. Quinn et al., *Reflected Best Self Exercise,* Report (University of Michigan—Center for Positive Organizational Scholarship, 2003).

6. Kwame Nkrumah, "Ghana Is Free Forever," speech given at independence, Ghana, March 6, 1957, http://www.bbc.co.uk/worldservice/focusonafrica/news/story/2007/02/070129_ghana50_independence_speech.shtml

7. David LaPiana, *The Nonprofit Strategy Revolution: Real-Time Strategic Planning in a Rapid-Response World* (Nashville: Fieldstone Alliance, 2008).

CHAPTER 8: THE LAW OF COMPARATIVE ADVANTAGE

1. Comparative advantage is defined as "the ability of a firm or individual to produce goods and/or services at a lower opportunity cost than other firms or individuals. A comparative advantage gives a company the ability to sell goods or services at a lower price than its competitors and realize stronger sales margins." "Comparative Advantage," Investopedia, accessed September 2015, (http://www.investopedia.com/terms/c/comparativeadvantage.asp). "Having a comparative advantage is not the same as being the best at something. In fact, someone can be completely unskilled at doing something, yet still have a comparative advantage at doing it." "Comparative Advantage: An Economics by Topic Detail," Library of Economics and Liberty, accessed September 2015, http://www.econlib.org/library/Topics/Details/comparativeadvantage.html.

2. Keith Robinson and Angel L. Harris, *The Broken Compass: Parental Involvement with Children's Education* (Cambridge: Harvard University Press, 2013).

3. Keith Robinson and Angel Harris, "Parental Involvement Is Overrated," *Opinionator,* April 12, 2014, http://opinionator.blogs.nytimes.com/2014/04/12/parental-involvement-is-overrated/.

4. Daniel M. Cable et al., "How Best-Self Activation Influences Emotions, Physiology and Employment Relationships," Harvard Business School Working Paper No. 16-029, September 2015.

5. Interview with Jooa Julia Lee, October 15, 2015.

CHAPTER 9: ON THE PRECIPICE OF CHANGE

1. Claude M. Steele, *Whistling Vivaldi: How Stereotypes Affect Us and What We Can Do* (New York: W. W. Norton, 2010).

CHAPTER 10: GO AHEAD, DROP THE BALL

1. Irene van Staveren, "The Lehman Sisters Hypothesis," *Cambridge Journal of Economics* 38, no. 5 (2014): 995–1014.

2. "Men Deliberately Do Housework Badly to Avoid Doing It in Future," *The Telegraph,* July 14, 2011, http://www.telegraph.co.uk/men/the-filter/11215506/Men -deliberately-do-housework-badly-to-avoid-doing-it-in-future.html.

3. Christopher Muther, "Instant Gratification Is Making Us Perpetually Impatient," *The Boston Globe,* February 2, 2013, http://www.bostonglobe.com/lifestyle /style/2013/02/01/the-growing-culture-impatience-where-instant-gratification -makes-crave-more-instant-gratification/q8tWDNGeJB2mm45fQxtTQP/story.html.

4. Narayan Janakiraman, Robert J. Meyer, and Stephen J. Hoch, "The Psychology of Decisions to Abandon Waits for Service," *Journal of Marketing Research* 48, no. 6 (December 2011): 970–984, http://opim.wharton.upenn.edu/risk/library/J2011JMR _NJ-RM-SH_psychology_of_decisions.pdf.

5. Kenneth Tobin, "The Role of Wait Time in Higher Cognitive Level Learning," *Review of Educational Research* 57, no. 1 (Spring 1987): 69–95.

CHAPTER 11: CLARIFY WHO DOES WHAT

1. Carolyn O'Hara, "What New Team Leaders Should Do First," *Harvard Business Review* (blog), September 11, 2014, https://hbr.org/2014/09/what-new-team -leaders-should-do-first.

2. Interview with Jessica DeGroot, December 9, 2014.

3. Kenneth Matos, *Modern Families: Same- and Different-Sex Couples Negotiating at Home,* Report (Families and Work Institute, 2015), http://www.familiesandwork .org/downloads/modern-families.pdf.

CHAPTER 12: BELIEVE IN TEAM

1. Marlia E. Banning, "The Politics of Resentment," *JAC: Journal of Advanced Composition Theory* 26, no. 1/2 (2006): 67–102, 71, http://www.jstor.org/stable/20866722.

2. Robin J. Ely, Pamela Stone, and Colleen Ammerman, "Rethink What You 'Know' About High-Achieving Women," *Harvard Business Review* 92, no. 12 (December 2014): 101–109,https://hbr.org/2014/12/rethink-what-you-know-about-high-achieving-women.

3. Max Schireson, "Why I am leaving the best job I ever had," *Max Shireson's Blog,* August 5, 2014, http://maxschireson.com/2014/08/05/1137/.

4. Joan C. Williams, "Sticking Women with the Office Housework," *The Washington Post,* April 16, 2014, http://www.washingtonpost.com/blogs/on-leadership/wp /2014/04/16/sticking-women-with-the-office-housework/.

CHAPTER 13: RECRUIT A VILLAGE

1. Laura Vanderkam, "Working Mothers Who Make It All Work," *The Washington Post,* June 19, 2015, http://www.wsj.com/articles/working-mothers-who-make-it -all-work-1434712370.

2. Quentin Fottrell, "Most Americans don't care about living near family," *Market Watch,* August 27, 2013, http://www.marketwatch.com/story/most-americans-dont -want-to-live-near-relatives-2013-08-26.

CHAPTER 14: DONE IS ANOTHER PERSON'S PERFECT

1. *Global Diversity and Inclusion: Fostering Innovation through a Diverse Workforce,* Report (Forbes Insights, July 2011), http://images.forbes.com /forbesinsights/StudyPDFs/Innovation_Through_Diversity.pdf.

2. Thomas Barta, Markus Kleiner, and Tilo Neumann, "Is There a Payoff from Top-Team Diversity?," *McKinsey Quarterly,* April 2012, http://www.mckinsey.com/insights/organization/is_there_a_payoff_from_top-team_diversity.

3. Lu Hong and Scott E. Page, "Groups of Diverse Problem Solvers Can Out-perform Groups of High-Ability Problem Solvers," *PNAS* 101, no. 46 (November 16, 2004): 16385–16389, http://vserver1.cscs.lsa.umich.edu/~spage/pnas.pdf.

4. Forbes Insights, "Global Diversity and Inclusion: Fostering Innovation through a Diverse Workforce," 11.

5. Barbara Annis and Keith Merron, *Gender Intelligence: Breakthrough Strategies for Increasing Diversity and Improving Your Bottom Line* (New York: Harper Collins, 2014), 9–11.

6. Ibid.

7. Deborah Arthurs, "Women Spend THREE HOURS Every Week Redoing Chores Their Men Have Done Badly," *Daily Mail,* March 20, 2012, http://www.dailymail.co.uk/femail/article-2117254/Women-spend-hours-week-redoing-chores-men-badly.html.

8. Sarah M. Allen and Alan J. Hawkins, "Maternal Gatekeeping: Mothers' Beliefs and Behaviors That Inhibit Greater Father Involvement in Family Work," *Journal of Marriage and Family* 61, no. 1 (1999): 199–212.

9. Judy Wajcman, *Managing Like a Man: Women and Men in Corporate Management* (Philadelphia: Pennsylvania State University Press, 1998).

10. Monologgruppen, "A Tale of Two Brains," YouTube, published February 28, 2011, accessed July 1, 2014, https://www.youtube.com/watch?v=3XjUFYxSxDk&feature=kp.

11. Marshall Gans, "Leading Change: Leadership, Organization, and Social Movements," in *Handbook of Leadership and Practice: A Harvard Business School Centennial Colloquium,* edited by Nitin Nohria and Rakesh Khurana (Boston: Harvard Business School Press, 2010), 509–550.

12. *The New Dad: Take Your Leave,* Report (Boston: Boston College Center for Work & Family, 2014), 3, https://www.bc.edu/content/dam/files/centers/cwf/news/pdf/BCCWF%20The%20New%20Dad%202014%20FINAL.pdf.

13. Pamela Stone, *Opting Out?: Why Women Really Quit Careers and Head Home* (Berkeley: University of California Press, 2007), 78.

CHAPTER 15: AFFIRM WITH GRATITUDE

1. "Emotional Deprivation," The Free Dictionary, accessed July 3, 2015, http://medical-dictionary.thefreedictionary.com/emotional+deprivation.

2. Valerie Purdie-Vaughns, "Why so few black women are senior managers in 2015," *Fortune,* April 22, 2015, http://fortune.com/2015/04/22/black-women-leadership-study.

3. Jessica Bennett, *Feminist Fight Club: An Offical Survival Manual (for a Sexist Workplace)* (New York: Harper Wave, 2016).

4. *Feeling Different: Being the "Other" in US Workplaces,* Report (New York: Catalyst, January 16, 2014), http://www.catalyst.org/knowledge/feeling-different-being-other-us-workplaces.

5. Victoria L. Brescoll, "Who Takes the Floor and Why: Gender, Power, and Volubility in Organizations," *Administrative Science Quarterly* 56, no. 4 (December 2011): 622–641.

6. Barbara L. Fredrickson, "The Role of Positive Emotions in Positive Psychology: The broaden-and-build theory of positive emotions," *American Psychologist* 56, no. 3 (March 2001): 218–226.

7. Elizabeth Weil, "Married (Happily) with Issues," *The New York Times,* December 1, 2009, http://www.nytimes.com/2009/12/06/magazine/06marriage-t.html?pagewanted=all&_r=0.

8. Robert A. Emmons and Michael E. McCullough, "Counting Blessings Versus Burdens: An Experimental Investigation of Gratitude and Subjective Well-Being in Daily Life," *Journal of Personality and Social Psychology* 84, no. 2 (2003): 377–389, 377, http://greatergood.berkeley.edu/pdfs/GratitudePDFs/6Emmons-BlessingsBurdens.pdf.

9. Adam Grant and Francesca Gino, "A Little Thanks Goes a Long Way: Explaining Why Gratitude Expressions Motivate Prosocial Behavior," *Journal of Personality and Social Psychology* 98, no. 6 (2010): 946–955, http://www.umkc.edu/facultyombuds/documents/grant_gino_jpsp_2010.pdf.

CHAPTER 16: DON'T BUY THE STEREOTYPE

1. Interview with Roger Trombley, January 15, 2015.

2. Lowe's Home Improvement, "Lowe's Commercial Valspar Reserve," YouTube, published April 29, 2014, https://www.youtube.com/watch?v=kHw0-QaGYVs.

3. Ross D. Parke and Armin A. Brott, *Throwaway Dads: The Myths and Barriers That Keep Men from Being the Fathers They Want to Be* (New York: Houghton Mifflin Company, 1999), 91.

4. Shira Offer and Barbara Schneider, "Revisiting the Gender Gap in Time-Use Patterns: Multitasking and Well-Being among Mothers and Fathers in Dual-Earner Families," *American Sociological Review* 76, no. 6 (2011): 809–833, 813, http://www.asanet.org/images/journals/docs/pdf/asr/Dec11ASRFeature.pdf.

5. American Psychological Association, "Multitasking: Switching Costs," accessed January 2016, http://www.apa.org/research/action/multitask.aspx.

6. Dan Gilbert, "The Psychology of Your Future Self," TED video, filmed March 2014, https://www.ted.com/talks/dan_gilbert_you_are_always_changing?language=en.

7. Steve Connor, "The hardwired difference between male and female brains could explain why men are 'better at map reading,'" *The Independent*, December 3, 2013,www.independent.co.uk/life-style/the-hardwired-difference-between-male-and-female-brains-could-explain-why-men-are-better-at-map-reading-8978248.html.

8. Jennifer Senior, *All Joy and No Fun: The Paradox of Modern Parenthood* (New York: Ecco, 2015), 79–80.

9. Pamela Stone, *Opting Out?*, 62.

10. Sarah M. Allen and Alan J. Hawkins, "Maternal Gatekeeping: Mothers' Beliefs and Behaviors That Inhibit Greater Father Involvement in Family Work," *Journal of Marriage and Family* 61, no. 1 (February 1999): 199–212.

11. Jay Fagan and Marina Barnett, "The Relationship Between Maternal Gatekeeping, Paternal Competence, Mothers' Attitudes About the Father Role, and Father Involvement," *Journal of Family Issues* 24, no. 8 (November 2003): 1020–1043.

12. Michael E. Lamb, "The development of father-infant relationships" in *The Role of the Father in Child Development,*3rd ed., edited by Michael E. Lamb (New York: Wiley, 1997), 104–20.

13. Meaghan O'Connell, "I Am the Slacker Parent," *New York*, February 26, 2015, http://nymag.com/thecut/2015/02/i-am-the-slacker-parent.html.

14. Eyal Abraham et al., "Father's Brain Is Sensitive to Childcare Experiences," *Proceedings of the National Academy of Sciences of the United States of America* 111, no. 27 (June 2014), http://www.pnas.org/content/111/27/9792.abstract.

15. Ibid.

16. R. Kirk Mauldin, "The Role of Humor in the Social Construction of Gendered and Ethnic Stereotypes," *Race, Gender & Class* 9, no. 3, (2002): 76–95, http://www.jstor.org/stable/41675032.

17. Dovemencareus, "2015 Commercial-#RealStrength Ad | Dove Men+Care,'" YouTube, published January 20, 2015, https://www.youtube.com/watch?v=QoqWo3SJ73c.

18. Nissan, "Nissan 2015 Super Bowl Commercial | 'With Dad,'" YouTube, published October 17, 2013, https://www.youtube.com/watch?v=Bd1qCi5nSKw.

CHAPTER 17: HAPPINESS MOTIVATES EVERYONE

1. Robin Lally, "A Wife's Happiness Is More Crucial than Her Husband's in Keeping Marriage on Track, Rutgers Study Finds," *Rutgers Today*, September 12, 2014, http://news.rutgers.edu/research-news/wife%E2%80%99s-happiness-more-crucial-her-husband%E2%80%99s-keeping-marriage-track-rutgers-study-finds/20140911#.VqmPePkrKM8.

2. Interview with Christine Carter, September 10, 2015.

3. Pantene, "Not Sorry | #ShineStrong Pantene," YouTube, published June 18, 2014, https://www.youtube.com/watch?v=rzL-vdQ3ObA.

4. Karina Schumann and Michael Ross, "Why Women Apologize More Than Men: Gender Differences in Thresholds for Perceiving Offensive Behavior," *Psychological Science* 21, no. 11 (November 2010): 1649–1655, http://pss.sagepub.com/content/21/11/1649.abstract.

5. Jennifer Santoleri, speech given at Allegis annual employee awards program, Baltimore, MD, May 1, 2015.

6. http://www.right.com/wps/wcm/connect/right-us-en/home/thoughtwire/categories/media-center/For+Many+Workers+the+Boss+Emails+Never+Stop.

7. Sonja Lyubomirsky, Kennon M. Sheldon, and David Schkade, "Pursuing happiness: the architecture of sustainable change," *Review of General Psychology* 9, no. 2 (2005): 111–131, http://sonjalyubomirsky.com/wp-content/themes/sonjalyubomirsky/papers/LSS2005.pdf.

CHAPTER 18: WHY WE NEED MEN

1. Scott Page, *The Difference: How the Power of Diversity Creates Better Groups, Firms, Schools and Societies* (Princeton: Princeton University Press, 2007).

2. Claudia Dreifus, "A Professor's Model, Diversity-Productivity," *The New York Times*, January 8, 2008, http://www.nytimes.com/2008/01/08/science/08conv.html.

3. *Statistical Overview of Women in the Workplace*, Report (New York: Catalyst, March 3, 2013).

4. Deborah L. Rhode, "Perspectives on Professional Women," *Stanford Law Review* 40, no. 5 (1988): 1163–1208, 1187.

5. Scott L. Coltrane, *Family Man: Fatherhood, Housework, and Gender Equity* (New York: Oxford University Press, 1997).

6. James B. Stewart, "A C.E.O.'s Support System, AKA Husband," *The New York Times,* November 4, 2011, http://www.nytimes.com/2011/11/05/business/a-ceos -support-system-a-k-a-husband.html.

7. Ibid.

8. Fortune Magazine, "Ursula Burns, 'Chill out a little bit,'" YouTube, published October 17, 2013, https://www.youtube.com/watch?t=80&v=j6lup0CGQfc.

9. *The Global Gender Gap Report,* Insight Report (Geneva: World Economic Forum, 2014), http://reports.weforum.org/global-gender-gap-report-2014.

10. *Women. Fast Forward: The Time for Gender Parity Is Now,* Report (EY, 2015), 5, http://www.ey.com/Publication/vwLUAssets/ey-women-fast-forward -thought-leadership/$FILE/ey-women-fast-forward-thought-leadership.pdf.

11. Ashton Kutcher, "Ashton Kutcher's Facebook Page," published March 8, 2015, accessed May 17, 2015, https://www.facebook.com/Ashton/posts/10152568462597820.

12. Ashton Kutcher, "Stop Gender Stereotyping: Provide Universally Accessible Changing Tables in All Your Stores," *Change.org* (petition letter), accessed May 17, 2015, https://www.change.org/p/bethechange-provide-universally-accessible-changing -tables-in-all-your-stores.

13. Scott Behson, "The Rise of the Hands-On Dad," *Harvard Business Review* (blog), June 13, 2014, http://blogs.hbr.org/2014/06/the-rise-of-the-hands-on-dad.

14. Healthy Families Act of 2015, HR 932, 114th Cong., 1st sess., (2015).

15. "Paul Ryan's Full Statement on His Conditions for Serving as House Speaker," *Time* (video), October 20, 2015, http://time.com/4080753/paul-ryan-house-speaker -full-statement/

16. Ross D. Parke and Armin Brott, *Throwaway Dads,* 129–130.

17. Boston College Center for Work & Family, *The New Dad: Take Your Leave,* 3.

18. Try This: Christopher Shea, "Male CEOs With Daughters Treat Women Better," *The Wall Street Journal,* March 3, 2011, http://blogs.wsj.com/ideas-market/2011 /03/03/male-ceos-with-daughters-treat-women-better/.

19. Scott Behson, "The Smartest Thing I Heard at the White House Summit on Working Fathers," *Father, Work and Family* (blog), June 21, 2014, http:// fathersworkandfamily.com/2014/06/21/the-smartest-things-i-heard-at-the-white -house-summit-on-working-fathers.

20. Andy Hines, "Is 2014 'Year of the Dad?,'" *The Daily Beast,* June 9, 2014, http://www.thedailybeast.com/articles/2014/06/09/is-2014-year-of-the-dad.html.

21. Dan Mulhern, "Dan Mulhern Responds to NEWSWEEK's Cover on the 'Beached White Male,'" May 1, 2011, http://www.newsweek.com/dan-mulhern-res ponds-newsweeks-cover-beached-white-male-67651.

22. Ibid.

23. *The Hartford's Millennial Parenthood Survey* (The Hartford, 2014), http:// www.thehartford.com/sites/thehartford/files/millennial-parenthood.pdf.

24. Alyssa Croft et al., "The Second Shift Reflected in the Second Generation: Do Parents' Gender Roles at Home Predict Children's Aspirations?," *Psychological Science* (June 2014): 5–6.

CHAPTER 19: THE FOUR GO-TOS

1. Sharon Meers and Joanna Strober, *Getting to 50/50: How Working Couples Can Have It All by Sharing it All* (New York: Bantam Dell, 2009).

2. Katharine Zaleski, "Female Company President: 'I'm Sorry to All the Mothers I Worked With,'" *Fortune,* March 3, 2015, http://fortune.com/2015/03/03/female-company-president-im-sorry-to-all-the-mothers-i-used-to-work-with.

3. Sandrine Devillard, Sandra Sancier-Sultan, and Charlotte Werner, "Why Gender Diversity at the Top Remains a Challenge," *McKinsey Quarterly,* April 2014, http://www.mckinsey.com/insights/organization/why_gender_diversity_at_the_top_remains_a_challenge.

4. Catalyst, *Statistical Overview of Women in the Workplace.*

5. Feminist Majority Foundation, "Empowering Women in Business," accessed August 22, 2014, http://www.feminist.org/research/business/ewb_myths.html.

6. Sophia Breene, "13 Mental Health Benefits of Exercise," *The Huffington Post,* March 27, 2013, http://www.huffingtonpost.com/2013/03/27/mental-health-benefits-exercise_n_2956099.html.

7. Ibid.

8. Ibid.

9. Ibid.

10. Souha R. Ezzedeen and Kristen G. Ritchey, "Career Advancement and Family Balance Strategies of Executive Women," *Organizational Dynamics* 38, no. 4 (2009): 270–280, http://yorkspace.library.yorku.ca/xmlui/bitstream/handle/10315/6295/HRM0013.pdf?sequence.

11. Ibid.

12. Sylvia Ann Hewlett, "The Real Benefit of Finding a Sponsor," *Harvard Business Review* (blog), January 26, 2011, http://blogs.hbr.org/2011/01/the-real-benefit-of-finding-a/.

13. Selena Rezvani, "How to Negotiate," *The Shriver Report,* January 12, 2014, http://shriverreport.org/how-to-negotiate-selena-rezvani/.

14. Alex Crippen, "Warren Buffett's $100,000 Offer and $500,000 Advice for Columbia Business School Students," *CNBC,* November 12, 2009, http://www.cnbc.com/id/33891448.

15. *The Global Social CEO Survey* (BRANDfog, 2014), 5, http://brandfog.com/CEOSocialMediaSurvey/BRANDfog_2014_CEO_Survey.pdf.

16. Jan Bruce, "The Truth about Sleep," *Forbes,* March 25, 2014, http://www.forbes.com/sites/janbruce/2014/03/25/the-truth-about-sleep.

17. Lisa F. Berkman et al., "Managers' Practices Related to Work-Family Balance Predict Employee Cardiovascular Risk and Sleep Duration in Extended Care Settings," *Journal of Occupational Health Psychology* 15, no. 3 (July 2010): 316–329, http://www.ncbi.nlm.nih.gov/pmc/articles/PMC3526833/.

18. "Lack of Sleep 'Damaging Mothers' Lives'," *Daily Mail,* accessed January 2016, http://www.dailymail.co.uk/news/article-107866/Lack-sleep-damaging-mothers-lives.html.

CHAPTER 20: FINAL FRONTIER

1. Katy Steinmetz, "Help! My Parents Are Millennials: How this generation is changing the way we raise kids," *Time,* October 26, 2015, http://time.com/help-my-parents-are-millennials-cover-story/.

2. "Motherhood Today: Tougher Challenges, Less Success: Mom's Biggest Critics Are Middle-Aged Women," *Pew Research Center* (Social & Demographic Trends),

May 2, 2007, http://www.pewsocialtrends.org/2007/05/02/motherhood-today-tougher
-challenges-less-success/.

3. "More Research Says Helicopter Parenting Backfires," *NY Daily News,* June 2, 2015, http://www.nydailynews.com/life-style/research-helicopter-parenting -backfires-article-1.2243512.

4. U.S. Census Bureau, "Current Population Survey, Annual Social and Economic Supplements, 1994 to 2015," accessed January 2016, https://www.census.gov/hhes /families/files/graphics/SHP-1b.pdf.

5. Katherine Bowers, "A Mother's Work: Special Report," *Working Mother,* March 19, 2014, http://www.workingmother.com/special-report/mothers-work -special-report.

6. Judith Warner, *Perfect Madness: Motherhood in the Age of Anxiety* (New York: Penguin, 2005).

7. Ibid., 299.

8. Rachel G. Lucas-Thompson, Wendy A. Goldberg, and JoAnn Prause, "Maternal work early in the lives of children and its distal associations with achievement and behavior problems: A meta-analysis," *Psychological Bulletin* 136, no. 6 (November 2010): 915–942, http://dx.doi.org/10.1037/a0020875.

CHAPTER 21: FREEDOM

1. Joan Williams, *Unbending Gender: Why Family and Work Conflict and What to Do about It* (New York: Oxford University Press, 2000), 6.

2. Carol Hymowitz, "Behind Every Great Woman," *Bloomberg Businessweek Magazine,* January 4, 2012, http://www.businessweek.com/magazine/behind-every -great-woman-01042012.html.

3. Ibid.

4. Gretchen Livingston, "Growing Number of Dads Home with the Kids: Biggest Increase among Those Caring for Family," *Pew Research Center* (Social Demographic Trends), June 5, 2014, http://www.pewsocialtrends.org/2014/06/05/growing -number-of-dads-home-with-the-kids/.

5. Virginia Rutter and Pepper Schwartz, "Gender, marriage, and diverse possibilities for cross-sex and same-sex pairs," in *Handbook of family diversity,* edited by D. H. Demo, K. R. Allen, and M. A. Fine (New York: Oxford University Press, 2000), 59–81.

6. "Women Call the Shots at Home; Public Mixed on Gender Roles in Jobs," *Pew Research Center* (Social & Demographic Trends), September 25, 2008, http://www .pewsocialtrends.org/2008/09/25/women-call-the-shots-at-home-public-mixed-on -gender-roles-in-jobs.

7. Arlie Hochschild, *The Second Shift,* 223.

8. Sheryl Sandberg, "Why We Have Too Few Women Leaders," TED video, filmed December 2010, 4:08–4:10, http://www.ted.com/talks/sheryl_sandberg_why _we_have_too_few_women_leaders?language=en.

9. Sandy Beach, "Drop the Rock Alcoholics Anonymous Talk," Palm Desert Roundup (June 1976).

INDEX